THE HAUNTING OF
VANCOUVER ISLAND

THE

HAUNTING

OF

VANCOUVER

ISLAND

SUPERNATURAL ENCOUNTERS
WITH THE OTHER SIDE

SHANON SINN

TOUCHWOOD

Edited by Alexandria Stuart
Cover and interior design by Pete Kohut
Cover photo by Evan Dalen/Stocksy United

LIBRARY AND ARCHIVES CANADA CATALOGUING IN PUBLICATION

Sinn, Shanon, author
The haunting of Vancouver Island : supernatural encounters with the other side / Shanon Sinn.
Includes index.

Issued in print and electronic formats.
ISBN 978-1-77151-243-5 (softcover)

1. Haunted places—British Columbia—Vancouver Island. I. Title.

BF1472.C3S56 2017   133.109711'2   C2017-903004-3

TouchWood Editions acknowledges that the land on which we live and work is within the traditional territories of the Lkwungen (Esquimalt and Songhees), Malahat, Pacheedaht, Scia'new, T'Sou-ke and WSÁNEĆ (Pauquachin, Tsartlip, Tsawout, Tseycum) peoples.

We acknowledge the financial support of the Government of Canada through the Canada Book Fund and the Canada Council for the Arts, and of the province of British Columbia through the British Columbia Arts Council and the Book Publishing Tax Credit.

PRINTED IN CANADA

26 25 24 23   7 8 9 10

To all the spirits of Vancouver Island

PAST

PRESENT

FUTURE

When they had assembled for a council again, one of the men said, "The ghosts of the dead must have got her. You know, when a village is abandoned the ghosts always come and look at the houses."
—Franz Boas, "Legends of the Nuu-chah-nulth," *Indian Myths & Legends from the North Pacific Coast of America*, 1895

CONTENTS

☠ ☠ ☠

INTRODUCTION

VANCOUVER **ISLAND IS AN ENTITY** of its own. Anyone who
lives here or visits here can sense that it has a unique per-
sona. The fog rolls in from the sea and the island suddenly becomes
shrouded in mystery, cloaked in a blanket of otherworldliness. The
air we breathe feels charged, the nights have an aura of power, and
we do not feel alone on the beach or in the woods. For thousands
of years, those who lived on Vancouver Island accepted as fact that
it was haunted. As settlers built cities and tried to cast aside their
own age-old belief in the supernatural, our urban centres spawned
countless new tales of hauntings and of the spirit world.

For those who believe in ghosts, there is this ironic idea that if
you die before your time, you will somehow be granted immortal-
ity. To the non-believer, there is a fear that death is either not the
end, or that happiness is not guaranteed in the next world. Some
take the position that the stories are fairy tales for children, even
though they continue to be told in every culture on Earth. Every
year, thousands of people will die and become a ghost story. Their
exact numbers are impossible to determine, because the subject is
rarely taken seriously.

Many people badly want to believe in ghosts. Others choose
not to, no matter what they have experienced or heard. So, stories
become semi-comedic at one end of the spectrum and completely

dismissive at the other. A balanced perspective is rare. When it comes to tales of the unexplained, some writers willingly add extra parts to the story, essentially altering it for dramatic purposes. Others do not attempt to check facts, but still promote the legend in a journalistic way without the authority to do so.

I will present these stories with the same accuracy and attention to detail that I would use if I were writing any other news report or historical account. I have done this out of respect for the subject, because I know people have these experiences. I know this because I have had them myself. I believe in ghosts, yet I am also a skeptic.

Some are quick to dismiss ghost stories as fantasy, but this is an outdated mode of thought. In 2005, Bryan Farha of Oklahoma City University and Gary Steward Jr. of the University of Central Oklahoma conducted a study on paranormal beliefs by polling 439 university students. They discovered that "as people attain higher college-education levels, the likelihood of believing in paranormal dimensions increases." A 2009 Pew Research Center survey found that eighteen percent of Americans claimed to have been in the presence of a ghost. Twenty-nine percent said they had been in touch with someone who had died. People experience hauntings—that is indisputable—but their causes remain a mystery.

In some cases, low-frequency noises are believed to create hallucinations in certain people. The *Guardian* reported in 2003 that engineer Vic Tandy had found sound waves at frequencies lower than could be heard by a human at two haunted sites. These, he proposed, caused hallucinations and fear. Some could argue that the subjects merely became more aware of what was already there, while others might propose that this is the cause of many ghost sightings.

Dr. Sam Parnia in *What Happens When We Die: A Groundbreaking Study into the Nature of Life and Death* cited several journal articles in his book that suggest a person's consciousness can exist outside of their body. The insinuation is that this could possibly be beyond death.

Many believe that DNA memory could give us access to ancestral knowledge as well, something that has recently been proven in mice. In 2015, Aaron Kase listed several studies that support these theories in "Science is Proving Some Memories are Passed Down from Our Ancestors." In a sense, this is physical proof that we can communicate with the dead.

There will be scientific discoveries and technological advances we cannot fathom in the decades ahead. Science will one day be able to explain exactly what a spirit is. Ghosts will either be proven to be the souls of the dead, or other phenomena that has the potential to destroy our belief in life after death. Perhaps the explanation will be somewhere in between, like the idea of the *tulpa*.

Tulpa is a Tibetan/Indian Buddhist word used to describe an entity that exists because someone began to believe it did. In theory, this could be caused on purpose or by accident. If such an idea was ever proven, it could suddenly explain everything from visions of the Virgin Mary to fire-breathing dragons. What would happen when a whole society believed in a particular entity like a god or goddess? What about in the case of a haunting? What if an entire neighbourhood believed the abandoned house down the street was haunted? Could the building acquire a resident spirit as a result?

In physics, there is a term called "the observer effect." As soon as a person watches something, they become a part of it, essentially changing it in some way. In its most obvious form, this is by using equipment; in a more subtle way, it is simply by being there. What if that observer watched that thing from a discriminatory perspective? Or with the intention of changing it? This is suddenly a similar idea to a belief in magic, spells, and curses. Many cultures, for example, have a concept called "the evil eye." The term is a metaphysical way to describe the process of looking at something, in this case another person, with the desire to change it. Physical existence might be far more complex than we had ever imagined.

Science accepts that energy cannot be destroyed. This is called "the law of conservation of energy." Energy cannot be added to or taken away from. What if there is an undetected layer of energy that remains bonded to the physical world when a being dies? Or a rare phenomenon where the energy does not break apart after death, as it should? If one believes in other dimensions—as many modern scientists, including Stephen Hawking, do—then there are other possibilities as well, in addition to philosophical or religious explanations.

My point is that the possibilities are endless. We simply do not know what hauntings really are. We do, however, know that a huge percentage of people have had experiences with them.

Those who fear the idea of ghosts often claim that anyone who has had these experiences is "crazy." If the incidents are the result of mental illness, then it is disappointing that people in this day and age would react so harshly. Individuals have left homes, jobs, and partners due to experiencing what they believed to be paranormal events. If mental illness is the cause, this should be a reason to explore these claims, not ignore them.

There are others who believe that all of these accounts are lies. For this to be true, there would need to be millions of people involved in the hoax, all in an effort to convince skeptics that something make-believe was actually real. Framed that way it sounds preposterous. Yet, unfortunately, it is rare to come across a tale that can be trusted fully because so many people are willing to lie or embellish second-hand stories to suit their own agenda.

Being human, we all have flawed perspectives. In cases of oral storytelling, the facts are changed slightly even if it was never the intention. As most encounters are never recorded when they occur, they become damaged as they are passed from one person to another. For this reason, a ghost story is difficult to take at face value, even for someone like me who has had experiences of his own.

One of my earliest childhood memories was of a strange cloud in the basement of our North Saskatchewan home. The room inexplicably filled with a greenish fog that slowly rolled together and transformed into a human-like shape. My ears rang, and my body froze. I tried to breathe. It was something I did not want to see. Somehow, I broke the spell and ran. My mom told me that I was imagining things. Later, as an adult, I would learn that she had unexplained experiences herself.

Over the years, I sometimes awoke to see that green cloud hovering over me. Not just in one home either. I slowly came to believe, as I got older, that the cloud was a figment of my imagination. I was half asleep. It was not real. It would be years before someone else saw it at the same time as me.

As teenagers, my buddies and I would often go to a place called the St. Louis Ghost Light near my hometown. This site has appeared in documentaries, newspapers, magazine articles, books, YouTube videos, and on the news. Groups have studied the ghost and have proposed theories to explain it that range from swamp gas to headlights in the distance.

The St. Louis Ghost Light is one of Canada's most famous ghost stories. Most of the people I grew up with in Prince Albert, Saskatchewan, have seen it. Whole groups of people have seen it at the same time. In 2014, Canada Post featured the haunting on one of its stamps and posted the story online. The legend is that a railway worker was killed on the tracks near the town of St. Louis close to the South Saskatchewan River. The area is mostly farmland, but there is a tree-lined dirt road where the tracks used to run. Nowadays, fences with "No Trespassing" signs restrict access, but back then the road was wide open.

I have seen this light a hundred times or more, usually with other people. It often returns over and over again during the same night. Sometimes, it looks like a large single headlight. At other times, the light is red and sways back and forth. One story claims this is the conductor looking for his head.

I have witnessed these lights during the day, and I have seen them while walking along the road in both directions. I have observed them in the distance and I have seen them up close. It is not headlights and there are no swamps nearby. To me, the explanations are even more whimsical than believing in spirits of the dead.

Some places incite peacefulness: temples of worship, well-tended gardens, New Age healing rooms. The St. Louis Ghost Light had the opposite effect; it was unsettling. Car stereos turned on or off by themselves. Sometimes vehicles wouldn't start. The air burned electric. The experiences left an impression on me that I have carried ever since, long after I left the prairies for the West Coast.

I first came to Vancouver Island in 1995. I immediately fell in love with the region's primordial spirit and the eclectic people who call the island home. Over the years, I would leave to work or travel, but I would always return to Vancouver Island, which had somehow become a part of me.

I continued to have experiences I couldn't explain. Some were easy to push aside as an overactive imagination, while others felt more like spiritual encounters.

While living in Nanaimo in 2001, I had a particularly transformative moment. I would still wake up sometimes to see a green cloud floating above me. It seemed similar to the experience I had as a child or, possibly, it was even the same entity. It would slowly dissipate as I woke up fully. For this reason, I became more and more convinced that it was not real. One night, I opened my eyes to see the cloud hovering above me near the ceiling. I watched it with detached amusement. Suddenly my girlfriend, who had been asleep beside me, started to gasp in distress. I asked her what was wrong. "Don't you see that green cloud?" she asked. The hairs stood up on the back of my neck. All of those years of doubting were erased in a single moment. I never saw it again. It felt like whatever it was just needed me to know that it was real. I became much more spiritual after that, for a little while anyway.

The same year, I was transferred to a downtown Vancouver department store as a loss prevention manager. My job was to put systems in place that would prevent loss, to train or manage people making arrests, and to personally arrest those committing criminal offenses. Over the next several years, I also attended Douglas College in nearby New Westminster to get a criminology certificate. This would help me become a police officer, which seemed like a natural career progression at the time. Understanding legal systems and preparing legal documents were important skills to acquire. They made me look at things critically. Unfortunately, thinking this way pulled me away from a belief in ghosts once more. In retrospect, my goals seemed easier to achieve by becoming more conformist. It was disappointing then, when I discovered the building I worked in was haunted.

Many of my co-workers had experiences there, particularly when we received unexplained motion alarm call-outs at night to certain areas of the store. The most extreme thing that ever happened to me was a door slamming in my face when I could see that there was no one in the hallway in front of me. This was during a call-out where I was the only person in the store. Many staff reported similar incidents. One woman working before the store opened said she had seen a lady in a red dress. The apparition had disappeared in front of her.

Writing has always been a strange obsession for me, so I started a blog about loss prevention. Approaching Halloween, I published a post about the store being haunted. The article was the first ghost story I had ever shared online, and it became more popular than anything else I had written.

In 2007, I finally completed my criminology schooling. I was about to apply to several police forces in the region when I received a message from the Canadian military informing me that I had been accepted into the infantry as a reservist. This was a complete surprise. Years earlier, for many reasons, I had felt compelled to go to Afghanistan, but I did not agree with the conflict in Iraq. After Canada officially took this same stance, I had volunteered to serve in 2003. I had not heard back. Suddenly, four years later, I was in.

I was sworn into the army and began to get my primary military qualifications on weekends. The following summer, I took a leave of absence from my job and left British Columbia for more training. By 2009, I left my job and was in Edmonton attached to the Princess Patricia's Canadian Light Infantry preparing to deploy to Afghanistan as a part of Operation Athena. This was another seven months of training. There were only a few reservists attached to the Battle Group and I was one of them. These were coveted positions among reservists, as it meant a more classic military role as opposed to convoy protection or security positions. I would have done my part no matter what, but I am grateful to have had the experiences that I did. They have left me thankful for every little thing I have.

We returned home in the spring of 2010. Almost as soon as I was back in Canada, I was diagnosed with testicular cancer. I was operated on, but it spread into my abdomen. I underwent chemotherapy in 2011. The side effects—many of them extremely rare—were horrendous. I went from 91 kilograms (200 pounds) to less than 68 kilograms (150 pounds). I had no energy and was short of breath. I was useless to the military and could no longer work as a loss prevention manager.

Trying to find purpose while sick, I started to blog about folklore and legends and volunteered part-time at the Nanaimo Museum as a research assistant. I also joined the British Columbia Ghosts

& Hauntings Research Society (BCGHRS), a group I found online and was impressed with. I liked them because the members were more grounded than any group I had ever come across. They followed the Paranormal Studies and Inquiry Canada (PSICAN) guidelines and were an official member group. PSICAN focuses on documentation from a level-headed, skeptical perspective. There are strict rules to follow when conducting an investigation: trespassing is forbidden, professionalism is paramount, and trying to prove that a ghost has a logical explanation is the first task. The BCGHRS group following these mandates was small and conducted very few investigations, but I appreciated—and still do—communicating with others who are skeptical believers.

Still not recovering very fast, I was medically released from the military in 2014. Thankfully, the release provided me with two years of schooling. It looked as if I could only possibly do a part-time desk job, so I chose to study writing. Living back in Nanaimo, I enrolled at Vancouver Island University (VIU) in the Creative Writing Program and continued to post some of my writing online.

One of the posts I published on my blog, Living Library, was about the Banshee, the Irish shrieking ghost. As they had before, people responded positively to the content. To meet the needs of my audience, I started to research hauntings and ghosts more exclusively. One wildly popular post was a list of haunted locations on Vancouver Island. Another was about haunted locations in Victoria. Around this time, the Nanaimo Museum asked me to do research for its October Lantern Tour, which was composed of historic ghost stories and other dark tales from the area.

It became more and more apparent that there was an appetite

on Vancouver Island for homegrown ghost stories and that no one was telling them. Sure, there were the more popular tales like the April Ghost, the *Valencia* Phantom Ship, or Beban House's boy with the red ball, but there were so many other stories that were only well known in certain areas, such as the Headless Woman of Mount Sicker, the Skull-Faced Bishop, or the Ahousaht Witch. Without intending to, I became the only person on Vancouver Island collecting the island's ghost stories in a serious way. I suddenly realized that it was something I had started to do twenty years earlier. Slowly, a book on Vancouver Island's hauntings started to form.

As I began to recover physically, I explored more and more places across the island. I was required to report to the military base in Esquimalt and the Veterans Affairs office in Victoria as well. Every trip, I would visit one or two reportedly haunted locations. As I slowly got better, I got into paddle boarding and paddle surfing. These sports introduced me to new places as I fought to regain my health and find a new sense of purpose. I would explore the locations that were believed to be haunted and meet people who would tell me more and more stories. I had collected friends all over the island since the mid-nineties, and many of them helped with tips or introducing me to others. Some of these friends appear in the stories I am about to share.

For those who are unfamiliar with Vancouver Island, some perspective is necessary. To visit here is to step into another world not quite like anywhere else I have ever been. The cities still have an outpost-like air to them, and there are many wilderness areas that continue to feel both ancient and sentient.

Located off the west coast of British Columbia, the island is 460 kilometres (290 miles) long and roughly 80 kilometres (50 miles) wide, making it 32,134 square kilometres (12,407 square miles). This makes Vancouver Island larger than the state of Hawaii, the island of Sicily, and over fifty other countries in the world. It has a population of fewer than 800,000 people, with almost half living in the Victoria region on the southeast tip of the island. Another 100,000 people live in the mid-island Nanaimo region. Overall, Vancouver Island is sparsely populated. Once outside of the urban areas, much of the island is only accessible by logging road, boat, or floatplane.

Mostly forested, Vancouver Island has many inlets, mountains, rivers, and waterfalls. The coastline is inhospitable, especially on the west side of the island, where many places are accessible only by boat when seas are calm. The west coast has thick rainforest and is considered rugged terrain by even the most ambitious outdoor enthusiast. Many areas are home to old-growth forest; some individual trees believed to be over a thousand years old and some whole forest areas thought to be over seven hundred years old. The tallest known tree in Canada is located on Vancouver Island and stands at 95 metres (315 feet) tall. Wildlife is abundant, including wolf, cougar, bear, elk, and deer. There are also many species of large birds, including eagle, owl, raven, and waterfowl, such as the heron. The coastline is home to many species of whales, such as the grey and killer whale, as well as sea lion, the giant Pacific octopus, and several shark species, including the six-gill shark and occasionally the great white shark.

Vancouver Island has a very dynamic history, which I will explore in greater detail throughout this book. First Nations people thrived here for thousands of years. Many groups conducted Viking-like raids, destroying and killing whole villages, enslaving the suitable survivors, and claiming spoils of victory. Later, settlers came in search of resources. Much of Vancouver Island was colonized and developed in the pursuit of coal and timber, both rough trades that introduced new waves of immigrants in the decades to follow. Coal mines in the Nanaimo region claimed over six hundred lives, including 150 people in a single disaster in 1887. The gold rush brought a cowboy culture to the island as well, which often resulted in bloodshed and hangings. Many early settlements wouldn't last. In *Ghost Towns and Mining Camps of Vancouver Island*, T.W. Paterson claims that there are at least twenty-eight abandoned ghost towns on the island. Most of these have been reclaimed by the forest and are almost impossible to find.

The port settlements on Vancouver Island were often chaotic places with high rates of crime, a thriving prostitution trade, and disease. Fishing along the coast was and continues to be dangerous; with the waters claiming many ships and lives. The west coast of the island is part of the infamous Graveyard of the Pacific.

If one considers that ghosts are often believed to be the result of a tragedy, then there is no shortage of explanations for the many sites people believe are haunted.

There are several smaller islands around Vancouver Island as well, including the Gulf Islands and the Discovery Islands. These islands are accessed by ferry and are often considered a part of the Vancouver Island region. For these reasons, I have included stories from some of these locations as well.

It is important to me that this book truly represents Vancouver Island. The more populated regions have the most stories, but there are tales from all over the island. Some are urban and others are rural. There are stories from reserves and accounts from logging roads. Some are from castles, inns, and cemeteries. There are reports of spirits on mountaintops, beaches, and those that appear on the water. There are also traditional tales from each of the three First Nations groups who call Vancouver Island home: the Coast Salish, the Nuu-chah-nulth, and the Kwakwaka'wakw. When it comes to the subject of ghosts and spirits, they have a fundamental belief in the spirit world, which allows us to look at ghosts through a lens many of us are not used to. Some topics have multiple perspectives, even within the same community, so those included here should be seen as samples and not an exhaustive exploration.

In some cases I have taken liberties while describing apparitions to increase readability. Many historical reports would say something to the effect of "a woman in white," which, as a reader, I found dissatisfying. As the act of manifestation is essentially the climax of many of these stories, I wanted to paint a clearer picture of the entity where I felt it was needed. I did my best based on the information I had at my disposal and my imagination. These particular sections may stick out to you as being different, but should not detract from the seriousness of the research.

As each chapter is an exploration of a haunting or other spirit-world event, they have been handled in different ways. Some of them are tales taken from newspaper reports or other sources. Many of the stories are a fusion of oral and written material or are accounts from people I have interviewed. Where I have seen a problem with a story, I will point it out. When I am convinced of the storyteller's authenticity, you will be able to tell. The chapters begin at the south end of the island and make their way northward up the island.

This book is written from an investigative perspective. What you will read in these pages is as close to the truth as I know it.

View of Oak Bay from the Chatham Islands.
PHOTO BY SHANON SINN

THE SPIRIT
OF THE WOLF

CHATHAM ISLANDS

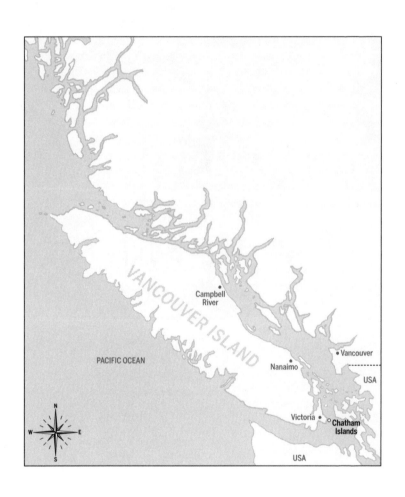

I N 2012, CAMPERS REPORTED A lone wolf on one of the Chatham Islands east of the city of Victoria. Conservation officers initially dismissed the sightings as mistaken identity, thinking it was more likely that a dog had been abandoned on the small island. While coastal wolves have been known to swim short distances, it seemed unlikely one would have travelled the five kilometres (three miles) from Victoria, but there was nowhere else it could have come from.

According to news sources, Songhees First Nation members and conservation officers soon confirmed that the skittish animal was a wolf. Discovery Island, where it was originally noticed, is part marine provincial park and part Songhees reserve land. The wolf has since been spotted on the other Chatham Islands as well. The Songhees dubbed the canine Staqeya, meaning "wolf" in their Lekwungen dialect. They believe it is sacred.

I've always felt a special connection to wolves. First Nation members have told me that the wolf is my spirit animal. As a soldier in Afghanistan, I kept a patch of a wolf on my pack. Wolves have a code of honour absent in many animals; they are monogamous, loyal, take care of their sick, and will die for one another. Yet they have been persecuted for thousands of years, often to the point of extinction, out of an unsubstantiated fear that they are dangerous.

I was intrigued. How could a wolf exist by itself for so long in such a small area? And where did it come from? The nearest wolf pack was in the vicinity of Shawnigan Lake, 44 kilometres (27 miles) northwest of Victoria. To come from that direction, the wolf would have had to cross multiple heavily populated municipalities and highly trafficked roads before making the swim. I felt compelled to investigate further.

In 2015, my opportunity finally came. I pitched the story to one of my professors as an idea for an online magazine story. I would first research the wolf, and then I would go to the island to dig deeper and try to take a picture. With my military and outdoor experience, I knew I could get the story without being intrusive to the wolf.

A few weeks later, the twenty-five foot *Amanda Anne* ploughed through the frigid February waters of the Strait of Juan de Fuca. Approaching the fog-shrouded islands at night, Chief James Swan from Ahousaht (a First Nations village north of Tofino) and I agreed that trying to get ashore in the dark would not be safe. We decided to put down anchor in a semi-sheltered spot and wait for dawn.

I first met James in the army during infantry training. Our friendship is rooted in the belief that the natural world is a spiritual kingdom deserving respect. When I told him I wanted to write a story about Staqeya, he volunteered to take me in his boat.

The night was cold but the stars were bright. The sound of singing frogs carried across the water. Eventually, the sun rose, and the rain, which had arrived in the dark, stopped. The tide ripped past, but the water was otherwise calm. We drank our tea and started to move along the shoreline, looking for signs of Staqeya. Our plan was to search by boat first, as she had most often been seen from shore.

On the water we met a lone kayaker, photographer and environmentalist Cheryl Alexander. She showed us a picture of Staqeya that she had taken earlier. I recognized the arbutus-lined shoreline and light-coloured wolf from news story images. The wolf was originally reported to be a female, but the image she had of Staqeya was of a male. I was surprised.

After exchanging contact information, James and I continued on our way. We hadn't seen the wolf from the water, so we decided to head ashore after we found a safe spot to put down anchor. James rowed a small dinghy, while I travelled on my stand-up paddleboard with gear on my back. We landed ashore. I got out of my wetsuit and into camping clothes.

After a short walk, James and I found a bluff where it looked like a large mammal had been resting. A trail through the tall grass led to a patch where the undergrowth had been bent flat to the ground. We knew it was the wolf. No large land mammals had ever been reported on any of the islands and pets were not allowed. We found wolf feces in the area as well. Some of it looked several months old, while one sample looked less than a day old.

James had other commitments back in Victoria, so he hiked back to our landing spot, rowed back to the *Amanda Anne*, climbed aboard, and disappeared from sight. We thought I had a better chance of seeing or hearing the wolf alone. James promised to return the following afternoon.

I was left on the small island by myself, but judging from everything I had seen, Staqeya was there with me.

According to the *Times Colonist*, the wolf had mysteriously shown up on the island shortly before Songhees Chief Robert Sam passed away following a stroke. Conservation officers had intended to trap and relocate the animal on the provincial park side of

Discovery Island. This was the only area in the Chatham Islands that was not reserve land. Staqeya ignored the bait. The Songhees—who had not been consulted about the plan—insisted that the wolf be left alone. They issued statements saying that Staqeya's arrival was directly connected to Chief Robert Sam's passing. Like me, he had a kinship with wolves.

The idea defied contemporary conventional beliefs, but the explanations offered by various officials to news stations did as well. One conservation officer put forward the idea that the animal had swum from the Olympic Peninsula in Washington State, roughly forty kilometres (twenty-five miles) away—an impossible distance from a region that had not been habituated by wolves in over a hundred years. Another proposed that the wolf had wandered through the city of Victoria, and still another that it had hitched a ride on a logging barge. As the wolf had repeatedly demonstrated it feared humans to the point of avoiding food-laden traps, none of the theories seemed likely.

The Songhees' belief resonated with me. An island-hopping wolf in the vicinity of Victoria was unprecedented, and by all accounts, Chief Robert Sam was a great man. In a 2017 *Maclean's* story, Songhees Tourism Manager Mark Salter said, "there are [Songhees] members who find solace in the fact that he's returned in the spirit of the wolf to protect the island." To them, the wolf is significant.

I searched the shoreline for hours. There was sand in only a few places, and mud was scarce. Eventually, my persistence paid off. I found a single paw print clear enough to show up in a picture.

I headed back to my campsite and set up my summer tent. My supplies were limited because of weight. I was tired, and the

Staqeya mysteriously appeared near Victoria in 2012.
PHOTO BY CHERYL ALEXANDER, WILDAWAKE IMAGES. INSTAGRAM: @CHER_WILDAWAKE

temperature was dropping dramatically. Fires were not allowed on the islands.

I kept looking toward the bluff where James and I had found the impressions in the grass. I suddenly noticed what appeared to be a large white rock in the grass, where there hadn't been one a moment before. An eerie feeling overcame me. The shape was too big to be a bird. I began to wonder if I was mistaken, as it remained motionless. After about ten minutes, it quickly vanished. I had seen Staqeya. He had been watching me, and I had been watching him.

I cooked pasta on a small pocket stove as the day faded to night. There were low clouds instead of stars. The seals on the rocks began to speak like humans, frogs sang, and an owl called into the enfolding night. These were joined occasionally by the haunting howl of a lone wolf. I felt as if I had stepped into the otherworld.

I used my wetsuit as a mat to keep me off the ground inside my tent. I crawled into my sleeping bag still wearing long johns, socks, and a wool hoodie. I made an awkward pillow out of various items as the rain started to drum against the top of my tent. I drifted in and out of sleep and dreamt of wolves.

First Nations on Vancouver Island have many legends about wolves. In the time of myth, wolves, like all animals, had transformative powers allowing them to shapeshift from a human to an animal and back again. The Coast Salish, the Kwakwaka'wakw, and the Nuu-chah-nulth all have stories of wolves abducting humans and bringing them to the land of the wolves. Franz Boas recorded several of these in the late nineteenth century, which he published in *Indian Myths & Legends from the North Pacific Coast of America*. The abducted person was always treated well in this other realm, but would eventually be sent back to the human world with supernatural abilities after a certain period of time. In one Kwakwaka'wakw tale, this occurred after the man began to grow hair on his back where his wolf wife had often "held him in her embrace." He returned to the human world with a name the wolves had given him, meaning that he had become a part of their family, or pack if you will.

The wolf is associated with spirits of the dead particularly. Boas shared a K'omoks Coast Salish story, about a man who searched for the land of the wolves after they had abducted his daughter. To find them, he had to pass through a lake where "the dead dwelt" and ask them for directions. Upon entering the land of the wolves, the father discovered his daughter had already married the chief's son and had become one of them. He left for home after four days, satisfied that his daughter was happy. The man discovered upon his return that he was really gone for four years. Because of the marriage, he and his descendants had become relatives of the wolves. For a successful deer hunt, all they had to do was ask the spirits of the wolves to help them.

Boas shares a Nuu-chah-nulth story about wolves that has an even more direct connection to the land of the dead:

> Thereupon [the wolves] took him off the box and placed him beside the chief. Then the Wolves [sic] dragged in a dead person. They wrapped the corpse in a Wolf skin, laid it down by the fire and began singing, keeping time by beating on their sides and their haunches. Then the dead person rose and staggered around. But the longer they sang, the surer he stepped and finally he ran just like a Wolf. One of the Wolves gave him his cape and another one taught him to run. Then the chief said to [him], "Now you see what becomes of the dead. We make Wolves of them."

The wolves carried the man back to the human world, gifting him with a powerful arrow, which had the ability to both kill and raise people from the dead when it was pointed at them. The man was also given permission to use the wolf song and dance he had witnessed, and told to pass it on to his "daughters and their husbands, and all their descendants."

I woke from a fitful and dream-filled sleep. I made tea as the sun came out and started to warm me. It was a beautiful morning for February. I laid my gear out to dry, repeatedly looking toward the shoreline and bluff I had seen Staqeya on. I then packed my bags before setting off to finish exploring the island. Instead of the shore, this time I entered the thicker parts of the forest.

The woods were thick with shadows, with beams of light piercing the canopy overhead. Wolf scat, seal fur, and bird bones were abundant. There were scratch marks on the trail as well. Still aware that there were no pets or other animals on the island, I knew I was getting an education in spotting wolf signs in the wild. Everywhere I went, it felt as if I was being watched. I slowly made my way to an old abandoned lighthouse, then to the island's highest point, before making my way back to the campsite.

The time was approaching for James to pick me up. I began to tighten up my gear as I prepared to leave. As anticipated, the *Amanda Anne* came into view and James laid on the horn. I threw on my wetsuit, grabbed my bags, and headed into the water and onto my board.

I paddled to the boat and climbed aboard. I stared at the shoreline as we pulled away, hoping for another sighting. I could still feel Staqeya watching me. I did not want to leave. I had not been able to get a picture, but my experience had been profound. I found tracks, scat, trails, heard him howl multiple times, and even saw him in the distance. Four years after he was first spotted on the unlikely islands, the sacred wolf was still alive and well.

In the months that followed, ignoring Songhees and park official requests, several boaters brought dogs onto Discovery Island. They did so even though there were signs requesting that they stay off First Nations land, and others stating dogs were not allowed anywhere, including the park. The park had been officially closed after Staqeya reportedly demonstrated curiosity toward dogs, likely as a possible food source. As of 2017, the Conservation Officer Service is still assessing how dangerous Staqeya is and whether or not to reopen the park.

Cheryl Alexander continues to document Staqeya and take photos of him from the water. In the process, she has become the loudest non-Songhees ambassador for his protection. As for the Songhees, to them Staqeya is sacred. Not just because he is living in the most unlikely of places, but also because Chief Robert Sam has returned to them in the spirit of the wolf, to protect them and the islands he calls home.

The Victoria Golf Club and surrounding area.
PHOTO BY KEVIN OKE

The Apparition
of Spring

OAK BAY

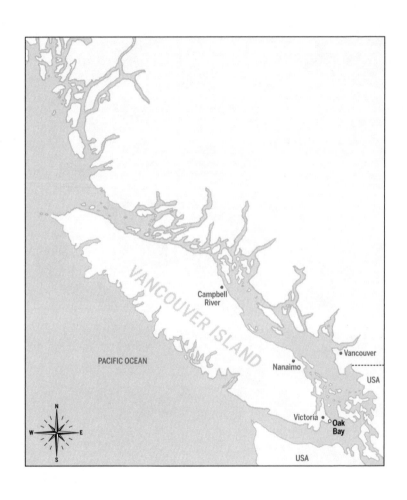

N EAR THE CHATHAM ISLANDS, THE *Amanda Anne* slowly passes Oak Bay's oceanfront golf course. The rocky cliff face marks the site of one of Canada's most documented hauntings. The apparition of the "April Bride" has been seen by countless people on or around the Victoria Golf Club's property.

In the summer of 1936, Doris Gravlin was the young single mother of a five-year-old boy. Doris and the boy's father, Victor Raymond Gravlin, married on March 8, 1929, but the couple had been separated for two years.

Victor had once worked as a sports writer for Victoria's *Daily Colonist*, but left for health reasons in 1934. Much later, writers Charles Lillard and Robin Skelton would assert that he was a "mean-spirited" drunk, and that the health claim allowed him to save face. Whatever really happened, Doris and Victor split up the same year. Doris took their then three-year-old son and moved in with her parents.

Despite the hardship, Victor and Doris were still in contact. Neither of them became involved with other people. Victor also lived with his parents. According to witnesses, his only ambition was to have Doris and his son back in his life. Some said he was willing to do anything to make this happen.

In *The April Ghost of the Victoria Golf Links*, Charles Lillard and Robin Skelton reported that: "According to gossip at the time, Victor, who had been winning his battle with the bottle, phoned

Doris and asked her to meet him." Some believed that they were going to get back together.

Doris was last seen wearing a knitted dress, a blue coat with silver buttons, a grey hat, and white kidskin shoes. The last thing the popular auburn-haired woman said to anyone was, "I'll be back in a while." It was already dark when she stepped out.

According to the *Daily Colonist*, just one hour later, residents near the golf course reported hearing a scream, "sometime after nine o'clock."

Lillard and Skelton claimed that the couple would often walk through Oak Bay's majestic golf course, sometimes taking a more scenic route along the ridge overlooking the ocean. On Sundays, they would first go for tea at the Oak Bay Beach Hotel located on the other side of the course before making their way back.

Walking out to Gonzales Point was an indirect, though more romantic, route to their destination. The water-and-mountain view was—and still is—especially stunning. In 1936, with less light pollution than today, the stars would have been clear and bright. At night, the grounds were peacefully removed from the lights and sounds of the city.

Tuesday, September 22, was the last time anyone saw either of them alive. This was the night of the autumn equinox, a detail I have never heard mentioned. It is a sacred time for some, going back to ancient Rome and the cult of the wood goddess Pomona. Nowadays, neopagans celebrate the equinox as a festival of thanksgiving, claiming their traditions can be traced back to antiquity. In an unknowable world of spirits, this date might be more important than one might think. Not every murder becomes a ghost story.

Doris' body was found the following Sunday near the seventh hole of the course. Clearly, she had been murdered. Foliage had been used to cover the young mother's body. Coroners later concluded that she had been strangled. There were marks on her throat and across her body. Her hat and coat were missing, and so were her shoes. Victor was nowhere to be found. For reasons no longer known, Doris Gravlin's body was sent to Seattle to be cremated.

A month later, Victor was found tangled in some seaweed just off shore, near to where Doris' body had been found, but closer to the ninth hole. Doris' missing kidskin shoes were found inside Victor's pocket. Her coat and hat were never recovered.

No one knows what really happened, but the deaths were ruled a murder-suicide. It should have been a closed case, but the Victoria Golf Club, and Gonzales Point in particular, would forevermore be synonymous with murder—and soon with ghosts as well.

The first sightings are said to have occurred shortly after, but the earliest account on record took place sometime before April of 1964, when it appeared in the *Daily Colonist*. A lone fisherman was casting from a boat near shore as the sun was setting. An inexplicable feeling of "not being alone" suddenly came over him. The man turned toward shore to see a woman in "old-fashioned" clothing standing on the ridge above him. Immediately, he sensed something wasn't right.

The woman was close, but she did not make eye contact. He would later say that he wondered why she looked so sad. She stared straight out to sea as if he wasn't there.

Suddenly, the woman began to make her way down the ridge toward the water. She moved quickly in his direction, but as she neared the beach, she disappeared. The fisherman claimed he saw her "melt away."

According to *The April Ghost of the Victoria Golf Links*, the same woman has been seen walking across the golf course as well. In some cases, where people reported feeling strange sensations, she would look toward them and make eye contact. What struck people as strange was the woman's old-fashioned attire at the affluent golf course.

The spirit believed to be Doris Gravlin does not interact with people during the day. Her appearance at night, however, is quite different.

In the dark, the apparition has been reported in a white wedding dress, or as a source of light. She has been known to torment people, intentionally scaring them or chasing them away. Local folklore even goes so far as to claim that Doris Gravlin hates seeing couples together, and those that see her are cursed never to marry.

A young man and woman reported spotting her one night in the mid-1960s. The teenagers had trespassed onto the golf course as a dare, as they'd both heard stories of the ghost.

The couple had only walked a short distance before stopping dead in their tracks. A figure they believed to be Doris Gravlin appeared in front of them. She wore a dress, but her form was an illuminated grey colour.

She travelled with otherworldly grace. Her bare feet skated across the grass and over the rocky ledge without touching it. "She moved with much more ease than a human," they were quoted as saying in the *The April Ghost of the Victoria Golf Links*.

Missing Since Tuesday

Victor Gravlin and his wife, Doris Gravlin, missing from their respective homes since last Tuesday, are being sought throughout Greater Victoria. Mr. Gravlin is described as being in his middle-thirties, about five feet eleven inches tall, weight about 135 pounds, medium build and of a nervous temperament. Mrs. Gravlin is thirty years of age, five feet six inches tall, weighing 130 pounds, with auburn hair, and large brown eyes. Last Tuesday she was wearing a knitted dress, blue coat with silver buttons, and a grey hat.

A 1936 *Daily Colonist* article reporting Doris & Victor Gravlin missing.

The couple watched in disbelief as she headed toward Gonzales Point. They hadn't thought they would actually see the apparition. Frozen in place, they watched the woman as she stood looking out toward the sea. Eventually, they left in fear, but only after watching her for several minutes.

In the late 1960s, a larger group of teenagers snuck onto the course in the hopes of finding the lady. One of the girls later said an icy chill suddenly shrouded her as her surroundings became eerily silent. In front of her, the form of a semi-transparent woman appeared. She estimated that the woman stood less than five feet tall.

No one but her had seen the apparition, but it was enough to convince the others to return a second night. This time, they all saw her: "At first I thought I could see right through her, but after staring for a while I realized she was opaque," claimed one of the witnesses in *The April Ghost of the Victoria Golf Links*. Another said that the features were hard to make out, but that it was definitely a woman.

After viewing her for about five minutes, some of the teenagers started to get brave. They approached the woman, but she disappeared. When they turned around to leave, she suddenly reappeared behind them. The group fled in fear, later reporting the incident to Victoria's *Daily Colonist*.

According to the paper, another group of friends had a similar experience. One man became frightened of the apparition and tried to run away. Whatever direction he turned, however, the apparition was blocking his escape. He would later say, "Her whole body was shadowy at the edges . . . She looked sad—my God how sad she looked!" The other witnesses watched in helplessness as the man tried to flee, but the woman kept disappearing and reappearing in front of him. Suddenly, she was gone.

"A human being cannot appear and disappear in different places in the twinkling of an eye!" The same witness said. "I know what I saw! I saw the ghost of the murdered girl!"

In the 1970s, two *Victoria Daily Times* reporters decided to seek out the apparition themselves. Neither of them expected to encounter anything. After a short stakeout, one of the men saw a swirling white mass close to the beach. They both tried to look at it through binoculars, but the form melted away. Just as quickly, they were embraced with a merciless chill that froze them to the bone. One of them claimed to see a light resembling a "shooting star." Interestingly, others had reported seeing a ball of light as well.

In many cases, witnesses hadn't even stepped onto the golf course when they saw the ghost. To a couple walking along Beach Drive, the apparition appeared as a beam of light. To the woman, it looked like a glowing female in a white sheet. The entity was so bright that the couple could see it "a hundred yards" off the side of the road, down close to the water. They later agreed that the presence radiated an eeriness that unsettled them both, but the man tried to downplay the incident, saying that it must have been lights from a building on the golf course. As they walked away, they kept looking back to see if it was still there. It was.

The man and woman quickly shared the story with friends, who in turn told them of the golf course's ghost story. In a state of partial disbelief, the young man returned to the course the next day, only to confirm that there'd never been a building at the spot where they'd seen the light. Neither of them had previous knowledge about the haunting.

A story recounted in several books, including *The April Ghost of the Victoria Golf Links*, is even more unnerving.

Two men drove along the lonely road toward Oak Bay Beach Hotel. As they pulled up to the first crosswalk, the driver noticed there was a young woman in a white dress standing at the side of the road. She was fixed in place with her head down. Long dark hair covered her face. The driver stopped the car to let her cross. After an uncomfortable pause, she delicately made her way across the road and stepped into the darkness of the golf course. The men later agreed that the incident was strange. The driver pulled ahead and continued to drive. They had stopped talking.

It was a short distance to the next crosswalk, where the tenth and eleventh holes intersected. The man slowed to a stop. There, standing on the side of the road, was the same barefoot woman in a white dress. She stood stoically in place, but her eyes seemed to be fixed on the golf course across the road. The driver stopped once more to let her cross. The men began to feel a deep sense of terror, as the woman in white moved across the road—unnatural and graceful at the same time. They sat open-mouthed for a long moment, before quickly accelerating away.

As they came to a third intersection, closer to the hotel, the men were horrified to see the same woman standing at the side of the road, waiting for the car to stop so she could cross. "For god's sake, don't stop!" the passenger yelled. The driver sped through the intersection without stopping. Neither man spoke about the incident for "some time" afterward.

By the mid-1970s, the ghost had garnered many different names: the April Ghost (due to several springtime encounters), the Watcher, the Oak Bay Ghost, and the Ghost of Golf Course Point.

The story had become so popular that Jean Kozocari—a mediumistic witch who would later write *A Gathering of Ghosts* with Robin Skelton—decided to investigate the haunting with a number of her associates.

The first night the group staked-out the golf course, three of them said they saw a white figure gliding over the grass. They described the illuminating person as moving in a "smooth, yet not jerky," way. A moment later, they began to second-guess themselves as the apparition had vanished.

The group returned on another evening. It was a warm, windless summer night. An unusual cold wind suddenly howled and tugged at them as soon as they got out of their vehicles. A pressing, terrifying, supernatural energy whipped up against them; one woman began to scream. They joined hands and formed a circle, chanting blessings into the night. During "the attack" at least forty cars drove by the rattled investigators. Three of the vehicles' headlights had illuminated an unnatural figure running through the grass. It later confused them why the other headlights had not.

The ritual had shaken most of the group, so they retreated to the cars. Kozocari said she felt one of her investigators grab onto her hand. She later remembered thinking that whoever it was must have been terrified, as the hand was cold as ice. Almost as soon as she had this thought, she noticed that all of the group was hurrying to the cars ahead of her and that she'd fallen behind. As she realized this the hand faded away.

During the 1980s, Brigid Skelton (daughter of writer Robin Skelton) and a group of teenagers shakily reported seeing Doris Gravlin as well. Later, several University of Victoria students also reported seeing her. Two more people in a car saw her along the same stretch of road. These sightings were recounted in the *Times Colonist* and *The April Ghost of the Victoria Golf Links*.

According to Robert Belyk in *Ghosts: True Tales of Eerie Encounters*, one of the most amazing accounts took place in 1998. During the month of October, the Old Cemeteries Society of Victoria had been giving Halloween ghost tours. A bus drove groups of tourists around Victoria, showing them some of the city's sites that are reputed to be haunted. One of the stops, of course, was Victoria's Golf Club—the April Ghost had become more popular than ever. Tour guide John Adams stood with his back to the course as he told the group the story of the haunting. Faces dropped; eyes went wide. People started to shift from side to side nervously.

Adams finished telling the tale. He later told Belyk he was disappointed the group had appeared distracted while he was speaking. Baffled, he told them to head back to the bus. No one moved.

"We saw her!" one of the tourists said. "We saw the ghost!"

The group told Adams that a woman in a white dress had been gliding through the shrubs behind him. They described her as "shimmering." Some of them were sure the sighting was a hoax set up by the Old Cemeteries Society. Adams convinced them this hadn't been the case.

Adams told Belyk that he had added the account to other reports he'd been documenting. The April Ghost had become interesting to him as more and more people said they had seen her. Eventually, he started a company called Ghostly Walks, which offers tours of haunted sites downtown. He also began to promote ghost tourism throughout Victoria.

Not as many people see the apparition anymore, but the sightings haven't stopped completely. A young woman left a comment on my blog about a woman in white she had seen on Beach Drive near McNeill Bay. The woman was dripping with water, so the witness thought she was the ghost of a lady who had drowned. She suddenly disappeared when another car drove by. The commenter said she "looked sad and maybe lonely." As the sighting was not on the golf course, some would question whether or not it is the same spirit or another one. I think it is close enough that it is unlikely it would be a different apparition, but this is speculation.

Many people have claimed to see the April Bride, but even so, there are questions that remain unanswered. If these are sightings of a restless spirit—as so many people believe—then why does she wear a white wedding dress at night and an old-fashioned suit during the day? Is she Doris Gravlin? The details seem to indicate she could be. If she is, why does she stare out to where Victor's body was found? Witnesses have said she looks like she is waiting for someone and appears sad. Has she forgiven him? One theory is that Victor wasn't the killer. If this is true, maybe she is upset the man she loved was blamed for her death? Either way, if this is Doris Gravlin, her heart must have been broken when she was killed.

The phantom is able to interact with people, move from place to place, and can alter her appearance. Because there are so many claims, the Apparition of Spring is Victoria's most famous ghost. There's even an urban legend about her. As seen in 2003 on the once-popular TV show *Creepy Canada*, some believe she can be summoned, but for what purpose remains unclear. If a person is brave enough to go to the seventh tee at night, the apparition will appear. All that brave soul needs to do is ring the bell, and wait.

The Honourable John Tod, born in 1794 in Scotland.
IMAGE C-08882, COURTESY OF THE ROYAL BC MUSEUM AND ARCHIVES

THE WOMAN IN CHAINS

OAK BAY

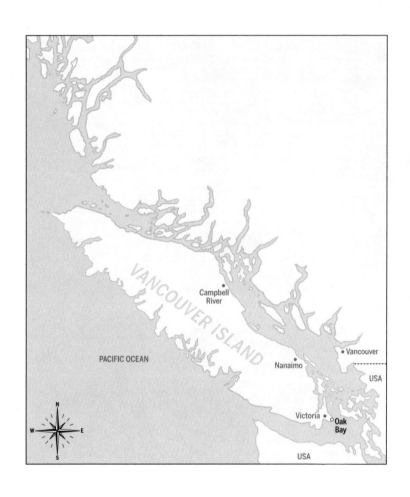

FORT VICTORIA WAS BUILT IN 1843, on the southernmost tip of Vancouver Island. The island was a rough place at the time, inhabited by colonizers, fortune seekers, and First Nations people.

When the fort was first founded, officials declared that it would serve more than just one purpose: borders were still in flux following America's independence from the British Empire, so its placement was primarily strategic. The fort's presence would declare to foreigners and to native-born alike that Vancouver Island belonged to the British Empire. The Hudson's Bay Company (HBC) would spearhead the project. It had been granted the rights to Vancouver Island's resources for ten years, with the explicit condition that it helped Britain colonize it. For this purpose, the fort would also establish a permanent harbour for resource exploration and serve as a company trading post to resupply inland outposts as well.

According to the online *Dictionary of Canadian Biography*, John Tod was a fur trader for most of his life. Born in Scotland, he immigrated to Canada in 1811 as an employee of the HBC. At fifty-six, he came to Vancouver Island looking for a place to settle. Most of the early homesteaders on Vancouver Island were Hudson's Bay Company men who had been rewarded with land for their services.

Tod had been married more than once before he settled in Victoria and already had several children. He arrived at Fort Victoria with Sophia Lolo—a woman of mixed First Nations ancestry—who

Fort Victoria in 1843. Model on display at the Royal BC Museum.
PHOTO BY SHANON SINN

is believed to have given him seven more children. They were not formally married until 1863 after one of Tod's former wives passed away.

Tod's was a large rural parcel he intended to use for farming until he retired. As this was long before Oak Bay became a part of the Greater Victoria area, his land was over a hundred acres and reached out toward the rocky shoreline. When the Tod House was first built in 1850, there were only a few hundred white settlers in the Victoria area, some coal miners at the north end of the island at Fort Rupert, and a handful of settlers elsewhere.

The house—now the oldest standing home in British Columbia—was built facing the Chatham Islands. Coincidentally, it's close to Victoria's Golf Club as well.

Upon his arrival, Tod was nominated as one of Vancouver Island's first legislative council members, a position he held for several years.

The *Dictionary of Canadian Biography* records indicate that he was well read and musical, but also that others considered him "vulgar" and "not generally liked." During the period before his death in 1882, Tod was openly involved with the spiritualist movement—a practice that allowed communion with the dead. He was known to have participated in séances.

Reports of the Tod House being haunted begin as early as the 1920s. The one-storey structure is now unassuming compared to many of Victoria's large older homes, but its reputation brought it renown throughout the province. By the late 1940s, so many people had witnessed activity in the building that several newspapers reported it, and the CBC aired a story.

In 1949, the *Daily Colonist* reported unexplained activity, such as cabinets opening on their own, objects moving, and a biscuit barrel suspended on a hook that would sometimes "swing" for hours. During one Christmas season, all of the decorative holly on the walls was taken down and thrown into the middle of the room. The cellar door was also seen opening by itself by several witnesses.

In *Ghosts: True Tales of Eerie Encounters* Robert Belyk said that one owner of the home—Mrs. Turner—would later claim she would wake up in the middle of the night with a feeling that someone was in the room with her. Additionally, her cat would sometimes hiss, growl, and arch its back for no reason. Mrs. Turner often felt as if someone was walking behind her. She would later say that neither she nor her daughter would spend the night in the master bedroom alone as it gave them an unsettled feeling.

The *Daily Colonist* reported that Lieutenant-Colonel T.C. Evans and his wife purchased the home in the 1940s. Mr. Evans told the paper that he was "never much disturbed by the manifestations."

As Belyk tells the story, Mr. Evans was a retired colonel. During the war the couple had gotten into the habit of inviting serving military personnel to stay during their weekend leaves. Mrs. Evans put two of the men into the old master bedroom for the night. In the morning the room was empty. The men had fled.

When the servicemen returned, they spoke of a horrific night. Most startling of all, one of the men claimed to have seen an apparition in detail.

The man awoke with an ominous feeling. There was a sense that he was not alone. He remembered having heard the sound of rattling chains. Half asleep, the guest peered into the darkness of the master bedchamber.

Hard eyes glared from out of the inky blackness. Accusing. Unblinking. A bedraggled woman stood in the shadows. Tangled hair twisted across her face and down her shoulders. Her arms slowly stretched toward him with curling grasping fingers that danced in unison. There were iron bands around her wrists and ankles.

He watched wide-eyed from his bed, completely paralyzed and unable to move.

The figure appeared to be First Nations. Her eyes were sad and pleading. Long black hair framed her face like a cape of darkness. She reached for him. Closer. Her mouth forming words he could not hear.

Then, she was gone.

When the guest grabbed his belongings and fled, the other man, just as terrified, followed behind. It is not known if he saw the apparition as well.

According to Belyk's account, Mr. Evans hired contractors in 1947 to help him with some much-needed renovations. One of the projects was the addition of a furnace near the front of the house. While digging a deep pit for the equipment, the contractors unexpectedly came across the corpse of a woman in chains. She was believed to have been one of John Tod's wives.

The *Daily Colonist* reported that an anatomist was called in who said the body had been soaked in lime. Most terrible of all, the woman's head was completely missing. It was determined that the body was likely an Asian woman, though it was difficult to say for sure. Her bones were so badly decomposed that they crumbled when they were touched. *Daily Colonist* stories to follow claimed the activity in the house ceased with the removal of the body.

Promoting Victoria as a haunted city, some modern versions of the story have claimed that the haunting activity actually increased. This is not true. In 1949, Mr. and Mrs. Evans told the *Daily Colonist* that the activity ceased when the body was taken away. The reporter said he had the impression they missed the ghost. When asked if she had ever been afraid, Mrs. Evans told him that she was, "always more frightened of newspapermen and researchers than of manifestations from the spirit world."

Pioneer Square in Victoria, formerly the Quadra Street Cemetery.
PHOTO BY SHANON SINN

VICTORIA'S
GRAVEYARDS

VICTORIA

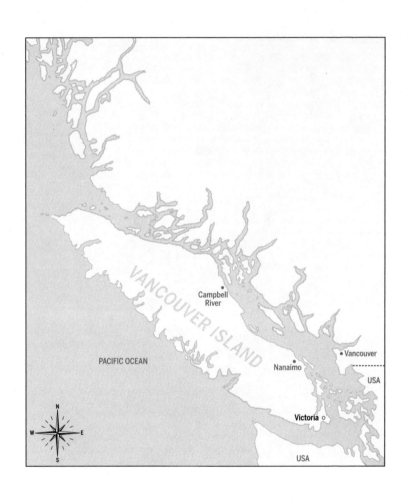

PACIFIC OCEAN

VANCOUVER ISLAND

Campbell
River

Nanaimo

Vancouver

USA

Victoria

USA

N
W—E
S

FORT VICTORIA'S FIRST GRAVEYARD HAD been small. It quickly filled up and was abandoned for a larger burial area in 1855 known as the Quadra Street Burial Ground or Cemetery. Shortly after the Quadra Street Cemetery opened, the fort's graves were dug up and moved to the new site by a prisoner chain gang. British Columbia's gold boom in 1858 changed everything. Over the span of a few weeks, Victoria's population went from a few hundred people to well over five thousand. With over a thousand people interred at the Quadra Street Burial Ground by 1873, an additional location was established: the Ross Bay Cemetery.

Unlike the original cemetery grounds, the Quadra Street Burial Ground—now called Pioneer Square Park—and the Ross Bay Cemetery are both reputed to have resident spirits. The tales of the two ghosts said to haunt Pioneer Square have been distorted by time, though both are rooted in truth. The stories involving the more recently used Ross Bay Cemetery are far less evolved.

The "White Lady," as she was called in her early days, was seen near the Quadra Street Cemetery as far back as December of 1861. The *British Colonist* reported sightings of her by at least three different witnesses, one who said he'd seen her on two separate occasions.

The ghost of the young woman was dressed entirely in white. She was plain looking, with hair that hung loosely about her shoulders. She didn't walk across the path in front of them, they said, but glided as if her feet could not touch the ground. As suddenly as the woman appeared, she faded into nothingness. In one moment she was there, and in the next she was gone.

The reporter who wrote the story was not convinced there had been a ghost, but he acknowledged that one of the witnesses was so frightened by the incident his teeth chattered while he recounted it.

In *Favourite Stories from Lantern Tours in the Old Burying Ground*, the Old Cemeteries Society of Victoria said the spirit was identified as Adelaide Griffin, wife of Benjamin Griffin. They also claimed that she began to be seen around the Quadra Street Burial Ground around this time as well.

Following their arrival from San Francisco during the gold boom, the Griffins opened the Boomerang Inn, one of Victoria's earliest drinking establishments. Unfortunately, Adelaide died a few years later on July 25, 1861. The *British Colonist* stated that she'd been thirty-one years old at the time (though some records, such as the *Find a Grave* website, indicate she may have been thirty-five). Following her death, Ben—as he's often called—began to practice spiritualism: he participated in séances and is believed to have tried to contact her.

The Old Cemetery Society of Victoria says the spirit was sometimes called "the White Lady of Langley Street," because that was where she had been seen. The narrator on *Creepy Canada* claimed that Adelaide still haunts Pioneer Square Park and that she's even been photographed.

The second spirit said to haunt Pioneer Park was recognized immediately, as he was first seen at his former home—near the graveyard—on Meares Street. Richard H. Johnson had often challenged politicians, military leaders, and the people of Victoria alike.

His spirit would have been easily recognizable as he was of African descent. He had also been a captain of the Victoria Volunteer Rifles and was a well-known proponent of race equality.

The original sighting of him was covered in the October 21, 1871, edition of the *British Colonist*. The new owners of Johnson's old home had just taken possession when the incident took place.

After Johnson's death, the house had been rented out until it sold. It's important to mention that the people who lived there during the rental period said that they had no experiences at all. One of the men interested in buying the property claimed, however, that he had experienced such a chill looking at the home that he made up his mind not to buy it. Neighbours added they had heard someone walking on the veranda when no one was in the house.

Mr. Deas, who the *British Colonist* identified as the purchaser of the house, claimed he saw what appeared to be a crackling fire that arched and sent off unexplainable sparks across the room. Deas said that he then saw an apparition he knew to be Johnson. The look on the spirit's face conveyed "great sadness."

A young female servant gave the most frightening account of all. She said that she had seen a "black" man's face hovering outside of her window. The scared girl managed to throw a blanket over the windowpane, but the face passed through the material unabated and continued to stare at her as she shivered on her bed in fear.

The stories spread like wildfire. Two days later, the *British Colonist* tried to dismiss the original account by saying it was just a case of mistaken identity, that it was an African-descended man holding a lantern outside of the window. Clearly, the new owners were not enjoying the attention and wanted to recant their accounts. Few people bought their sudden change of heart, however, as it was easy to see the shift for what it was. Instead, like many other ghost stories, the tale began to take on a life of its own. As Johnson was buried near the home in the Quadra Street Burial Ground, a story emerged that he had been seen there as well.

Sadly, the story has been twisted in recent years to say that Johnson had committed suicide by cutting his own throat with a straight razor. At a time when crime was rampant in Victoria (Johnson had already been robbed at least once in that home), such a death would be covered in the paper and would have aroused suspicion. Suggesting Johnson took his life because the "all black" Victoria Rifle Pioneer Corps (VPRC) he served with disbanded in 1865 lacks merit as well.

Johnson had been a captain in the VPRC, composed entirely of freed African American men, in 1861. The unit had often been publicly treated poorly by some of Victoria's haughty citizens. Records indicate that Johnson was a brilliant man with a lion-hearted spirit. His letter to the editor of the *British Colonist* following the racial disgrace of his men is semi-legendary to some civil rights historians. So too, is the impeccable dress and drill of his troops, as is the speech he gave to governors James Douglas and Arthur Kennedy, in the face of those same racial discriminations. This story is well told by Peggy Cartwright in *Black Pioneers in Gold Rush Days*. Like the rest of his men, Johnson had lived through much harder times as a slave. He was an intelligent, articulate, natural leader who always led by example.

The *British Colonist* never mentioned a suicide; the Christ Church on Pandora Street performed the funeral rites without hesitation. The final hole in the suicide story is the fact that Johnson didn't die until 1870, five years after the Rifles are recorded as disbanding. And for those who would later say that Johnson killed himself in the house, there's another contradiction as well: the former captain wasn't even living in the house when he died, but passed away in the rural location of Metchosin outside of Victoria.

Be that as it may, recent stories say that Johnson's apparition appeared to the new occupants of his former home while simultaneously drawing his thumb across his throat, re-enacting—or attempted to communicate the cause of—his untimely death. It has even been said that Johnson repeated this same gesture when he appeared to people in the graveyard.

In December of 2003 an episode of *Creepy Canada* aired that propelled the Quadra Street Cemetery story to a whole new level. At least three people on three separate occasions, the narrator claimed, had seen the ghosts of Adelaide Gordon Griffin and Richard "Soap and Water" Johnson together in the graveyard at the same time. What was even more spectacular was the fact that they had appeared during full daylight. Johnson, the narrator concluded, always ran his thumb over his throat just to let people know that he had killed himself. Meanwhile, Adelaide would suddenly appear to stare intently at those same people until they fled in fear.

Truthfully, both of the apparitions only appeared at night. Adelaide was never said to have interacted with anyone, and Johnson may have only been seen for the year or so following his death. While the evolution of a ghost story can tell us a lot about the nature of these types of tales, it detracts from the original account, and in the case of Johnson, can defame the character of a person who might otherwise have been remembered for living an exemplary life.

While the Quadra Street Pioneer Cemetery has made online lists as one of the "most haunted" cemeteries in the world, the Ross Bay Cemetery has received a lot less publicity. The grounds are believed by many to be haunted as well, but the stories are less evolved, which, as noted, might not be a bad thing.

The oceanside graveyard is elegantly laid out, established, and historic. The south side is nestled up against a picturesque view of the mountains and sea. Deer graze beneath cemetery markers and old gnarled trees. The sea air instils a deep sense of peace.

The primary spirit believed to haunt the Ross Bay Cemetery is Isabella Ross herself, the fascinating woman that the grounds are named after.

Isabella was a French-Ojibwa woman from Ontario. She had come to Fort Victoria with her husband Charles and several children in 1843. Charles worked for the HBC and had been tasked with the construction of the fort. Unfortunately, Charles died in 1844. He was buried in the fort's graveyard and then moved to the Quadra Street Cemetery by the chain gang. After his death, Isabella took the children and ran a farm in what is now the state of Washington. She later returned to Victoria around 1853, buying ninety-nine acres of land around what would become Ross Bay.

The new farm was difficult to maintain, so Isabella sold portions of the land in the decades that followed. One of these parcels would be bought by the city of Victoria in around 1872 for use as a cemetery. Other portions of Isabella's original parcel also became part of the graveyard over time.

Isabella died in 1885, in the care of the Sisters of St. Ann, and was buried in what was originally an unmarked grave.

Times Colonist reporter Richard Watts shared an interesting story about Isabella. The 2013 article said that raiding First Nation warriors attacked Isabella's family when they were on the mainland, likely looking for easy spoils. Isabella picked up "a pike" and fought off the attackers in order to protect her children. Quoting Isabella's great-great granddaughter, Old Cemetery Society historian Fern Perkins, the article went on to say that Isabella impressed her attackers. They said that white men must be strong to be able to "keep" such a woman.

The story of Isabella's apparition is incredibly vague. Like many other coastal spirits, she is usually said to stand near the shore and stare out over the water. The sightings seem to indicate that she's an older woman dressed entirely in black. A surviving photograph of her in the BC Archives collection might explain this image—actual or imagined. In the 1860s picture, Isabella is dressed as a woman in mourning. It was common for a woman to dress as a widow for the rest of her life at the time, especially if she never remarried. Seeing her dressed in black is an interesting piece of lore, as apparitions in dark clothing are usually not seen as good, while Isabella is someone who is both loved and admired.

An old-style wooden marker, a recreation of the original, was placed in 2015. It says that Isabella died on April 23, 1885. It mentions that she was British Columbia's first woman landowner, but not that she had Ojibwa ancestry.

People have claimed to see other apparitions in the Ross Bay Cemetery, including an unidentified older couple, some children, and a lady who is said to be looking for her lost child. David Fee, a man who was gunned down on Christmas Eve outside of St. Andrew's Cathedral in 1890 is also said to haunt the grounds. Emily Carr, however, is Vancouver Island's celebrity ghost. The revered British Columbia artist lived from 1871 to 1945.

Carr's grave is somewhat of a shrine, as she's become a role model to many artists—especially women—for breaking traditional societal expectations of females. Notably, Carr's art and writing often included First Nations content. Her marker reads:

> Dear Mother Earth!
> I believe I have always specially belonged to you. I have loved from babyhood to roll upon you, to lie with my face pressed right down on to you in my sorrows. I love the look of you and the smell of you and the feel of you. When I die I should like to be in you uncoffined, unshrouded, the petals of flowers against my flesh and you covering me up.
>
> Emily Carr

There are always gifts of flowers, flower petals, pinecones, and even art supplies left by admirers around the gravesite.

The story of Carr's apparition in the cemetery is vague. Her ghost, however, has also been reported at several other locations around Victoria. Emily Carr House where she grew up is believed to be haunted—some say by the spirit of her mother. Staff members at the James Bay Inn have claimed to see her apparition on their premises as well. Nuns had cared for Carr at the inn when

Emily Carr in her studio, 1936.
IMAGE D-06009, COURTESY OF THE ROYAL BC MUSEUM AND ARCHIVES

it was briefly a care home during her last few years. The staff has stated that she is responsible for poltergeist activity in the bar and throughout the building. People who have witnessed Carr's apparition claim to recognize her from images they have already seen.

Emily Carr's epitaph at the Ross Bay Cemetery.
PHOTO BY SHANON SINN

The most unusual tale involving Carr's spirit took place at St. Ann's Academy during the 1990s. It was reported in the *Times Colonist* and other publications, such as *Historic Haunted America* by Michael Norman and Beth Scott.

A heated debate had arisen about what should be done with the old academy. Some people thought it should be destroyed, while others said that it should be saved. Somehow, Carr's name was brought into the discussion. While she was alive, some said, she enjoyed drawing the academy's buildings. Others claimed she had liked to visit the nuns who resided there.

One dusk, a white dove landed atop the golden cross adorning the tower. Carr appeared at the same time. She stood saint-like in the tower surrounded by light, as the ghost of a pet monkey she had in life simultaneously stroked the side of her face. The impression of the Catholic artist who had seen her was clear: Carr was so upset the building's fate was in turmoil that she had returned to make things right. After a few moments, the image dissipated.

As strange as the story sounds, James Fry, a TV producer, claimed to have also seen her in an upper-floor window during a separate incident. In an effort to get the full story, the producer apparently tried to get an interview with the ghost. Surprisingly, she did not cooperate.

Fortunately, the property was saved in 1997 and underwent a $16-million restoration. Though Emily Carr's connection to the property is speculative at best, there are still stories of her ghost wandering the grounds of St. Ann's Academy to this day.

Bishop Charles John Seghers.
IMAGE A-01767, COURTESY OF THE ROYAL BC MUSEUM AND ARCHIVES

THE SKULL-FACED BISHOP

VICTORIA

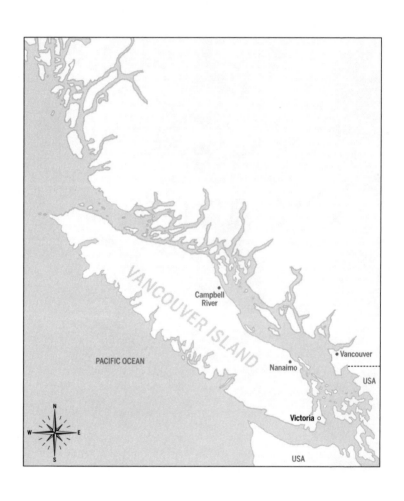

WAVES OF PEOPLE ARRIVED IN Victoria during the gold rush of 1858, numbering in the tens of thousands: Americans, Australians, Polish Jews, Italians, Chinese, Eastern Canadians, Britons, Hawaiians (Kanaka), and others. Many of the people were only passing through, but thousands of opportunists following the prospectors stayed at the fort, turning Victoria into a city overnight. Drinking establishments and brothels sprang up everywhere. A jail soon followed. Then came the places of worship.

The Quadra Street Cemetery was located beside a small church. Most of Victoria's first prayer houses were little more than temporary gathering places. Grander buildings followed in the decades to come. The still-standing synagogue on Pandora Street was built in 1863, making it the oldest in Canada. The Presbyterians also had a congregation as early as 1866, but didn't complete the still-used St. Andrew's Presbyterian Church until 1889. The Anglican Church of Our Lord was built in 1876 and is still used today. Chinatown's first Tam Kung Temple was built that same year. Many more churches would be constructed in the 1890s, including the Catholic's new St. Andrew's Cathedral (not to be confused with the similarly named Presbyterian church).

St. Andrew's Cathedral was believed to be haunted as early as 1890. Construction had only just begun on the new cathedral, when a lone gunman shot and killed an innocent man—David Fee—as Christmas Eve Mass was letting out. According to court records, during the subsequent trial, the defendant's lawyer argued that his client had mistaken David Fee for "a ghost." The site was believed to be haunted by the murdered bishop buried there.

Charles John Seghers: Priest and Bishop in the Pacific Northwest 1839-1886: A Biography by Gerard G. Steckler provides a well-researched overview of the bishop's life and death. Born in Belgium in 1839, Charles Seghers attended a college that was founded to provide America with English-speaking clergymen. He responded to an appeal for the colony of Vancouver Island, arriving in Victoria in 1863. By 1873 he was named Bishop of Vancouver Island.

In 1886, Seghers decided to go on a mission to the remote regions of Alaska, "spreading [the] Divine Saviour's gospel among the heathen." He brought with him two other priests, an Irish assistant, and a French-Canadian labourer. The goal was to travel overland from the Yukon River in order to reach a particularly remote village before the Protestants did. The trek would be a vigorous November journey through harsh weather and over rough terrain. Used to hardship, the priests led by Bishop Seghers embraced the assignment as a matter of faith and duty. They set sail, landed in Alaska, and then started their overland journey almost immediately.

It wasn't long before Francis Fuller—the Irishman—began to demonstrate symptoms of "insanity." By today's standards, Fuller would have likely been diagnosed with paranoid schizophrenia. He heard voices, for example, saying that his travel companions were part of a conspiracy to kill him. When the French labourer disappeared, the priests believed that he had simply become tired of Fuller's increasing instability. In later years, reporters would speculate that he might have been Fuller's first victim.

Bishop Seghers believed he could control Fuller, despite the concerns of the other priests. Frustrated with the situation, the bishop sent the priests on a side mission while he and Fuller carried on with three First Nation guides. One of the guides left the party at a trading station. The remaining members continued on their way. Fuller began to act more and more erratic.

On the morning of November 28, 1886, Fuller shot Bishop Seghers through the heart as he leaned over to gather his gear. The man died instantly in front of the two horrified guides. Fuller immediately began to act even more bizarre, shaking one of the guide's hands while expressing to them that "the man" needed to be killed. The guides wrapped up the body and left to get help with Fuller accompanying them willingly.

The party reached the village that day. No one knew what to do with Fuller. He wasn't immediately incarcerated, but was instead sent to another village for the winter, away from two local white women who had expressed "terror" at being in his presence. Fuller continued to act strangely over the duration of the winter, apparently changing his story as to what had happened several times.

It wasn't until spring that the other priests learned of the bishop's death. By the time the body was recovered from the site of the murder, his face had been partially eaten by mice. Bishop Seghers' body was moved to the cemetery at St. Michael in Alaska and finally buried in July of 1887.

The trial against Fuller was disappointing, at least for those who'd revered the bishop. Unable to decide if Fuller should be hanged for first-degree murder, or if he was "not guilty" due to reasons of "insanity," the jury instead chose a compromise: Fuller was convicted of manslaughter, sentenced to ten years of hard labour, and fined one thousand dollars. People were outraged. They thought that the man was either guilty or he wasn't. Fuller had admitted to killing the bishop; his reasons for the act changed with each telling, but never his admission of guilt.

In 1888, the Catholic Church had the body of Bishop Seghers exhumed and brought home to Victoria. He was placed in an ebony casket with silver mountings and brought to St. Andrew's Cathedral. The *British Colonist* reported that Victoria gave the body a hero's welcome, and people lined the streets. Even the Navy participated in the ceremony.

There were rumours that Bishop Seghers had been shot through the head, so the casket was opened in private. The cause of death was confirmed as a bullet wound. At the time, the attending priests recorded that the body was in a state of decay, but also that the bishop was still easily recognizable. Bishop Seghers was then placed in a crypt alongside another bishop and a priest who had been appointed a bishop, but who had died before being consecrated.

The silver plate on Bishop Seghers' ebony coffin read: "Most Rev. Charles John Seghers. Died Nov. 28th, 1886: aged 47 years. R.I.P." He was finally buried in Victoria on November 16, 1888, at St. Andrew's Cathedral.

The first cathedral had been built in 1884, but a Gothic revival replacement was being constructed in 1890. Court records in the David Fee murder case indicate that the construction site needed to hire night watchmen because someone—or something—was playing "pranks" on the men at the location. It's uncertain exactly what was happening at the time, but the mischief had given rise to

St. Andrew's Cathedral on View Street in Victoria.
PHOTO BY SHANON SINN

two contrasting explanations. Some of the men believed that ghosts were to blame, while others felt vandals were coming into the area and moving items around at night. According to the *British Colonist*, there was at least one incident where a man was found inside the cordoned-off area by a night watchman and hit with a lantern.

While the building was taking place, an Irishman named Lawrence Whelan was accused of placing a Fenian Brotherhood flag up in the construction area. This was to demonstrate his support for the Irish in the United States who were protesting British rule in Ireland. Not surprisingly, labourers were ordered to take the flag down to the frustration of the Irishman. Witnesses claimed that Whelan said he would make whoever took the flag down "pay." What he meant by this would later be debated in court.

Hands must have been short on Christmas Eve, as Whelan was hired as the night watchman for the evening. He carried a shotgun as a deterrent. Witnesses testified that Whelan thought the gun was loaded with a type of shot that would scare a man away, but wouldn't hurt him. He had been drinking all night.

As Christmas Mass in the original Cathedral building let out, two men in white jackets and bowler hats exited, walking by Whelan. One of the men carried a toy trumpet that he sounded as they passed him. The man's name was David Fee. For reasons that remain unclear to this day, the Irishman lifted his gun and shot Fee in the torso. The young man fell to the ground and died in a matter of moments. Whelan initially ran away, but later turned himself in.

Prosecutors claimed that Whelan was upset over the flag incident and that he had shot the wrong man in retaliation by mistake. The intended target, they said, usually wore a white jacket. The evidence supporting this claim—including testimony—was especially weak.

Whelan's defence lawyer, on the other hand, said that the fear of ghosts was a factor in the killing of Fee. After the case was over, Whelan even went so far as to say that the devil may have come behind him and pulled the trigger. He claimed he didn't understand how the gun could have gone off.

According to the *British Colonist*, witnesses remained divided as to whether or not Whelan was afraid of ghosts. A letter to the editor at the time even brought into question whether or not the electric light on the corner had been on. The speculation, of course, was that Whelan could have easily mistaken the two men in white as ghosts if it had not.

In a coincidence too great to ignore, a jury sentenced Whelan with manslaughter, similar to Bishop Seghers' killer. The *British Colonist* said that Judge Begbie, the "Hanging Judge," was upset at the jury's light-handed approach. After a condemning speech, he sent Whelan away to serve a life sentence. Whelan was released after serving only ten years for good behaviour.

Victoria's Ghostly Walks tour guides claim that both murder victims have been seen at St. Andrew's Cathedral. Fee is sometimes described as being in a white clown-like jacket with a red pompom in the middle of it. Accounts during the trial said that the white jackets worn by the men had red "braids" across their chests.

The guides claim that Fee has been seen on Christmas Eve, near the site where he was shot. The sighting is rumoured to accompany the sound of a gunshot. Fee is also believed to haunt the Ross Bay Cemetery.

Bishop Seghers' apparition, on the other hand, is one of Vancouver

Island's most terrifying visages: a man in full priest attire glides across the cathedral's floor from out of the shadows. Sometimes he stands still and stares. His smile can be seen, even in the dark—that wide, toothy, piteous smile. As one's eyes adjust to the shadows, a chill creeps inside of a chest refusing to breathe. Instead of a face, or hair, or flesh of any kind, the apparition of the priest has a bare-boned smiling skull set upon his shoulders.

It is not exactly what one would expect from a man who has dedicated his life to spreading the word of God. The bare skull is odd too. The only reported damage to the bishop's face at the time was from field mice. As already noted, the *British Colonist* account of the funeral said that Seghers was recognizable in his coffin, suggesting his face had remained intact even though mice had eaten part of it. Why he'd appear without flesh on his face is a mystery. Like others, this story may have morphed over time as it was passed from one teller to another.

Perhaps the manifestation was an intentional choice on the part of the entity? If this is the case, then the spirit's motive must be to inspire fear.

Some believe that ghosts truly are the dead. These otherworldly beings are often said to exist because they have unfinished business in the mortal realm, or because they don't know that they have died. In either case, the ghost of Bishop Seghers would have to be attached to his physical body, as the murder occurred at a distant location. Additionally, the bishop had no connection to the cathedral he is now reported to haunt, as it hadn't even been built yet.

There is another possibility though. Perhaps a separate negative entity attached itself to Bishop Seghers' body? According to some schools of thought—including the Catholic idea of demons—such a dark being could have been connected to Fuller originally, or even to the land where the murder took place. Either way, beings such as these are sometimes said to persuade the weak to kill. If this was the case in the bishop's death, could this spirit have somehow been involved in the second murder as well? As already mentioned, Whelan claimed "the devil" may have pulled the trigger from behind him. The idea deserves consideration if nothing else.

As recently as 2008, another innocent man was shot and killed near the spot that Fee was. The *Times Colonist* reported that there had been a dispute at the Red Jacket nightclub across the street from the site of Fee's murder. The guilty man claimed in court that the killing had been accidental, a spillover from a dispute with another man. He said the victim hadn't been the intended target at all; in fact, no one had even seen him. Could the murder be yet another coincidence? Or does this tragedy have darker implications as well? Thankfully, in this case, the mastermind behind the attack was sentenced to life in prison, with no possibility of parole for fourteen years.

Bishop Seghers' body continues to rest in the crypt beneath St. Andrew's Cathedral, 125 years after he was first buried. The church has a beautiful stained-glass window that honours him as well. Some people believe that the bishop's spirit never found rest. The idea has existed for almost as long as he's been buried there, making the Skull-Faced Bishop another one of Vancouver Island's earliest recorded ghost stories.

Fan Tan Alley in Victoria's Chinatown.
PHOTO BY SHANON SINN

FAN TAN ALLEY

VICTORIA

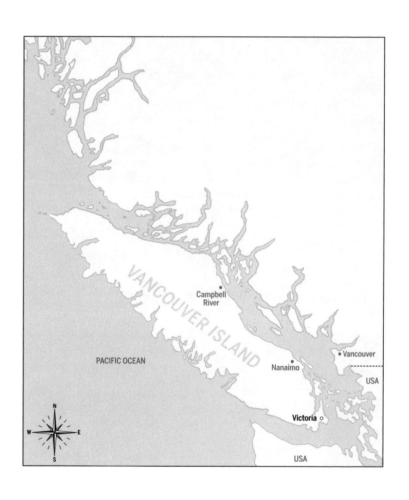

VICTORIA'S CHINATOWN IS ONLY A few blocks from St. Andrew's Cathedral. It is Canada's oldest Chinatown and the second oldest in North America after San Francisco's.

The gold rush brought the first waves of Chinese settlers to Fort Victoria. Soon, a community grew as more and more Chinese people arrived. Not unlike other parts of Victoria, violence was common. Murders often went unsolved.

One of Chinatown's most famous killings took place in 1889. Strangely, it is the apparition of the murderer people claim to see, not the young woman who was brutally slain.

The murder took place directly across from the Chinese Consolidated Benevolent Association building. The beautiful three-storey pagoda-roofed structure was built in 1909, twenty years after the killing. The crime took place where the main office of the Capital Regional District is now, at 71 Fisgard Street. Fire insurance maps from 1891 (two years after the murder) show that the street numbers were different then. By that time, the building had already been torn down and the lot had been converted into a garden.

The *Seattle Post-Intelligencer* called the crime the most "diabolic" of all of British Columbia's murders, and called the killer "a Chinese Jack the Ripper." The *British Colonist* said it was, "one of the most fiendish crimes ever perpetrated in British Columbia." Mayor John Grant offered two hundred dollars for the capture of the murderer or murderers through an ad in the paper. The Chinese and white communities were divided at the time, but the woman's brutal death united them in anger.

While covering the murder, the *British Colonist* called Chinatown "the vilest corner of our city," and referred to its residents in derogatory ways. Racial tensions were high. A war in China had killed over twenty million people between 1850 and 1864. The resulting famine caused many survivors to look for new lands to settle in. The need for cheap labourers or the promise of wealth brought many Chinese settlers to North America. By 1885, the Canadian government began to charge Chinese immigrants fifty dollars to enter the country in an effort to stem the tide. It was worse in the United States. The Chinese Exclusion Act of 1882 stated that no Chinese labourers could enter at all.

Most of the Chinese settlers were male. Capitalizing on the destitution in China, slave traders brought beautiful girls—or even babies—to ports like San Francisco and Victoria as prostitutes. In an article on the American History USA website, historian Dan Bryan said that the first waves of women sold for as much as $1,000 each. A *British Colonist* article from 1891 says that one woman was sold in Victoria for $1,330. In his 1873 book, *À la California: Sketch of Life in the Golden State*, Colonel Evans claimed Chinese prostitutes lived a life, "a thousand times more hopeless and terrible than the negro slavery of Louisiana or Cuba." The Victoria Chinatown website says that by 1888, a Presbyterian-supported charity was set up in Victoria to help Chinese and Japanese women leave the sex industry and escape their slavers.

The white neighbourhoods weren't any better. Victoria was well known for its brothels at the time. A journal entry from Eunice

Harrison, an early judge's wife, said, "there were red light districts in BC with literal red lanterns hanging from the gates." Elaborate brothels catered to the wealthy. White men wishing to pay less would venture down Chatham Street. Some would even wander into the wood and tin neighbourhoods of Chinatown.

The *British Colonist* said that the murdered woman, Yow Kum, was one of the most beautiful Chinese women in Victoria. Her owner, a woman named Ah Gee, had brought her to the city three years earlier from San Francisco, likely for prostitution. When the Americans wouldn't let the girl back into the country because of the Exclusion Act, she became the property of the brothel at 71 Fisgard Street. No one knew her exact age, but she was estimated to have been between sixteen and nineteen years old.

Yow Kum's job—like all Chinese slave girls—was to sit at a window and solicit passersby. There was a wicker-like screen over the window. A hole large enough for her to put her head through allowed men to see what her face looked like when she stuck her head out. She was also encouraged to try to verbally solicit them. If they liked what they saw, the men would then go to the door and pay the girl's owners. Generally speaking, if a woman like Yow Kum was not aggressive enough in attracting clients, she would be beaten or starved.

The paper said that Yow Kum had many young white male "friends." It was also reported that she had an aversion to Chinese men.

The killer, Ah Heung, was a regular client. Witnesses said that he visited Yow Kum every night. Heung lived next to the brothel, on the third floor. He made fifteen dollars a month working at the American Hotel on Yates Street. His age was not known either, but he was described as a young Chinese man.

The wife of the brothel owner, Ah Sum, was reported to have said in testimony that the two were always arguing, and that Ah Heung had proposed to Yow Kum twice. The girl would never have been released without fetching a fair price though, and Ah Heung was not a rich man.

Ah Heung would later state he was upset at having had to listen to Yow Kum soliciting white men from next door. He also admitted to being jealous.

On Sunday May 12 at 10:30 PM, Ah Heung picked up an 18-inch fish knife and ran down the stairs. He then pulled Yow Kum's head out of the wicker hole as far as it would go and hacked at the back of her neck three times. She screamed as her head was being cut off. Her body remained in the room, but the head dangled out of the window, held on by the remaining flesh.

The *British Colonist* said that witnesses put another man at the murder scene, but indicated that he only watched. Ah Sum—who claimed she was also watching through a crack in the wall—said that a third man held Yow Kum's hair. No other witness verified this. The third Chinese man, she said, had also wanted to marry Yow Kum. Ah Sum testified she had been told Ah Heung was going to poison her and her husband in order to steal Yow Kum.

Ah Heung would later confess to having acted alone. Blood on his left sleeve supported the claim that he held the young woman's head himself.

Ah Heung ran away before people flooded the streets. He threw the knife down (which was never recovered) and fled toward the American Hotel. Two days later, he was found hiding in one of the seven coal bins by the hotel owner's son. A passing policeman was called and he was arrested.

On May 31, Ah Heung was sentenced to death by hanging. His execution date was set for July 10. He administered this sentence on himself, however, on June 10 in cell number forty-five of the provincial jail, in "the southwest corner of the third tier."

On the day he committed suicide, guards observed Ah Heung being reverent and peaceful. He had shaved and taken a bath. When the guard went to retrieve the prisoner's dinner dishes he found that the man had hanged himself.

Ah Heung had made a noose from rope woven with strands of his undershirt. He then rolled his bedding together to make a platform to stand upon. Once he had the noose around his neck, he kicked this away and killed himself.

Fan Tan Alley is a short walk away from the murder scene, past the intently staring lion protectors at the Gate of Harmonious Interest. The alley is said to be haunted by Ah Heung's ghost, as it is one of the routes he could have taken fleeing the scene of the murder.

The dark and narrow alley was named after a gambling game that was once illegal. Hidden Fan Tan meeting rooms were accessed from the alley. Non-regulated—and later illegal—opium dens were as well.

Local stories abound. People hear footsteps behind them when no one is there. At other times, an invisible force shoves them. Tour guides and writers have said that people have also claimed to see a young Asian man covered in blood. There is a long knife in his hand. His face is twisted in agony. For a moment he is there, then he flees, fading as quickly as he has appeared.

Witnesses made these claims on *Creepy Canada*, but they sounded as contrived as other accounts. The show changed the names of both the killer and the victim, suggesting that the story was intentionally misleading. The alley itself would be an indirect route for someone running toward the American Hotel. The claim raises other questions as well. Why would Ah Heung's spirit be covered in blood, when he more-or-less just had blood on his sleeve when he was arrested? Why would he come back as a ghost while Yow Kum had not?

Chinese women like Yow Kum were sold for sex so cheaply that a man making fifteen dollars a month could use her regularly. Her life and death were tragic beyond comprehension. If ghosts are restless spirits, then why isn't she one of them? Could the building's later removal and transformation into a garden have something to do with her spirit finding rest? Why wouldn't all Chinese girls who were abused and forced into prostitution return as ghosts?

Interestingly, there is also a story in *A Gathering of Ghosts* by Robin Skelton and Jean Kozocari that sounds suspiciously like the spirit of a Chinese woman who had been used for sex.

Skelton lived in an old house in the Oak Bay area. At some point, everyone in the family—including a male houseguest who was living there—became aware that a spirit shared the home with them. Skelton believed that the entity was a "young girl," possibly Asian. This "shadowy presence" would often follow people through the home, standing very close to them, much as a servant would. One night, something woke up the male houseguest. A young woman was standing at the foot of his bed.

The form in the darkness is small statured, naked chested, and has soft curves. She is not very old, but not a child either. Long dark hair flows past her cheeks and across her shoulders. High cheekbones and emotionless lips are beneath dark Asian eyes, unreadable in the shadows. Her arms are at her sides, but they slowly raise, palms up as she offers herself.

Chinese prostitute on display in a pen, San Francisco, ca. 1880.
UNKNOWN PHOTOGRAPHER

Heart racing, he reaches over to the lamp beside his bed and turns the light on. The girl is gone. For a long moment, he stares at the place where she has just been. It was a bad dream. Nothing more. He reaches over and turns the lamp off to go back to sleep. She is still there. He cannot breathe. He scrambles to turn the light back on. She is gone once more. He leaves the lamp on for the rest of the night, struggling to go back to sleep.

The next morning, the houseguest told Skelton what had happened. As Skeleton and Kozocari called themselves exorcist witches, what they describe afterward would normally not appear in a book about ghosts. Shortly after the houseguest's experience, Skelton, Kozocari, and two other spiritualists claim they spoke with the spirit, telling her that what she had done was inappropriate. Skelton said the ghost was never that bold again.

Skelton proposed that the young woman had been a Chinese servant. Many of the grand houses kept servants for menial tasks, such as cleaning and gardening. Was the girl expected to perform sexual favours for the master of the house as well? Sexual abuse toward female domestics was the norm in the late nineteenth century, and Chinese women had even fewer rights than other women. It is definitely possible.

Four Mile House in View Royal.
PHOTO BY SHANON SINN

The White Lady of Thetis Cove

VIEW ROYAL

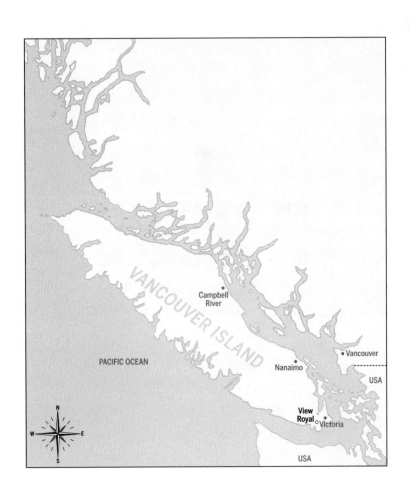

GHOST STORIES DESCRIBING A WOMAN in white are told all over the world. From South America to Australia and Thailand to Russia, the apparition of a lone woman wearing a white flowing dress has been passed on from one generation to the next. Consistent with many of these tales is betrayal or abandonment by a husband or lover. The common theme is that the haunting occurs in a rural or secluded area as well. Doris Gravlin's spirit is one such example. Another is the White Lady of Thetis Cove, a legendary spirit that has a connection to one of British Columbia's oldest buildings.

The Four Mile House is located in View Royal, a suburb of Victoria. The biggest challenge investigating the story was the family associated with the spirit. They had been tellers of tall tales, which had been passed on to different owners of the building and to historians. Almost everything about the Four Mile House's past turned out to be false: Peter and Elizabeth Calvert were not the original owners of the inn; they did not meet on the semi-legendary ship the *Norman Morrison*; their daughter's name was Mary, not Margaret; and likely no great-aunt—who the White Lady was supposed to be—ever died on the property. Worse yet, storytellers not understanding the term "great-aunt" slowly turned the ghost from a younger woman into an old lady.

The tale of the apparition was real though. Dyke Point, the rocky cliff on the north side of Thetis Cove, had been unofficially named White Lady Point by the *Daily Colonist* sometime before 1921. It is also true that the deceased was believed to be a sister of Peter or Elizabeth Calvert, the couple most heavily associated with the Four Mile House's early past. The inn has several other ghost stories attached to it, and its history is intimately linked to the legend of the White Lady.

During the 1870s, advertisements in the *British Colonist* invited Victorians out to the Four Mile Inn, as it was called then, for rural retreats. For those without transportation, a coach would pick them up at the Adelphi Building on Government and Yates streets. The drive would take Victoria's elite away from the squalor of the city into beautiful Craigflower country for picnics, refreshments, and regular shooting matches. The advertisement had been placed by an enterprising new innkeeper, Peter Calvert, a man determined to make a name for himself.

According to census records, Peter had been a grocer in 1861 living with his brother William in a boarding house in Yorkshire, England. By 1867 however, he was in Esquimalt and had come into money. Esquimalt Bay was much deeper than Victoria's harbour so it was used by the Royal Navy and as a place to offload larger ships. The *British Colonist* reported that Peter played a billiards match for twenty-five dollars at a bar informally referred to as "Howard's." Terry Reksten in *More English than the English* describes it as a rough place. Sailors, soldiers, and men carving out the land frequented the establishment, where they drank heavily, fought, and gambled. Peter lost what would be four hundred dollars in today's currency by one shot.

Peter was charged with assaulting a drunken woman who had tried to enter the home he was staying at two years later. The *British Colonist* reported that the woman claimed Peter had left her for dead. Eighteen-year-old Miss Elizabeth Montgomery testified on Peter's behalf, however, saying that Peter had "gently" laid the woman in the ditch. The *British Colonist* referred to the house as "Mrs. Cook's" a place where drunken people weren't welcome. The judge dismissed the charges, saying that if the woman had died Peter and Elizabeth would have faced more serious charges. They married shortly thereafter.

Unlike Peter, Elizabeth had actually been aboard the *Norman Morrison* in 1853 with many of Vancouver Island's first settlers, but she had only been two years old at the time. Records indicate that her father had travelled to Vancouver Island as one of the Hudson's Bay Company's original workers, but he died in 1860. Elizabeth's mother likely remarried and became Mrs. Cook, though the evidence is conflicted. Peter was staying at Mrs. Cook's, where Elizabeth also lived, in 1869, but whether he was a boarder or already courting Elizabeth is not known. Birth records show that their first daughter was born in 1870.

That same year, an advertisement in the *British Colonist* for the Four Mile Inn said that Peter recently leased the premises, and that he would "furnish the best accommodations anywhere in the colony outside of Victoria." The Four Mile Inn was located on a thin strip of land separating the Esquimalt Harbour and Portage Inlet. The well-used road went directly past Peter's newly acquired building.

In 1872, Peter saw a more promising opportunity further down the road at Parson's Bridge Hotel (the Six Mile Inn) and moved locations. The hotel had boat access, whereas the Four Mile Inn was "a four-minute walk" from the water. This meant that customers could be dropped off more readily by water with greater amounts of luggage. The site also had easier access to freshwater, a valuable commodity in those days. Besides offering wines, liquors, and cigars, Peter also advertised fishing, shooting, and boating.

The *British Colonist* said there was a dispute in 1877 over the ownership of the retail licence for the Parson's Bridge Hotel. Strangely, it was with Mr. Morais, the man who had taken over the licence at the Four Mile Inn. Technically, both men held the licence for the Parson's Bridge Hotel and had applied for renewal. The court was not impressed, and closed the hotel impermanently, adjourning the case for five months. A few days later, Peter Calvert was involved in an accident. The shaft of his buggy broke at Sangster's Plains (now Colwood) and he was thrown. The paper reported that Peter received serious head injuries and died a few days later.

Surrendering to pressure to leave Parsons Bridge Hotel, Elizabeth made the exchange with Mr. Morais, taking her five young children back to the Four Mile Inn.

It couldn't have been easy at first, but Elizabeth was determined to make the Four Mile Inn great. In 1878, she advertised that the inn had been renovated and refurnished. Whereas most ads at the time had the hotel proprietor's name in small print at the bottom, hers said "Mrs. Calvert" in large letters beneath "Four Mile House." It was a bold statement for a woman at the time.

The hotel offered excursions from Victoria and was a day-trip destination for the leisure steamship *Lenora*. In 1881, the *West Shore Periodical* said that it was "the prettiest wayside inn in British Columbia." An 1890 *British Colonist* article said, "The hotel is stylish and picturesque with its snow white fences and well-tended gardens." By 1892, the inn boasted a new dance hall.

Stained-glass image of the White Lady.
PHOTO BY SHANON SINN

Marriage records indicate that Elizabeth remarried twice. The first was in 1879 to Peter's brother William. Sadly, the paper reported that William passed away from a lengthy illness in 1884. Elizabeth then married a blacksmith named John Conway in 1885. By this time, the inn had become a community of its own with over a hundred livestock, several buildings across the road, and many workers. According to the death record, Elizabeth passed away in 1893 at forty-two years of age. She left behind seven surviving children.

The *British Colonist* informed the public that the management of the inn had become the responsibility of son Joseph Calvert and his older sister Mary Gouge. Tragedy returned in 1905, however, when both Joseph, and Mary's husband, Bertrand, died on the premises only a month apart. The deaths were reported in the paper. Mary was forced to manage the hotel alone.

The Four Mile Inn thrived for over a decade. The hall advertised "social hops," "grand balls," and dances. When prohibition came to British Columbia in 1917, the inn became a private residence and boarding house. There were several attempts to reacquire a liquor licence in the 1920s and 30s, but the newspaper reported that an encroaching urban neighbourhood rallied against it. Mary eventually moved to a nearby house on View Royal Avenue, where she passed away in 1950.

An 1881 woodcut image from the *West Shore Periodical* shows that the inn originally looked different than it does today. The building was remodelled in a Tudor style during the 1920s. These renovations were likely in anticipation of a liquor licence approval that was never granted.

The business eventually reopened in 1940 as an inn under new management. Its new name advertised in the *Daily Colonist* was "Ye Old Four Mile House." The business failed by 1941, but opened once more in 1946 as That Old Lantern Inn. The building changed hands again and eventually closed, falling into disrepair. According to the Four Mile House website, Graham and Wendy Haymes bought the building in 1979 and restored the inn to its former glory.

The owners have made several statements over the years about the building being haunted and about the White Lady of Thetis Cove apparition as well.

The newspaper reported that multiple people—besides the five already mentioned—have died on the property, including two unnamed babies and one-year-old Minnie Calvert. In 1891, Mr. Newton—who had lived at the Four Mile Inn for eighteen years— passed away. Sixty-seven-year-old long-time resident George McKiel died on the property in 1926. George had been married to another

Calvert daughter, Fanny. A skeleton with a pistol in its hand was found in the woods near the building in 1908. The unidentified man was believed to have been a suicide from the year before.

On the Four Mile Inn website, the Haymes claim that a woman in a full-length gown has been seen in an upper-storey window. They believe this to be Mary Gouge, who died in her home nearby. The woman, who they and others incorrectly call Margaret, looks down at the garden and appears to be happy.

There is also an account in Belyk's *Ghosts: More Eerie Encounters* of a man in an old-fashioned suit sitting in the restaurant. A waitress saw him sitting alone before they opened for the day. She went to ask Wendy Haymes how he had gotten into the building, only to discover that no one was there. The waitress said he was wearing a "1940s-style suit" and a black trench coat. The man was of European descent and had dark hair that was receding. There was also an open briefcase on the table in front of him. Wendy's mother claimed to have seen this man as well. Others said that they had also seen him out of the corners of their eyes. This rash of sightings happened when renovations were taking place.

On the Four Mile House's website, there are other paranormal incidents listed, such as the sound of a spoon tapping against a teacup, "a voice softly calling," and the echoes of footsteps upstairs. There are also claims of items going missing and reappearing in the same spot later. These types of incidents are commonly reported in buildings where apparitions have been seen. When I asked the staff about recent activity they reported that there hadn't been any "lately."

Portage Park separates the Four Mile House from the shoreline of Thetis Cove. A well-maintained path cuts through the trees toward the shore. The pebble-and-mud beach faces the Olympic Mountains and tiny Richards Island. Fisgard Lighthouse is also visible. Early accounts, such as surviving letters from pioneer Eleanor Caroline Fellows, indicate that the area was the site of Esquimalt First Nations' remains, but that navy officers disrespectfully collected anything they could find as souvenirs.

To the north of the beach is Dyke Point. Ship activity in Esquimalt Harbour is visually obstructed on the beach. If someone wanted to watch ships enter and exit the harbour, then Dyke Point would be where they would sit or stand.

Legend says that an apparition of a woman in white used to be seen standing on that point looking out to sea, waiting for her seafaring husband to come home. Her hair is tossed back from her face. A white gown catches the ocean breeze and floats slowly around her body. Wide eyes stare vacantly over the water with unblinking diligence, lonely and pleading.

According to the Four Mile House's website, Mary Gouge's son Wilf claimed that the ghost was one of his great-aunts who had died in the inn. He said she had succumbed to a lengthy illness and that she'd been buried on Dyke Point. Confused by the term "great-aunt," later tellers of the tale have sometimes said that the lady was an older woman, but this isn't necessarily true.

Census records indicate that Peter and William's sisters stayed in England. John Conway left the Four Mile Inn after Elizabeth's death. I was unable to find any record of his relatives coming to Vancouver Island from Pennsylvania. This leaves two possible candidates for the White Lady: Elizabeth Montgomery's two sisters, Annie and Margaret.

Annie Montgomery was the youngest sister. She married a

farmer named Colin Cameron, had several children, and passed away in her home on Yates Street in 1901. The forty-two-year-old woman was buried at the Ross Bay Cemetery.

Margaret Montgomery was born in 1853, the same year the *Norman Morrison* arrived. She died in 1872 from a heart disease she'd suffered since childhood. Margaret was only nineteen years old and was buried at the Quadra Street Burial Ground. The *British Colonist* said that "Miss Montgomery" was very respectable and that both of her parents were dead. A third mention, however, said that she had died at her "mother's" house on Douglas Street. This mother's name was Mrs. Cook, who was likely the same woman Elizabeth had been living under in 1869. The early directories listed Mrs. Cook as a washerwoman.

If the White Lady of Thetis Cove is the spirit of a dead aunt, then Margaret is the most likely candidate even though she is buried elsewhere. Unless there had been a falling out, she would have spent time at her sister's inn. In all likelihood, Elizabeth would have tried to introduce Margaret to prospective partners, many who would have been ship officers.

It is unlikely anyone from the inn would have been buried at White Lady Point, as they would have been buried in graveyards at the time. The point also had a cabin on it, suggesting burial away from the shore would have placed the grave in someone's yard.

The White Lady of Thetis Cove is another ghost story that is more fiction than fact. Several years ago, Wendy and Graham Haymes commissioned a stained-glass window depicting her and the tragic tale she represents. Today, the image is proudly displayed in the Four Mile House's pub. A White Lady drink is served in her honour as well. It's made with coffee, Baileys Irish Cream, and Frangelico liqueur.

Robert Dunsmuir passed away while Craigdarroch Castle was being built.
PHOTO BY SHANON SINN

COAL BARONS
AND CASTLES

GREATER VICTORIA REGION

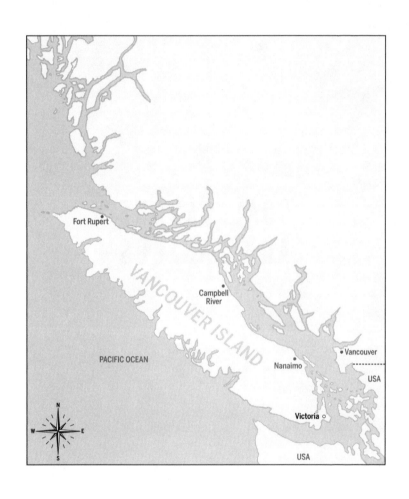

VANCOUVER ISLAND HAS TWO CASTLES. Both of them were built by the Dunsmuir family and are said to be haunted.

The Dunsmuirs were Vancouver Island coal royalty at the turn of the century. Their wealth was carved out of the island itself and their meteoric rise and fall reads like the script of a movie. Unlike the occupants of the Four Mile Inn, the lives of the Dunsmuirs have been well documented in books like *The Dunsmuir Saga* by Terry Reksten, *Alex Dunsmuir's Dilemma* by relative James Audain, and *Black Diamond City* by Jan Peterson.

Robert Dunsmuir and his wife, Joan, left Scotland with their two young daughters in 1850 aboard the *Pekin*. After an eighteen-day stay at Fort Vancouver (now located in Washington State), the family boarded another ship, the *Mary Dare*, and sailed toward their ultimate destination of Fort Rupert. Dunsmuir's uncle, Boyd Gilmour, had been hired by the Hudson's Bay Company (HBC) to establish a coal mine there, and he had volunteered last minute to help him.

Set in the northeastern corner of Vancouver Island, the fort was a remote outpost where coal was being mined by a handful of determined and gritty settlers. When Dunsmuir's three-year contract ran out in 1852, Governor James Douglas asked the mining families to move to Nanaimo, located centrally on the island, where a more promising coal vein had been discovered. Robert Dunsmuir willingly accepted. Eventually, his would be the only family from the original group to stay on.

Nanaimo was an unpopulated trading post called Colville when they arrived. By 1853, the HBC had erected the Nanaimo Bastion fort to protect the company's interests. According to the 1857 census, Nanaimo grew to a 30-cabin, 132-resident settlement within five years of the Dunsmuir's arrival. The name would change to Nanaimo—an anglicized attempt to name the settlement after the displaced Snuneymuxw First Nation—in 1860.

The following decade brought more settlers to Nanaimo. Many of these were men who had come to work the mines. Others imported different trades or came to grow food. These immigrants slowly increased the settlement's numbers. The HBC's land lease ran out in 1859. As a result, independent businessesmen began to take an interest in the coal industry. In 1869, Robert Dunsmuir found the coal vein that would eventually make him the wealthiest man in British Columbia. While out searching for coal, he had noticed some of the black rock in the roots of an overturned tree. His discovery would bring even more settlers and migrant workers to the area.

By 1871, mining laws had begun to change. New regulations meant that Dunsmuir needed a company of ten men or more to access 2,500 acres of land, versus five hundred men as an individual businessman. In response, Robert formed Dunsmuir, Diggle & Company, made up of partners including his sons Alex and James, and a son-in-law, James Harvey. Once the company was legally recognized, all of the men relinquished their rights to the coal.

By the end of 1875, Robert Dunsmuir's mines were producing fifty thousand tons of coal per year. By the 1880s, he became involved in politics, first representing Nanaimo and then the province. While in provincial office, he was instrumental in building the

E & N Railway that would eventually connect Nanaimo to Victoria.

Dunsmuir moved to Victoria in 1885 and began the construction of Craigdarroch Castle on a hill overlooking the city. Popular legend has it that before they left Scotland, he had promised Joan that once he was successful in Canada he would build her a castle. Unfortunately, he never saw the castle completed. He died on April 13, 1889, a year before the building was finished.

When Robert had left Nanaimo his son James had taken over the mining management while his son Alex managed the San Francisco office in California. The family assets had grown to include the railway, natural resources like iron and timber, real estate, other businesses, and even a theatre.

Robert Dunsmuir's outdated will left everything to his wife, Joan, which was a serious blow to his two sons who were managing the businesses. It came as a surprise to the brothers, as they were expecting to inherit the business they had been running. Joan and the female members of the family squandered the fortune by living luxurious lifestyles. She also used her authority to contradict her sons in their professional and personal lives. Alex couldn't marry the woman he loved, for example, until business matters had settled ten years later. Joan had disapproved of his fiancée because she had a child and had been previously married. Alex died shortly after their marriage in 1900.

Alex left his assets to his brother, James. This divided the family again. James' sisters and mother tried to sue him for what they believed should have been their share. The case was scandalous at the time, as James had followed in his father's footsteps and had become the premier of British Columbia. He and his mother never spoke again. Joan died in Craigdarroch Castle in 1908. At the last moment, James decided to attend the funeral. He is said to have hung his head and wept.

Without revenue, the Dunsmuir daughters were forced to sell Craigdarroch Castle. The land around it was subdivided and sold as well. The castle became first a private residence, then a college, a military hospital, and a music conservatory before finally being restored and converted into a historical tourist attraction, which it is to this day.

After Joan had died, James and Laura Dunsmuir moved into their recently finished Hatley Castle in 1910. James passed away ten years later in 1920, but Laura continued to live in the building until her death in 1937. The government purchased the castle and used it as a military college until 1995. It has operated as a public university ever since. Hatley Castle is a popular filming location; most notably it was the site of Professor Xavier's School for Gifted Youngsters in the X-Men movie franchise.

There have been many stories involving Craigdarroch Castle over the years, though the Historical Society has not been as public about these as Hatley Castle's caretakers have. Still, people have made claims to writers and to online sources as well.

Craigdarroch Castle has made numerous online lists of haunted sites in Victoria. People claim to have seen the ghost of a Victorian-era maid, a man in a "bowler" hat, a little girl in the basement, and the leg of a man walking up the servant stairs (the only portion that would be visible from that angle). Stories of the apparitions of two soldiers—apparently from the days when the castle was a veterans' hospital—have circulated as well.

Hatley Castle was the jewel of James Dunsmuir's private estate.
PHOTO BY SHANON SINN

Many people have claimed to be able to feel Joan Dunsmuir's presence in her sitting room. The room has always felt strange to me as well, as if some unseen presence really was there.

Robin Skelton and Jean Kozocari in *A Gathering of Ghosts* said that people have claimed that items had been mysteriously moved throughout the castle, candle wax or perfume could be smelled, gusts of cold air could be felt, and a piano could sometimes be heard. Many of these stories were likely invented over the years, just because a castle—any castle—*should* be haunted, especially when it looks like it might be. Craigdarroch Castle does have a certain haunting appeal. It was used as a set, for example, for the 2016 movie *The Boy* starring *The Walking Dead*'s Lauren Cohan.

The castle's main stories involve an apparition of a woman seen on the stairs between the ballroom and the third floor. The *Province* reported that she was dressed in a white gown, but accounts are usually less detailed. Skelton and Kozocari originally published the most well-known sighting of her in *A Gathering of Ghosts*, which has since been retold in over a dozen publications.

In the late 1970s, a repairman called medium/witch/author Jean Kozocari to tell her that he had seen a partial apparition at Craigdarroch Castle. The man had been sitting on a chair facing the stairs on the third floor and eating his lunch. Suddenly, he noticed a foot and the bottom part of a gown moving very slowly down the stairs from the fourth floor (ballroom) toward him. He couldn't believe what he had seen. The sighting was unusual, if only because he could only see the bottom "twelve inches" of her. The repairman said she moved slowly and silently. A noise distracted him. When he looked back, she had disappeared.

One of the Dunsmuir daughters, Marion, was likely the first person to die in the castle in 1892. The surviving image of her shows an attractive and elegant woman, regally seated upon a chair in front of a lavish Victorian cabinet.

Marion—Robert and Joan's third daughter—had met her husband Lieutenant Colonel Charles Houghton in Nanaimo. The militia had been called to the mining town when workers were threatening to strike. Houghton was the officer in charge.

According to Reksten in *The Dunsmuir Saga*, Houghton wasn't the man the Dunsmuirs had hoped. The officer, who was fifteen years older than Marion, was already secretly married with two children. He had abandoned them when he had been appointed to Victoria. His first wife—who Reksten says was a "high born" First Nations woman—died of a broken heart and the children

Marion Dunsmuir Houghton ca. 1880.
IMAGE A-02208, COURTESY OF THE ROYAL BC MUSEUM AND ARCHIVES

had subsequently moved to live with their grandmother. Superiors throughout Houghton's career reported that he was constantly drinking, lacked common sense, and was an incompetent soldier. He was transferred to Manitoba in 1881 to help put down the Louis Riel Rebellion. He took Marion with him. There, Houghton continued to demonstrate poor judgment as a soldier. During one skirmish in 1884, he "blundered about on a conspicuous white horse" and became separated from his troops. Reksten quotes a commanding officer that reported, "Lt. Col. Houghton is absolutely useless, and I wish I could find some excuse to get rid of him."

The couple lived in Montreal until Marion became ill in 1891. Houghton brought her home to Victoria where she died on February 13, 1892, in Craigdarroch Castle. She was only thirty-six years old. The couple never had children.

The *British Colonist* reported the funeral as one of the most "impressive ceremonies" of the day. A long "mourning" carriage and coach procession left Craigdarroch Castle for the Christ Church Cathedral where the ceremony was held, before proceeding to the Ross Bay Cemetery. One of the pallbearers was an elderly Sir Begbie, the "Hanging Judge,"—but all were esteemed men. Newspapers reported that Marion had been popular and that she had a large circle of close friends. The paper contained an exhaustive list of flower donors, with an apology saying that there were too many to name.

When Houghton passed away of throat cancer six years later, none of the Dunsmuirs attended the funeral. The man had barely been tolerated when Marion was alive; after her death, they learned about his prior marriage and children. Losing such a beloved family member as Marion had been hard enough. Realizing they had all been deceived must have been infuriating. Perhaps to the deceased woman most of all.

The air is cold. Faint music floats down from the fourth-floor ballroom. A woman slowly descends the stairs. Carefully. Deliberately. She should not be there. A long white skirt trails beneath a darker-coloured gown. The end of that skirt slides slowly across each stair, falling suddenly to the next stair as if "weighted" down by some unseen force. Small satin shoes touch gracefully upon those steps, pausing for a long moment before moving to the next one. The woman's hands hold onto the sides of her gown, pulling the fabric up enough so as not to trip her. Her dark hair is coiled upon her head. Ice-blue eyes stare down the stairs vacantly. She is alone, as if being presented to an unseen crowd, or to her own funeral.

Interestingly, the most popular sighting of her foot and dress was by a man sitting by himself. I can't help but wonder if other sightings of her are by men who are alone as well?

If Craigdarroch Castle was a symbol of power upon the hill, Hatley Castle was a rural hideaway far outside of the city. The road to Hatley passes the Four Mile Inn, crosses the Parsons Bridge, and is located even beyond Peter Calvert's accident site on the old Sangster's Plains.

In a 2004 episode of *Creepy Canada*, Friends of Hatley Park Society member Al Newton said that the oldest known ghost story happened shortly after the 1915 sinking of the *Lusitania*.

James' youngest son, James "Boy" Dunsmuir, had been eager to go overseas to join the war effort. He decided he did not want to wait for his unit to deploy from Victoria. Boy asked to resign so he could re-enlist in the British army. He was aboard the passenger ship when a German submarine torpedoed it. A secondary explosion followed before the sea swallowed the ship. A total of 1,198 people lost their lives. Boy's body was never found.

Newton claimed that shortly after Boy's death, his younger sister Dola saw his apparition in the gardens. As with most of *Creepy Canada*'s retellings, however, there are multiple problems with the dramatized portion of the tale: not everyone aboard the *Lusitania* died; Boy couldn't have been wearing a military uniform when he perished as he wasn't technically a soldier; and for that same reason no one ever received an army telegram. Be that as it may, the tale persists. Dola saw Boy's apparition in the garden and felt as if he had come to say goodbye.

Similarly, Reksten, in *The Dunsmuir Saga*, says that Boy's mother, Laura, had nightmares Boy was drowning in the sinking ship. She would wake up convinced that a hand had been slapping against her window, and that her son had been nearby.

James died a few years later as an old man; Laura died seventeen years after that. The castle's reputation for being haunted slowly emerged.

People have claimed to see James Dunsmuir's ghost over the years, but the sightings are rather reserved. He just watches, never saying anything or trying to interact with witnesses.

In 2012, Doug Ozeroff of Royal Roads University told CTV News that a Dunsmuir maid had once committed suicide by jumping out of an upper floor window. Apparently, the window has been found opened or closed without explanation ever since. While reviewing their footage, the CTV News team covering the story were surprised to find that they'd captured images they couldn't explain. A still camera had recorded a door slowly opening. Small whitish orbs crossed the screen at the same time. CTV's videographer Todd Harner—who is identified as a skeptic—said that he couldn't explain the patterns of white dots, while ruling out possibilities such as reflection and lint.

In the same news story, Ozeroff claimed to have seen a "red-bearded" apparition on the stairs outside. There was also a picture taken of a spirit holding a baby. This was what brought the news team to Hatley Castle in the first place. The picture isn't compelling, but this type of so-called evidence is commonplace when it comes to hauntings. If you need to circle part of a photograph and tell others what to look for, then it may be "pareidolia," the phenomenon of seeing an image where none exists.

The most persistent ghost tale of Hatley Castle is of Laura Dunsmuir herself. Originally told by Robert Belyk in *Ghosts: True Tales of Eerie Encounters*, the story is of a little old lady who would stand at the side of cadet's beds and stare at them until they woke up. In at least one case, the entity is said to have tugged on the young man's leg until he broke her grip.

The grip is strong, tugging persistently. The room is dark and the silence heavy. Someone is pulling him from his cot. He strains to see. Crouched at the end of the bed is an older woman. She is short and thick boned. Her brow is furrowed. He kicks his leg in panic, but the icy grip intensifies. His fingers grasp onto the sides of the metal-framed cot, trying not to slide off. His blankets have somehow been thrown aside. He can't cry for help. He can't even breathe. Her eyes stare down at him with pitiless fury he doesn't understand. He kicks harder and faster. Tears run down the sides of his face. He gasps. Suddenly, the old lady with the firm grasp has vanished. The air is cold as ice.

Castles have a reputation for being haunted. It comes with the territory. The same family attached to Vancouver Island's only two castles makes for an interesting study. Victoria has a booming tourist trade, with a portion of it leaning heavily on haunted locations. People want ghostly parks and places to eat, stay, or visit. The story itself becomes a commodity worth more than the truth. Why say a spirit has only been seen once if whole groups of people are hoping to see it several times a week? Unfortunately, it becomes harder to document actual sightings if many of them are made up. Most of the time, there was an actual sighting that was reported in the first place. Most subsequent encounters aren't real.

The late nineteenth and early twentieth centuries provide many of Vancouver Island's classic ghost stories, truly Victorian in nature. Interestingly, this matches the height of the belief in spiritualism, or communication with the deceased. This makes me wonder whether or not being open to communication with the dead might result in spirits being more active? There are countless contemporary stories involving Ouija boards where users have claimed this is the case. If spiritualism predisposes people to become ghosts or makes those that are trapped in the physical realm more interactive, then this might explain why many of the Dunsmuir homes have had activity in them.

The Judge's Wife is a memoir by Eunice Harrison that documents her life in British Columbia from 1860 to 1906. In the afternotes section, Eunice's son Victor said that many of the Dunsmuirs were Spiritualists. One of them, who had moved to England, was a "devout" believer and sent Eunice's husband several Spiritualist papers and materials. The afternote entry is given as a possible explanation to an apparition Eunice had seen in one of the Dunsmuir's former homes in Nanaimo.

Eunice's husband had recently been appointed judge of Nanaimo and North Vancouver Island. The couple rented James Dunsmuir's ten-bedroom house in Departure Bay. The area was rural then, and the house no longer exists, but the story is worth sharing. One night, Eunice was home alone studying Latin when she had an urge to look up. She noticed that the hallway door had somehow opened and that "a good child's face" was staring at her. The face disappeared. Eunice got up and looked into the hallway but there was no one there. She then checked on her children. They were all asleep as well. She continued to study for a while and then began to play the piano. Suddenly, she had the same feeling again and looked over toward the door expecting it to open. This time the door was closed, but she could see the same face looking at her through the glass, "floating as it were, with the child's sweet expression."

A neighbour later told Eunice that a young child had fallen down the servant stairs and been killed. In the same afternotes section, the editor mentions the deaths of two of James and Laura's children: Alexander Lee Dunsmuir—named after his uncle—had died at eight months old in 1887. The cause of his death was not recorded. Joan Olive White Dunsmuir (named after her grandmother) died in 1884 at four years old of "brain fever." Both of them are buried in the Nanaimo graveyard beside other Dunsmuir relatives, though Alexander's headstone is no longer visible.

If the kind-faced spirit was one of the Dunsmuir children, then it seems unlikely Eunice would describe an eight-month-old baby as a "child." The description would better fit four-year-old Joan Olive. Eunice never saw the apparition again.

A final Dunsmuir ghost story is recounted in James Audain's *Alex Dunsmuir's Dilemma*. Audain was one of James Dunsmuir's grandsons so he was privy to family stories. Published in 1964, the book is a fascinating account of Alex's eccentric life and early death.

After Alex passed away, his ailing wife Josephine travelled to Victoria in order to settle affairs with the family. While staying with James and Laura at their pre-Hatley "Burleith" home, she claimed Alex's apparition appeared to her several times. He told her to return to New York to undergo an operation she had been putting off. A maid Josephine confided in later shared the secret with the Dunsmuir family. Josephine left earlier than intended and got the operation, but she died eighteen months later.

Some have suggested the Dunsmuirs may have been cursed, either by betraying the wrong person in business matters or by taking coal from the Nanaimo vein, which according to elders' accounts in *Two Houses Half Buried in Sand* was sacred to the Snuneymuxw people. The family wealth was gone within two generations, and many of the family members met with untimely deaths. Robert's other daughter, Agnes, died the same year he did from typhoid, as did her husband right after. Their son, James Swan Harvey, was crippled in the First World War and eventually succumbed to his injuries many years later. Marion died shortly after Robert did, and Alex not long after her. Another of Robert's daughters, Effie, passed away in an asylum. Boy was killed during the submarine attack, and his sister Kathleen died in a café bombing in Paris in 1941. Rifts, illnesses, corruption, a market collapse, and mismanagement of family funds—the Dunsmuir fortune gradually disintegrated into nothing.

Tzouhalem totem by Master Carver and Elder Simon Charlie.
PHOTO BY SHANON SINN

CANNIBAL SPIRITS AND MOUNT TZOUHALEM

COWICHAN VALLEY

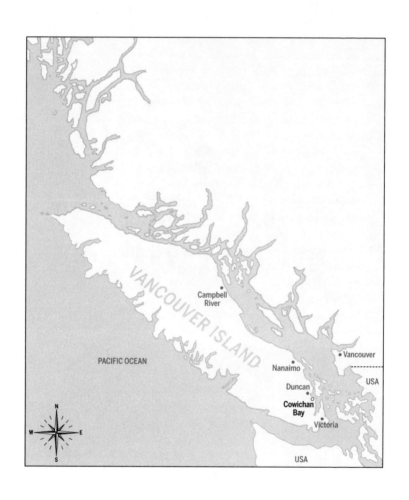

DUNCAN IS NESTLED IN THE Cowichan Valley, roughly halfway between Victoria and Nanaimo. At the east shore of the island near the small city is Mount Tzouhalem, named after an enigmatic First Nations chief who continues to inspire fear in whites and non-whites alike over 150 years after his untimely death.

Most of what is known about Chief Tzouhalem (Ts'uw'xilum, pronounced "zoo-hay'-lum") has been gathered from Cowichan First Nation oral sources. The Cowichan—like the Songhees—are Coast Salish. The term "Cowichan" is used to represent seven different villages that existed independently of one another before the government made them into a single band.

Tzouhalem grew up during a period of constant war. The Pacific Northwest First Nations people were known to conduct Viking-like raids as far south as Mexico. Men were killed in battle, while women and children were taken as slaves along with other spoils of war, such as tools, jewellery, and art.

In *The Terror of the Coast: Land Alienation and Colonial War on Vancouver Island and the Gulf Islands, 1849–1863*, Chris Arnett says that Chief Tzouhalem was raised during this tumultuous time of constant warfare by his grandmother, who was a mystic. Though his birthdate is never given, it is likely he was born before 1820. Tzouhalem's grandmother taught him sacred rites involving purification, prayer, and self-sacrifice as a means of acquiring gifts of power. To be a great warrior, he was to wash and rub himself every day with tree branches. He would go alone into the mountain forests until he met spirits willing to speak with him. When he had found a suitable spirit, he would make a pact that would make him the most powerful warrior on the coast.

Elders Johnny and Rosalie Seletze in *Two Houses Half Buried in Sand: Oral Traditions of the Hul'q'umi'num' Coast Salish of Kuper Island and Vancouver Island* (compiled by Chris Arnett) said that Tzouhalem's grandmother was motivated by revenge. Recorded in the 1930s by Beryl Cryer, the elders said that Haida from the archipelago of Haida Gwaii to the north had raided the Cowichan when Tzouhalem was a young child. He had been in the forest with his grandmother and had missed the attack. Many of the people were killed though, and his mother and baby brother were taken as slaves. One of the other slaves later escaped and brought the story of their fate back with her: the baby had cried so the raiders had thrown him into the water to drown. When Tzouhalem's mother began to weep they threw her overboard to die as well.

Tzouhalem's grandmother wanted him to be a warrior so he could fight the enemies of the Cowichan. She was determined that he would be greater than any other warrior on the coast.

Elder Qwulsteynum in *Two Houses Half-Buried in Sand* explained how some of Tzouhalem's power was acquired: there was a sacred hole on the side of Mount Tzouhalem that young men would reach their hand into. They would find an item inside that would indicate what kind of power they would have. A man who found goat hair or fish scales would be a hunter or a fisherman. Tzouhalem however, pulled out long black human hair. This was why he was good at killing people and "taking heads."

According to University of Victoria anthropologist Brian David Thom, this type of power seeking was common. In his thesis, *Coast Salish Senses of Place*, Thom explains that the spirit world is believed to be symbiotic with the natural world, and there is a prevailing belief that, to do anything well, one must have a connection to this "non-human world." If a person suffered hard enough or had been lucky enough to find one of the powerful supernatural beings— or *stl'eluqum*—that person could acquire supernatural powers. Presumably, the mountain had always been sacred. Thom shares a story of an old woman who also found her power generations before on Mount Tzouhalem.

For years, the old lady had climbed the mountain and ritualistically washed herself in a secret sacred pool. One day, she found a serpent-like being there. Her first instinct was to run, but the idea came over her that this could be the spirit being she had been waiting for. She stood and fought with the creature but lost consciousness. After an unknown amount of time, she woke up. As she began to gather materials for weaving, the old lady realized she had attained the knowledge to weave waterproof baskets. The story implies she was the first of many to carry this gift, and that she passed this knowledge on to future generations of her people.

According to Arnett, Tzouhalem's *stl'eluqum* was far more sinister. His purpose was to make war on his enemies, so he needed a spirit greater than any other warrior on the coast. The only *stl'eluqum* that could give Tzouhalem the power to crush all of his enemies was a cannibal spirit. This supernatural creature promised to accompany him into battle, teaching him a secret song and dance involving his "gun and knife." Part of Tzouhalem's power would come from eating human flesh, which presumably fed the cannibal spirit and gave it access to his body.

Many warriors had power songs they sang before battle, which put them into a "frenzied" state one could easily compare to that of the Norse Berserkers. Evidence suggests, however, that accessing this berserker-like possession through cannibalism was rare amongst the Coast Salish.

In *Aboriginal Slavery on the Northwest Coast of North America*, Leland Donald deconstructs the First Nation cannibalism ritual in greater detail: it was usually practiced on slaves or on those slain in battle to feed a particular supernatural being. When human flesh was consumed, the being—like Tzouhalem's *stl'eluqum*—would become one with the host. The ritual would likely be performed alone and away from the people. At a time of peace, the cannibal would return to their village in a possessed state, often needing to bite the first person they came in contact with. A slave would sometimes be sent out as a sacrifice in order to spare important members of the village.

There are three First Nation groups on Vancouver Island: the Coast Salish (predominantly along the inside of the island), the Kwakwaka'wakw (covering much of the north), and the Nuu-chah-nulth (found on the west side of the island). Donald proposes that the Kwakwaka'wakw and Nuu-chah-nulth used cannibalism (as recorded by multiple explorers and as told by elders), while the Coast Salish (other than those in the Comox region) usually did not. Elder Qwulsteynum also said this was not a practice used by the Salish but that it was more common for northern groups. The Kwakwaka'wakw even had a secret society dedicated to cannibalism called the *Hamatsa* (though some claim the ceremony was only symbolic, as it is today).

The practice of cannibalism may have been the reason Tzouhalem was banished from his village of Quamichan as a young man. Asked to leave, he took a group of followers and built a fortified compound at the mouth of the Cowichan River—which runs through present-day Duncan—near Mount Tzouhalem, which is on the north side of Cowichan Bay.

According to oral tradition, the young warrior continued to practice his rituals in a cave somewhere on Mount Tzouhalem. It is likely that Tzouhalem's warriors would have practiced these rituals as well.

Elder Rosalie Seletze, a relative of Tzouhalem, said in *Two Houses Half-Buried in Sand* that he would wear his hair long, fastened on top of his head with twigs and branches. Tzouhalem kept a live snake in his hair as well, which he claimed would help him kill anyone who disobeyed his orders.

Arnett and several others have documented oral histories of the events that led to the Battle of Hwtlupnets, which took place around 1840 (dates in the 1850s are sometimes inaccurately given). These stories often have differences, but the main points are consistent.

Messengers came and warned Tzouhalem that a large invading force was approaching from the north. This enemy force was made up of hundreds of the Kwakwaka'wakw and their Comox allies. An "unprecedented alliance" of Coast Salish warriors were gathered including Snaw-naw-as (Nanoose), Snuneyemuxw (Nanaimo), Stz'uminus (Ladysmith/Chemainus), Quamichan (Cowichan), Saanich (north of Victoria), Esquimalt, Songhees, and others, including Musqueam (Vancouver) and Squamish warriors from the mainland across the Strait of Georgia.

Tired of the constant raiding and killing at the hands of this massive northern alliance, the Coast Salish warriors had formed their own army months before—even though some of them didn't always get along. When the enemy's "armada" of canoes was spotted coming from the north, messengers were sent out, stealthily calling the warriors to fight.

Having already prepared by ritual, Tzouhalem and his men left by canoe to join the army gathering nearby, chanting power songs with every stroke of their paddles.

The Battle of Hwtlupnets may have been the largest Pacific Northwest battle ever fought on the coast. The trap was set in the bay north of Tzouhalem's fortress—between Duncan and Salt Spring Island—in the shadow of Mount Tzouhalem itself. There, a canoe full of warriors dressed as women paddled into sight of the northerners. They then feigned an attempted escape. The northern alliance took the bait and began to pursue the "women" in hopes of easy plunder.

Canoes ornately decorated with *stl'eluqum* and animal spirits swept in from at least two different directions and ambushed the enemy, first through gunfire and then through close-quarter fighting. With nearer access to trading forts, the Coast Salish had had superior guns and ammunition for over a decade, while the northern alliance had fewer places to acquire modern firearms. Chaos ensued. Bullets ripped through the Kwakwaka'wakw's cedar-rope armour, killing and wounding many and simultaneously defeating the manoeuvrability and speed of their paddle-propelled canoes.

The bodies of dying men fell into the Kwakwaka'wakw canoes or toppled into the water. The dugout vessels were simultaneously rammed as walls of spears were pounded into the enemy. The large canoes were suddenly hopelessly undermanned, as battle wounds incapacitated necessary paddlers. Like the other warriors, Tzouhalem and his men would have fought in their spirit-frenzied states, having called their *stl'eluqums* to assist them.

The smell of spent ammunition accompanied the echoing crack of gunfire bouncing off the mountainside. War cries carried over the saltwater as warriors drowned or were hacked apart by frenzied attackers. The fighting took place first on the water, and then on land as some of the enemy futilely tried to escape along the shores of the bay. The sound of stone-headed war clubs silenced the screams of the dying. The Salish warriors had lost loved ones to the northern raiders for years. Their fury was merciless. The battle was decisive. It is likely that few, if any, of the northern raiders survived, though some claim that a handful may have. The defeat would have destroyed the northern alliance's capacity to conduct raids on this scale for decades. By that time, colonialization would already be well underway, severely discouraging any more battles of this kind.

When Fort Victoria was first built in 1843—three years after the battle—many of the Salish had initially been happy. The post, they were told, would provide them with trading access to luxury items, such as ammunition, blankets, and non-traditional food staples like flour and sugar. Unfortunately, the new settlers never informed the local Salish that their lands were being claimed as well. Not understanding the concept of ownership as it applied to the colonials, some grazing animals were killed by Coast Salish hunters for a feast.

The fort ceased trading and demanded that those responsible be turned over, or that they receive compensation. The people were offended. An order was sent out to gather the same Salish alliance that had fought at the Battle of Hwtlupnets.

According to Arnett, Tzouhalem arrived leading the Quamichan warriors and took command of the forces. Following two days of failed negotiations, the Salish army unleashed a steady stream of gunfire upon the fort.

The fort's commander, a trader for the HBC, told his men not to return fire. He knew that they were in a precarious situation. His men could not fight off such a large army, which continued to grow in size by the day. Instead, he loaded a canon with grape shot and fired at an empty cedar house, blowing it apart. This had the result he had hoped for. Tzouhalem's army halted the attack and returned to negotiations. After a decision was made, the settler was compensated for the slain animals with a payment of furs.

In the years following the attack on Fort Victoria, little is known about Tzouhalem. He was recognized by the colony as the official chief of the Quamichan sometime before 1853. That year's census named him as the highest-ranking member of the Quamichan people. Another 430 Quamichan men were listed in the census along with a similar number of women, boys, and girls.

There are many local legends about Tzouhalem during this dark period. Despite being the chief, it is usually said that he was not allowed to live in the village because he kept killing people— including family members. He was either still banished or had been banished once again. Some claim that he stayed in a cave on the side of the mountain with a host of wives he had accumulated.

Mount Tzouhalem cliff face, with cross visible at the top.
PHOTO BY SHANON SINN

Given the number of people the cave would have needed to hold and limited access to resources this is unlikely. It is more probable that Tzouhalem would have continued to stay in the compound at Cowichan Bay. Early explorer Robert Brown said there was still a Coast Salish-owned fort there in 1863.

The cliff on the mountain that faces the bay has a cross on it today. Chief Tzouhalem is said to have thrown people, including wives, opponents, and priests, off this cliff to their deaths. If Tzouhalem brought people all the way up the arduous mountain trail only to throw them to their death, it could only have been for one of two reasons: this would have either been a spectacle for Tzouhalem's followers watching below, or it would have been for ritual purposes, possibly both. It is far-fetched to think Tzouhalem ever threw priests off this cliff though, as there would have been records of this having taken place, or of priests going missing. The church would have reported any missing missionary to officials who would have investigated.

By 1853, Tzouhalem had become a terrifying figure to the Coast Salish. Oral tradition says that by this time he had many wives taken from various villages after killing their husbands. The legends say he had fourteen at the time of his death, but also that he had much more than this at other times.

Arnett, in *The Terror of the Coast*, recounts the incident that led to Tzouhalem being killed: there was a woman living on Penelakut Island named Tsae-Mea-Lae who was married to a warrior named Shelm-tum. Tzouhalem wanted her, so in 1854 he went to the island in order to entrance her through song and dance. Seeing him coming, the villagers hid to avoid his powerful magic, and possibly plugged their ears as well. When Tsae-Mea-Lae didn't come out to greet him, Tzouhalem became confused and went into her house to find her. Tsae-Mea-Lae had hidden behind the door. As he entered, she grabbed him from behind and screamed for help. Shelm-tum came running to her aid, grabbed his axe, and cut off Tzouhalem's head.

Elder Rosalie Seletze in *Two Houses Half-Buried in Sand* said that the people of Penelakut kept the body but sent the head back to the Quamichan. Other versions claim that Tzouhalem's head was paraded by canoe up and down the coast by Shelm-tum so that everyone would know that the feared chief was finally dead. They had sent the body back but kept his head, conducting rituals over it to make sure he would never rise from the dead. As keeping heads from slain enemies was customary, it is more likely the Penelakut kept his head.

St. Ann's Catholic Church, with Mount Tzouhalem in the background.
PHOTO BY SHANON SINN

According to the BC Geographical Names website, Mount Tzouhalem appeared on maps as Tzohailim Hill as early as 1855, so may have been called this by colonists even before he had died. An inn was named after him in 1901, along with a road and several other places. In 1966, carver Simon Charlie added a detail of Tzouhalem to a totem pole now located in the library in Duncan. Interestingly, the totem pole has a snake behind Tzouhalem striking a protective pose.

According to a 2015 *Times Colonist* article, some claim that the first cross was placed on Mount Tzouhalem in the 1950s, while others say it was placed there in 1976 as part of a joint Easter ceremony by St. Ann and St. Edward's churches. The site of the cross offers a panoramic view of the Cowichan Bay. It can also be seen from across the valley. It is hard not to wonder if its placement at such a reputedly evil site contained exorcism-like considerations as well.

The cross has had a difficult history at this site. It was set on fire and vandalized several times. Then it was chopped down. A steel cross was erected in 1988. This was somehow thrown off the cliff in 2014. BC Local News reported that the Nature Conservancy of Canada—whose lands the cross had been sitting on—asked the public for feedback and found that eighty percent wanted to see the cross put back in place. This included Chief William Seymour speaking on behalf of the Cowichan People. As a result, a new cross was erected in 2015.

Even with the cross in place, the cannibal chief is believed to haunt Mount Tzouhalem to this day. In online forums, people often claimed to feel "watched" or inexplicably frightened walking along the trails. Caves on the mountainside are also believed to be inhabited by his spirit. On my Living Library blog post "Haunted Locations on Vancouver Island," one commenter said that she and her family, living near the base of the mountain, could hear "old drums in a native rhythm." They had also seen and heard many things that they couldn't explain. They were afraid to leave their home or open their windows at night. She also said that they took pictures inside their home that contained orbs, or balls of light.

There are claims people have seen Chief Tzouhalem's apparition, but those I have investigated are second-hand. Strangely, Tzouhalem is never said to manifest as a headless ghost. I find this detail interesting, especially because his body and head were separated after death.

On a Nanaimo forum (no longer in existence), a woman claiming to be Tzouhalem's great-great-granddaughter said that his apparition has been seen both on the mountain itself and walking down Tzouhalem Road past the graveyard of St. Ann's Catholic Church. The cemetery contains mostly First Nations Christians and wasn't built until fifty years after Tzouhalem's death, so it is a strange place for him to be. Others have also claimed that Tzouhalem haunts this area. The legend implies that Tzouhalem's ghost is looking for flesh, or possibly Cowichan Christian spirits to consume. The man who had inspired so much fear during his life continues to frighten people in death.

The night is chill. Wisps of fog roll across the forest trail. An owl calls into the darkness. Hairs rise up and down one's spine. Breathing becomes shallow and difficult. A sense of dread slowly twists up the narrow tree path. Unblinking black eyes shine from out of the shadows. He steps closer, out of an even darker place. His chest and face are bare, covered in scars and traced in patterns of blood. A snake writhes and dances around his head. Frothy bubbles of blackish red dribble down his mouth and chin, dripping slowly onto the forest floor. Fir branches are tied around his head and arms. In one hand is a long jagged-looking blade. In the other, held by fistfuls of hair, are several wide-eyed and open-mouthed severed heads. There is a choking rhythmic sound. The ghost of the cannibal chief is laughing.

Mount Sicker Hotel ca. 1925.
IMAGE 1997.10.3.1, COURTESY OF COWICHAN VALLEY MUSEUM & ARCHIVES

THE HEADLESS WOMAN
OF MOUNT SICKER

COWICHAN VALLEY

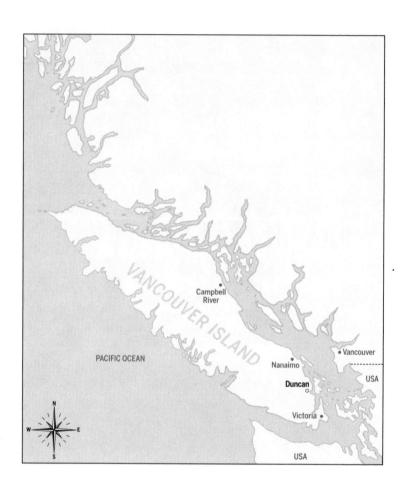

PACIFIC OCEAN

VANCOUVER ISLAND

Campbell
River

Nanaimo

Vancouver

Duncan

USA

Victoria

N
W — E
S

USA

FOR DECADES NOW, PEOPLE HAVE been claiming to see the apparition of a woman near the old Lenora townsite on Mount Sicker north of Duncan. There aren't any buildings left standing anymore—and the exact location is hard to find—but the ominous ghost story persists just the same.

The discovery of copper, silver, and gold in the late 1800s led to Mount Sicker (named after a local pioneer) being heavily staked by 1900. Three companies competed to mine the ore, eventually resulting in the failure of all of them. Without the mines, the townsites were quietly abandoned and slowly disappeared. Another company took ore from the mountain in the 1940s and 50s, but with modern technology there was no need to create a settlement so close to the mines.

At its height, the Lenora townsite (1900–1907) had a store, opera house, school, and hotel. The Mount Sicker Hotel was upscale enough that it was often used to entertain wealthy investors and newsmen. There was also a second community, Tyee (1901–1909), which had a smaller hotel, post office, and church. The church would have likely had a graveyard nearby.

Local newspaper stories suggest that the townsites were bustling places. Lenora's Mount Sicker Hotel was mentioned often. The mines were worked so hard that there were three shifts a day in the shafts. T.W. Paterson said in *Ghost Towns & Mining Camps of Vancouver Island* that the mountain's population was almost two thousand people at its peak. The Municipality of North Cowichan's *Guide To: Mount Sicker* says that there were seventy homes in the two villages combined.

Several years ago, when I first heard that Mount Sicker was haunted, the story was of a headless apparition, but others have since said that the ghost isn't headless at all.

According to accounts, she's usually seen on the old logging road near where the Lenora townsite used to be—but she's also said to wander other logging roads and the paved edges of Mount Sicker Road at the base of the mountain. A claim from a 2004 forum (no longer in existence) said that the woman's apparition even wanders through nearby farmer's fields.

One legend is that of a miner who found his wife cheating on him in the Mount Sicker Hotel. He killed her, either by accident—when he tried to kill the other man—or on purpose. The husband then cut the woman up and scattered her remains across the mountainside. Ever since, she's been searching for her missing head.

Old newspaper accounts do not support this domestic-murder story. The most brutal homicide took place on August 20, 1905. The *British Colonist* reported that a miner named Frederick Charles Breech took his 38.55 rifle and set out to kill the widow Mrs. Campbell and her suitor out of jealousy. Hotelkeeper Joseph Bebeau—"a quiet and inoffensive man"—went to investigate and was viciously shot and killed. Breech fled the scene, a manhunt commenced, and he committed suicide before he could be caught.

There were also mining fatalities during those early years. Additionally, the old tracks were treacherously steep and described as dangerous as well. Newspapers implied that people also died on them. All of these deaths would have been male—I have never come across any mention of a woman dying at either townsite, even from natural causes.

The Lenora site is now difficult to find. A logging company tore down what remained of the old buildings. There are supposed to be bricks in the area for confirmation—possibly some hidden ruins—but I've never been able to confirm anything definitive.

Accounts are consistent that the Headless Woman of Mount Sicker doesn't interact with people. She glides in front of them across the road where the Lenora townsite once stood or is seen walking in one of the other areas mentioned.

A 2004 Club Vibes online thread on real ghost stories had a second-hand account from a user named Beame. He said that the apparition had haunted his parents when they used to live in the area, but he did not elaborate. His claim was that the apparition was headless.

Larry Baker's comment on my blog, Living Library, in 2014 also corroborates the headless apparition story. He said that he and several others had visited the old hotel when there were still ruins left. All of them described seeing "something" on the remains of the hotel floor. His father described it to him as "looking through old glass." Larry said his uncle ran away and would never speak about the encounter again. His father's girlfriend, on the other hand, said that she saw a woman standing beside Larry in "a barrel-hoop dress." This woman was headless.

Also from 2014, a comment from a visitor calling himself Sam said he had never known the woman to be headless, but that he had heard of her. She would suddenly walk in front of vehicles on the dark road. Sam's "ex-girlfriend's father" claimed this had happened to him. The man had been driving when a woman appeared in front of his truck. He swerved to miss her, lost control of his vehicle, and got into a serious car accident that "wrecked all of his teeth." He then "climbed out of the wrecked truck to see if he ran the woman over, but he was all alone on the dark side of Mount Sicker."

The most convincing story appeared in the *Ladysmith Chemainus Chronicle* in 2011. An article by Ed Nicholson recounted a fellow *Chronicle* associate's experience. Rob Kernachan had said that he had actually seen the woman on Mount Sicker Road. Kernachan described her as a pale-looking young woman wearing a white nightgown. She was walking along the side of the road before "she just disappeared."

Stories of headless apparitions, like the Headless Horseman, are commonly told all over the world. Many times, the legend claims that the apparition is looking for its head. If this were the case, wouldn't Chief Tzouhalem be headless? And assuming these sightings really did take place, why would some accounts have her with a head while others claim she was headless?

A common detail in many ghost stories is that the apparition has no feet. Then there is the Craigdarroch Castle account where the worker only saw the lady's feet but nothing of the rest of her. Robert Belyk in *Ghosts: True Tales of Eerie Encounters* tells another, equally bizarre, tale. A couple in Victoria's Beacon Hill Park claimed they saw an apparition of a man from the waist down, only "half of the body."

Reports of partial entities or encounters that don't fit into a usual mould have a component that makes them somewhat more believable to me. When one also considers that some apparitions are very transparent and difficult to see, while others are said to be so solid they look like real people, it brings up questions that are difficult to answer. Whatever ghosts are, whether they are imprints we do not yet understand, visions from another realm, psychological in nature, or beings we can't usually see, the partial or transparent apparition

Reports of the apparition sometimes describe her as headless.
IMAGE BY DESERTROSE7

might exist only because we are incapable—in that moment—of seeing the entity clearly.

For some reason, the woman's ghost is sometimes seen as headless while at other times it is not. She will always be the Headless Woman of Mount Sicker to me, if only because that was the story I heard first. She is also the only headless apparition on Vancouver Island that I'm aware of.

She moves slowly through the darkness, across fields and along tree-lined roads far from the lights of civilization. The slender woman's legs and arms are bloodlessly pale. She wears an old-fashioned white nightgown that clings to her shapely body. At first, her face looks to be hidden completely in shadow, but as she steps more clearly into the space between the trees it is clear she has no head. She does not deviate from her path, but stumbles upon her way for several long moments. Then, she is gone. A wave of frigid air rushes past where she has just been. The night is deathly quiet.

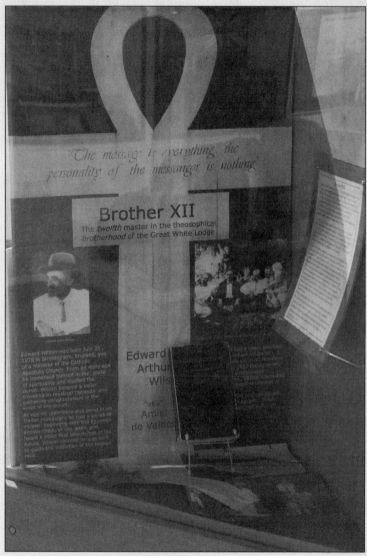

Brother XII display at the Nanaimo Museum.
PHOTO BY SHANON SINN

THE CURSE OF
BROTHER XII

CEDAR

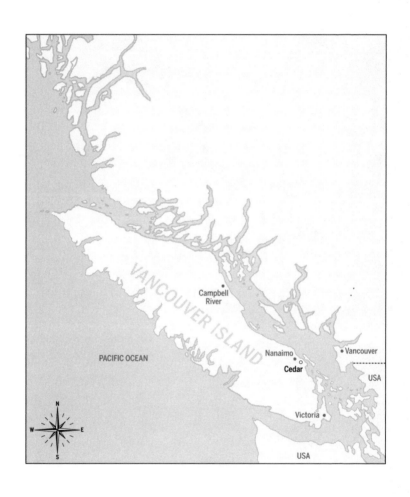

THE RURAL COMMUNITY OF CEDAR is just south of Nanaimo. It was once home to one of North America's most sensational cults. Much has been written about Brother XII—the infamous preacher of the 1920s and 30s. He was, after all, the charismatic leader of the Aquarian Foundation and later the head of a similar offshoot group. Edward Arthur Wilson—as Brother XII was legally named—would swindle hundreds of thousands of dollars from his most faithful followers. In the end, they would rise up against him and a battle would ensue involving legal proceedings, "psychic attacks," "black magic," protective First Nations magic, and assaults conducted by discarnate spirits. Brother XII would flee the battlefield with his closest of confidants—Madame Zee—but would perish on the run. Even the facts surrounding his death, however, have been contested to this day.

While the following events may sound fantastic, it's important to remember that, according to various sources, such as John Oliphant's *Brother Twelve*, all of the people involved believed these events actually occurred.

Historians concur that Wilson was born in England in 1878. His parents were members of a religious group that thought the biblical days of Revelation were at hand. According to later accounts from Wilson himself, he had always been gifted with the ability to communicate with spirits, including higher evolved beings and the dead. As an adult, Wilson eventually became a sea captain and travelled the world. During these travels he is said to have visited the holy temples of Egypt, India, Mexico, and China. He studied religion obsessively and subscribed to Theosophy—a blend of mystical and occult philosophies—in particular.

According to Oliphant, Wilson claimed he had a vision when he was in France in 1924. During this moment of enlightenment, he was told that he was one of the "Twelve Brothers" who had been tasked to help usher in a new age of enlightenment. These Brothers were all living men, but they were to be the tools of the ascended masters of a "White Lodge," tasked with helping facilitate this global change. Within three years of the vision, Wilson had dubbed himself Brother XII, and the Aquarian Foundation was established.

The headquarters of the Aquarian Foundation were located south of Nanaimo along a coastal region that included the Cedar area. The group would also—in its various forms—establish itself on nearby De Courcy and Valdes islands. The initial followers became frustrated with Wilson and brought him to court when they discovered he had been having extramarital affairs with some of his followers. He was also accused of using money that had been donated to the Aquarian Foundation for his own personal benefit.

In *Brother Twelve: The Incredible Story of Canada's False Prophet and His Doomed Cult of Gold, Sex, and Black Magic*, Oliphant says that the original group of followers thought that a "Black Adept" had possessed Brother XII. These Black Adepts were dark beings, similar in nature to the Christian version of demons. Apparently, a shift had come over Brother XII when he had attempted to perform an inner rite called the Sixth Initiation, which involved astral travel in order to obtain spiritual perfection. It was believed it was at this moment that Wilson shifted toward the darkness.

In a letter addressed to Wilson from one of his followers, it was stated that "imps"—small trickster or devil spirits—were seen circling him and an evil-faced monk's spirit was sometimes viewed in Wilson's presence.

Incredibly, Wilson was believed to possess the ability to spy on people remotely by leaving his body, pass through walls, listen to conversations through astral travel, and harness power in order to first fight the dark entities—and then later anyone who opposed him.

The Aquarian members began to have misgivings about Wilson as he seduced female followers, swindled people out of vast fortunes, and became more and more physically and verbally abusive.

The group finally brought Wilson to trial in 1928. The *Nanaimo Free Press* reported that he appeared to put a spell on a man named Turnball who testified against him. When Turnball was in the witness box he appeared to be attacked by a discarnate being, or spirit. Several people in the audience also fainted. The judge had a hard time speaking as well, so called for court to be adjourned for the day.

Jan Peterson said in *Harbour City: Nanaimo in Transition 1920–1967* that Wilson was being charged with stealing thirteen thousand dollars, "rape, assault, perjury, opium smuggling, and the sexual abuse of a 10-year-old girl." One of the key witnesses against Wilson disappeared in Seattle and is believed to have been murdered. As a result the case was dismissed, but the Aquarian Foundation was dissolved by order of the court in 1929.

Wilson's black magic and spiritual attacks had not been enough to stop the legal proceedings, but the disappearance of the witness and the failure of prosecutors created deeper levels of fear in those who entertained the idea of opposing him.

Oliphant describes an interesting ceremony in *Brother Twelve*: Wilson chose twelve disciples from his new group of followers and had each of them memorize lines—or incantations, if you will. Finally, on the evening of the ceremony, the group put on blue robes and travelled to De Courcy Island by canoe.

Wilson summoned spirits from "the four corners of the earth." At one point he yelled, "I now call fire down." A disciple threw water onto some branches, which immediately burst into flames.

The disciples would later say that during the ceremony they had been in awe of Brother XII's mastery over the four elements. One of them, however, would later theorize that Wilson had put white phosphorous into the water.

Another entry in the book describes how Wilson tried to kill his enemies with "black magic." First, Brother XII and two others would sit in a triangle. Then, he would imagine the person he intended to kill. Wilson then verbally cursed the victim while cutting the air with his hand. This gesture was supposed to "sever them from their physical bodies." Apparently, Wilson put curses like this on various government officials and legal representatives.

According to the *Nanaimo Free Press*, this second Aquarian-like group formed after the first one dissolved, and the patterns of abuse began to play out in a similar fashion.

In *Brother Twelve*, Oliphant says that Wilson's partner-in-crime, Madame Zee, put curses on outgoing mail and conducted hateful rituals. She often assigned harsh and demeaning physical labour to group members who challenged her authority. She even tried to kill a female member of the group using magic.

By the time these new followers were rising up to battle Wilson in court, a deep-rooted fear had taken hold of them. They had seen Brother XII's powers and had heard what had happened to the previous group members that had dared to face him. Due to this hysteria, the second court case was almost over before it had even begun.

Newspaper accounts claimed that new waves of psychic attacks were unleashed on this second group, similar to the first one. Some of them claimed to have been inexplicably paralyzed or to have been uncontrollably possessed by terror. Apparently, it had been conveyed to them that Wilson had put a curse on the witness box. As a result, all of the witnesses threatened to back out of the court case at the last moment.

According to Oliphant, one of the lawyers had in his possession a First Nations relic—a labret that had been worn by a medicine woman from Haida Gwaii, an archipelago north of Vancouver Island. The lawyer convinced the group members that if they held onto the item in the witness box no harm could come to them. The theory presented was that the magic was from the geographical area—that is to say, it was more *local* than Wilson's, so it was supposed to have more power. With this new magic in tow, every witness entered the box and testified with confidence.

When it became apparent that Wilson would lose the case (Oliphant writes that he had lost a "magic ring" that had been given to him by the masters), he fled British Columbia with Madame Zee in tow. They took all of the money—converted into gold—they'd taken from their followers. Before they left, however, Wilson smashed

Portrait of a Haida woman with a labret, from Captain George Dixon's 1787 visit to Haida Gwaii, an archipelago north of Vancouver Island.
PUBLIC DOMAIN, GEORGE DIXON

everything of value on the property he could get his hands on. As everyone else was in court, no one was around to stop him.

Edward Arthur Wilson, or Brother XII as he was also known, is believed by Peterson and many other historians to have died in Switzerland in 1934. Oliphant says this has been contested, however. Some people think the cult leader faked his death. For those who do not believe in the powers of servant spirits, psychic attacks, and black magic, this final act was just another con.

Wilson had convinced thousands of his followers to believe in the powers of the spirit world and in his ability to harness these beings. If these powers were real, then Wilson may truly have been "possessed" as many of his followers claimed. If on the other hand, he had no power, then the man had the capacity to fake anything.

Nanaimo Bastion & Harbour ca. 1910. Newcastle Island can be seen
in the background on the left, and Protection Island on the right.
IMAGE 1997 031 A-P2, COURTESY OF NANAIMO COMMUNITY ARCHIVES

KANAKA PETE, AXE MURDERER

NANAIMO AND NEWCASTLE ISLAND

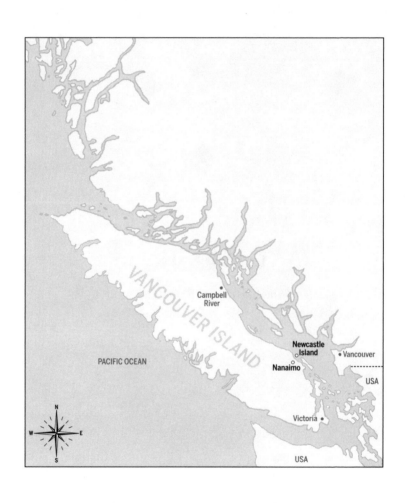

O N DECEMBER 4, 1868, AT two o'clock in the morning, Peter Kakua—a Hawaiian "Kanaka"—murdered his family with an axe. The victims included his wife, her parents, and his infant daughter. Peter was captured, tried, and hanged. With no one willing to claim his corpse, he was buried on a forested Nanaimo park island.

There are those who claim he resides there still.

Colville had become Nanaimo, and the gold rush that brought so many people to Victoria had ended. The year before, Canada had become unified into a single governed body. It would still be another year, however, before Robert Dunsmuir would find the coal vein that would make him rich.

The coal mines in Nanaimo had brought First Nations workers from the north, Americans seeking employment from the south, and toilers from many other nations by ship. These included Pacific Islanders. The men brought to Vancouver Island from Hawaii were often referred to as Kanakas, which sometimes had negative connotations, but means "free man" in Polynesian.

"Kanaka Pete" by W. J. Illerbrun was published in the *Hawaiian Journal of History* in 1971. Heavily researched, it is the most detailed account of Kakua's murders and trial.

Like many other Kanaka labourers, Peter had married a First Nations woman. Mary (Que-en) was from the Penelakut Nation, the same group who had killed Chief Tzouhalem fourteen years earlier. At the time of her death, the couple had been married for six years. It had not been a peaceful marriage. Peter had already served a three-month "hard labour" sentence for a vicious assault on Mary. In spite of the marriage's difficulty, Mary had given birth to an infant daughter—whose name is no longer known—shortly before the murder.

Mary tried to leave Peter in December of 1868. Her parents, Squash-e-lik and Shil-at-ti-Nord, had come to Nanaimo to bring her home. Peter was infuriated when he found out. He got drunk, returned to the small harbour cabin, and murdered everyone with an axe. The *British Colonist* reported that the scene was a "slaughterhouse." Court records indicate that his mother-in-law had been chopped in the back of the neck and that the baby's head was almost completely severed. The father had put up a fight and bit off one of Peter's fingers, but both he and Mary had still been hacked to death with the axe.

Illerbrun writes in "Kanaka Pete" that Peter claimed he remembered none of it. His defence, as reported by the paper as well, was that he had woken up the next day to find the gory scene. Instead of turning himself in, he began to make plans to flee. He showed the crime scene to another Hawaiian man the following evening. The man was horrified and went off to seek the constable. He was unsuccessful until the following morning.

By this time, Peter had paddled with another drunk to the far side of Newcastle Island. His plan had been to escape to the mainland, but the other man—a former American slave—had sobered up enough to protest. He did not yet know about the murders.

The heavily forested and sparsely populated island offered the two men a place to stop away from prying eyes. They built a beach fire and continued to drink.

It wasn't long before a search party spotted them. The group split in half. The first approached by canoe, while the second crept up on the men through the forest. Peter tried to escape but was apprehended. Illerbrun says he was brought back to Nanaimo and formally charged before being sent to Victoria for trial. He was then tried twice before separate juries as the judge had divided the murders. The killing of his wife could possibly be perceived as a crime of passion, but the other deaths were considered "a willful act."

Peter claimed he was not guilty. His lawyers asked for leniency as he had not been raised Christian and did not understand the ways of white men. This was a stretch, as Peter had already lived on Vancouver Island for fourteen years and Hawaiian immigrant murders were not common.

Most shameful of all was Peter's desperate attempt to put the blame on his wife and her family. He claimed that he had come home to find his wife having sex with her father in his bed. At best, it would be cavalier behaviour for a woman terrified of her husband. It was also outrageous. It wouldn't explain Peter murdering his baby or his attempt to flee either. It also directly contradicted his statements that he did not remember any of it.

As unlikely as this defence was, the court seemed to take it into consideration. The first jury decided Peter was guilty of murdering Mary, but recommended mercy. The second jury found Peter guilty as well, but asked that no mercy be given. The defence had failed to convince them that Mary's mother was a threat, as her body had been found in a place suggesting she had been hiding from the killer.

Peter was sent back to Nanaimo where he was incarcerated in the HBC's Bastion Fort. The *British Colonist* reported that he was hanged at seven o'clock in the morning on February 10, 1869, on a scaffold "within a dozen steps" from where he had committed the crimes. Peter offered no last words and accepted his fate stoically. The executioner was an unnamed convict who would receive a pardon for pulling the switch.

The people of Nanaimo, however, were presented with a dilemma. Neither the Penelakut nor the Snuneyemuxw wanted anything to do with the body. His defence of being non-Christian also prevented him from being laid to rest in any of the graveyards. It was decided he would be buried on Newcastle Island in the bay where he was captured—now called Kanaka Bay.

By 1899, Newcastle Island had become a site to quarry sandstone and mine coal. In a bizarre incident, a group of coal workers accidentally dug Peter Kakua up. The *Nanaimo Free Press* reported that the men opened the box not realizing it was a coffin. Inside they found a skeleton wearing a pair of leather shoes still in good condition. The body could be none other than that of the hanged man. He was moved a short distance away and reburied, where he is presumed to still be.

The most well-known sighting of Peter Kakua's ghost took place sometime before 1890 by James Hurst Hawthornthwaite (1869–1926), a regional political figure from 1901 to 1920. Before he was married, Hawthornthwaite had lived in an old cabin near the Bastion with Arthur Potts, an estate agent from another notable family. A story about the encounter was printed in 1958, years later, in the *Daily Colonist*: Mr. Potts woke up to what sounded like a fight taking place in the cabin. He ran into the living room to find Hawthornthwaite brandishing a fire poker. He asked Potts if he had seen where

Nanaimo Daily News Kanaka Pete cover story.
PHOTO BY SHANON SINN

the First Nations man "covered in blood and holding an axe" had gone. The men searched the home but found nothing. Years later, Hawthornthwaite relayed the incident "rather apologetically" to the chief of police. The chief was surprised that Hawthornthwaite did not know that this was either the cabin where the murder had taken place or one nearby. Hawthornthwaite chose to keep the incident otherwise private, but a few people knew about the encounter, eventually making the story public.

Bill Merilees in *Newcastle Island: A Place of Discovery* says that stories of Peter Kakua's ghost are often told to youth groups of Brownies and Cub Scouts camping on the island. Merilees elaborated in 2013 on Shaw TV. Peter Kakua, he said, wanders the island at dusk looking for young people to scare. Other versions claim he kills them.

Kanaka Bay is on the dark side of Newcastle Island, far from the lights of Nanaimo, moored boats, or campers tucked inside their sleeping bags. Those campers might hear a scream in the far distance, but no one else would.

The shadow of a large, hunched-over male moves slowly along the shore. His eyes are wide and unblinking, scanning side to side methodically, like a hunter's. His face wears a scowl. There is a long item in his hands. On one end is a dripping mess, on the other, a clenching and unclenching fist. The shadow stops suddenly. He hunches over more deeply, and moves cat-like toward his prey, one foot in front of the other, with jerking certainty.

The Bastion Fort, across the harbour from Newcastle Island, is also reportedly haunted. It's where Peter spent his last night.

The old HBC structure was completed in 1854, the same year Chief Tzouhalem was killed. The settlers were concerned about large groups of Haida or Kwakwaka'wakw raiders prowling the waters. According to the Nanaimo Museum, a "flotilla" of Kwakwaka'wakw canoes entered the harbour in 1855, causing residents to seek shelter inside the Bastion, but no fighting took place.

As the city grew, the protective structure became less and less necessary. It was almost demolished in 1891, but was saved and moved across the street. Thankfully, it was moved a short distance again in 1974 when the street was widened. Today, it is the only building of its kind left in North America.

Some historians have claimed that Peter Kakua was hanged on Protection Island at Gallows Point because other historic hangings had taken place there. This is not true. Across the harbour from the Bastion, Gallows Point is a site where two men, one Cowichan and the other Snuneymuxw, were hanged in 1853. In *Black Diamond City*, Jan Peterson says that the British ship the *Beaver* had tried them onboard for murdering a shepherd near Saanich. Called Tide Staff Point then, Gallows Point was the most convenient place to administer justice. It is generally believed that at least one of the men was innocent. Daniel Marshall in *Those Who Fell from the Sky: A History of the Cowichan Peoples* says that the Cowichan man was a slave handed over by the people to protect the man who may have been guilty. Gallows were constructed on the island near the ship, and the two men were executed. By the time Peter Kakua was hanged this site would have been impractical, as it would have required boating materials and men from Nanaimo for construction, and then the prisoner and witnesses as well.

Newspaper accounts confirm that Peter was executed in Nanaimo. An 1899 story in the *British Colonist* said that the scaffold was close to the cabin where the murder took place, which was also somewhere near the Bastion.

The Nanaimo Museum released a statement in 2004 saying that the Bastion was haunted. The claim was that tourists and staff had been reporting activity. Bill Poppy, who had been a bagpiper for the location for nineteen years, said he had heard things being moved, as well as footsteps above him when no one was there. The Bastion supervisor at the time, Jessica Krippendorf, stated she had heard whispering that stopped when she went to investigate. She had checked on a loud noise above her as well, only to discover that a nearly three-kilogram (six-pound) cannonball had been moved out of its case and was rolling across the floor.

I helped conduct research for the Nanaimo Museum's Lantern

Tours in 2013. These tours are offered in October and include ghost stories and other darker historic tales. Interpretation Curator Aimee Greenaway—who I reported to—told me that the claims the Bastion was haunted were true. Summer students had also found cannonballs out of place. No one could have possibly been upstairs when they had been moved.

There have been more whimsical-type reports as well. An out-of-town paranormal group stayed overnight in the Bastion in 2004. They later claimed they had evidence the building was haunted. The image of man's face had been found in a photograph in the grain of the wall's wood. With the popularity of "investigation"-style TV shows, this type of "evidence" became more and more popular in the early 2000s. The internet became flooded with images, where something vague would be circled and explained in detail by a paranormal team. This type of image—as I mentioned in the Hatley Castle report—is called pareidolia. This is what occurs when the mind tries to perceive a pattern where none exists. The group also claimed, however, that they had captured a light turning on and off on video. This was more compelling. The team said they would share the video online, but I do not believe they ever did.

If the Bastion is haunted, and if spirits of the dead really do cause these types of occurrences, then my best guess would be that it's Peter Kakua. His apparition has been seen at least once in the neighbourhood already. The murderer spent his last night in the Bastion, was hung outside, the killings took place nearby, and his remains weren't treated in a sacred way. All possible explanations for a haunting.

The Fire Hall and Fire Department, Nanaimo, B. C.

Historic Fire Hall No. 2 ca. 1910 (Building File: Nicol Street).
COURTESY OF NANAIMO COMMUNITY ARCHIVES

THE MYSTERY OF
NANAIMO'S OLD FIRE HALL

NANAIMO

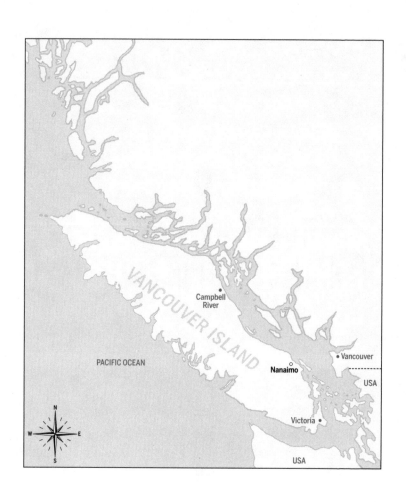

IRON OXIDE ART SUPPLIES STORE owner Willow Friday told me in 2014 that she never felt alone in the building her store was located in. "It's a good presence," she said, "it feels grandfatherly."

Not every haunting comes with apparitions fully manifesting. Sometimes, objects are moved without reason, odours—like burnt sandalwood—arrive without cause, and an overwhelming feeling of perpetually being watched prevails. Such is the case at Nanaimo's old Fire Hall No. 2.

The historic building is located on 34 Nicol Street—just south of the downtown area. Anyone driving through Nanaimo would recognize the iconic building, with its red brick Victorian Italianate tower—once used to dry off hoses—and castle-like appearance.

The upper level has been the Firehouse Grill since 2007, while the lower level has been Iron Oxide Art Supplies since 2014. The building hasn't served as a fire hall since 1967, but other restaurants and businesses have operated out of the old structure for years.

Willow sold art supplies out of the corner of a previous business before the idea for Iron Oxide presented itself. Art supplies were outselling everything else in her store, so Friday decided to open an art supply location in the lower level of the old fire hall. The activity began during renovations.

A hammer fell off a twelve-foot ladder and hit her harmlessly on the shoulder. Without registering why, Willow immediately said, "Thank you," as she felt that someone had guided the heavy item away from landing on her head.

As she worked beside her daughter Ocean and friends, Willow felt that there was a presence pushing her to work harder. When asked if it felt military-like, her response was, "Yeah, sort of."

The presence didn't seem to appreciate the pace others were working at, though. One friend had an item fall near him. Ocean had an open can of paint fall on her from a ladder. The presence, however, felt primarily motivational and positive.

There was a sense of serenity, for example, when the smell of burning "sandalwood" would suddenly permeate the air. Strangely, Willow was never able to locate the source of the smell.

According to the *City of Nanaimo Community Heritage Registry*, Fire Hall No. 2 was built in 1893. "The fortress-like crenelated roofline is particularly appropriate on the fire hall, a widely recognized symbol of protection." Iron Oxide's large doors were used for horses and equipment. The tower was added in 1914.

A 1968 radio series on now-defunct CHUB Radio called *Files of Yesteryear*, had an episode titled "The Beginning of the Nanaimo Fire Department" prepared by historian John Cass. His research found that the fire hall was designed by Mr. Honeyman and constructed by G.W. Frost. Honeyman had responded to a March 30, 1892, *Nanaimo Free Press* ad seeking proposals for a new brick fire hall. His plans were approved, the building was completed, and it became operational by September of 1893.

Many believe that ghosts are spirits who have met a tragic, or untimely, death. So I became curious if any of Nanaimo's firefighters had died in the building or in the line of duty while the hall was still being used.

Nanaimo has three recognized in-the-line-of-duty firefighter deaths. All of them spent time in the old hall, but none of their deaths occurred while the building was still being used.

The first death was Lieutenant Gordon Odgers who was fifty-six when he passed away. Odgers had joined the fire department in 1946 after returning home from military service overseas. According to the *Nanaimo Free Press*, while fighting a fire on October 20, 1974, Odgers had a heart attack and died on the scene. As a result, Odgers was recognized as Nanaimo's first fireman death. Odgers had worked out of Fire Hall No. 2 for twenty years and worked out of the new hall for seven more.

Bernard Moriez was a sixty-five-year-old volunteer firefighter when he was killed. Moriez had joined the fire department in 1938 when he was twenty-seven years old and stayed until his death. A large fire destroyed Nanaimo's Shell Oil plant gas and diesel storage tanks on September 7, 1977. Tragically, one of the resulting explosions killed Moriez who was trying to remove a vehicle from the yard. The *Canadian Coast Guard Association Newsletter* reported that the fire caused $3.8 million dollars in damage.

The *Nanaimo Free Press* said that Ian Michael Tychonick was found at the scene with burns to 90 percent of his body. Two days later, Tychonick was charged with arson and manslaughter. He never made it to court. He died from his injuries on October 20. The motives for his crime are still unclear, as Tychonick was not an employee of the plant. He had received a drinking and driving suspension earlier that night.

Barney Moriez Park near the scene of the fire is named in recognition of the fireman's sacrifice. Moriez had served thirty years in the old fire hall, but he hadn't worked out of the building for ten years either.

The third listed line-of-duty death was Captain Robert Owen who served in the Nanaimo Fire Department from 1966 to 1996. The *Nanaimo News Bulletin* reported that Owen was forced to retire due to heart disease attributed to service. He died fifteen years later, on August 17, 2010, at the age of seventy-two. His death was classified as in-the-line-of-duty, even though Owen hadn't taken a fire call in over a decade. Station A News Vancouver Island reported that the service was attended by firefighters from all over the province. Captain Owen likely only worked out of the old fire hall for the first year of his career. He had no connection to the building for the next forty-three.

Despite being Nanaimo heroes, none of the men seemed a likely candidate for a haunting. They didn't have a connection to the building at the time of death and they hadn't passed away on the property either.

I was surprised then, when I found a fourth firefighter death, one that had not been recognized as a line-of-duty death at the time. Amazingly, John Parkin had been the fire chief for over forty years. His service occurred almost exclusively out of Fire Hall No. 2. Additionally, the chief lived with his family above the fire hall on the upper level where the Firehouse Grill is now. I was even more surprised to learn he had died in the building. Fire Chief John Parkin seems the most likely candidate for the unexplained activity.

By today's standards, Parkin would be considered a line-of-duty-death without question. During the 1937 funeral ceremony, Reverend W.P. Bunt is quoted in the *Nanaimo Free Press* as saying that Parkin "died on active service."

The fire hall's distinct tower was added in 1914 as a means to hang hoses to dry.
PHOTO BY SHANON SINN

According to Jan Peterson in *Harbour City*, Parkin joined Nanaimo's Black Diamond Fire Department in 1889, four years before the new building was completed. He became chief in 1897.

Historian John Cass told CHUB that the whole fire department didn't move into Fire Hall No. 2 until 1894 after a fire destroyed Fire Hall No. 1. The Black Diamond Fire Department, which had been privately operated, became municipal in 1901.

The *City of Nanaimo Community Heritage Registry* (Parkin Block entry) says that Fire Chief John Parkin and his family lived above the fire hall. They used to host family dinners every Saturday night when "Youngsters used to amuse themselves by sliding down the fireman's pole."

In a presentation to the Nanaimo Historic Society in 1974, Fire Chief Albert Dunn spoke about the fire department's history. A March 1914 invitation to the Fireman's Banquet read like a long-winded poem, but it contained a portion about Parkin that is character revealing:

> Now there's Chief Parkin with trumpet in hand,
> Not big in size but a whale to command;
> Who faces the danger every fire he goes,
> But never fears as it's his duty, he knows.
> I speak for the boys when I wish this good wish
> That he may live long and enjoy times like this.

Albert Dunn also spoke about the connection Parkin had to the firefighting superhorses, Tom and Jerry. The horses were kept in the portion of the building that now houses Iron Oxide Art Supplies.

Older fireman still working when Dunn had joined the force told him the horses were so intelligent they used to trip their own harness lever with their noses (to put their harnesses on) when a fire call came. Apparently, the horses could tell by Parkin's voice on the phone whether it was an emergency call or not.

In January of 1937 Parkin led a fight against one of "Downtown's largest fires." The *Nanaimo Free Press* reported that he developed pneumonia after becoming drenched and being exposed to the harsh winter conditions. He died at the fire hall on February 25, 1937. He was seventy years old.

"Jack," as his friends referred to him, was highly respected by his coworkers and the community. The *Nanaimo Free Press* obituary from February 26, 1937, had the following to say about him:

> It will take a lot of canvassing to find a man capable of taking John Parkin's place. He knew every hydrant of the city; he knew the grade of every street, and he was never afraid to take his place on the front seat of the truck with the driver, sound the alarm, and tell him where to look out for "pot holes," and where to "turn her loose." He was never afraid of speed, and never afraid to take his place in the front ranks of the fire fighters. Jack Parkin had what it took to be a man.

Eighty years later, Chief Parkin might still be connected to the building that represented his passion to fight fires. The vigour of the unexplained activity became subdued after the renovations were completed. Following up with Willow while writing this section, she told me that she often still feels like there is someone watching over her.

"I don't know where he goes," she said, "but he isn't here all of the time."

Items still fall inexplicably from time to time—something that has also been witnessed by staff—including a "twelve-pound" (five-and-a-half kilogram) metal object that had been secured in the corner since the store opened. Willow believes these things happen when the spirit is present.

Not only was John Parkin still the fire chief of Fire Hall No. 2 when he died, he passed away in his family quarters inside the building. The old chief certainly fits the criteria for the "tragic death" prerequisite associated with many traditional ghost stories—even if he was already seventy years old when he died. That detail would also make him "grandfatherly." Perhaps Parkin is still on duty, making sure everything is still in order, always on guard, and ready to serve the community again if he is ever needed.

"I knew it!" Willow said when she heard Fire Chief Parkin's story. "That totally makes sense."

Built in the 1930s, the Beban House is often said to be haunted.
PHOTO BY SHANON SINN

THE
BEBAN HOUSE

NANAIMO

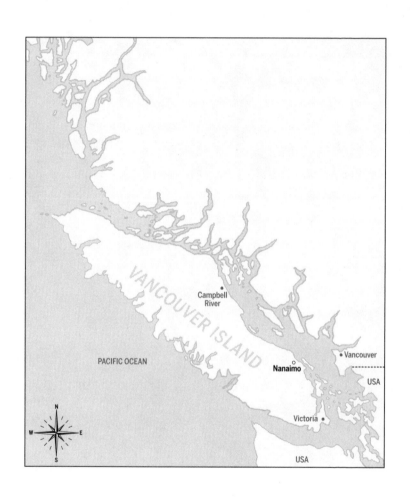

PRIOR TO TOURISM NANAIMO PURCHASING the old Beban House in 1997, it was a daycare. Children told caretakers stories of playing with a Chinese boy and his red ball. Adults reported activity in the house over the years as well, including RCMP members and office workers.

In *Harbour City*, Jan Peterson describes Frank Beban as a mine employee, a mill worker, and a horseracing entrepreneur. In 1906, he immigrated to San Francisco from New Zealand. He was twenty-four years old. One year later he moved to Vancouver Island to work in the mines for the Dunsmuirs. He married seventeen-year-old Hannah Hodgson in 1910 and had four children.

Beban inherited some money, which he successfully invested in several businesses including a lumber mill. According to City of Nanaimo records, he bought 160 acres in 1930 to use for horse stables. The Beban family tore down the old home and spent twenty-five thousand dollars to build a rustic-style log country house on the same site.

Valerie Green said in *If More Walls Could Talk: Vancouver Island's Houses from the Past* that Beban passed away in the upstairs bedroom. The year was 1952 and he was seventy years old. With the children already married and moved out, Hannah sold the property in 1956 to the City of Nanaimo for fifty-three thousand dollars. She passed away in Nanaimo in 1969.

The style of the Beban House was popular when it was built, but domestic buildings from the era were becoming increasingly rare. So in 1996, the home, garage, and grounds were added to the *City of Nanaimo Community Heritage Registry*. Tourism Nanaimo made the Beban House a tourist information centre in 1997. By this time, it was already believed by many to be haunted.

The Beban House has acquired a certain level of fame because of a story about a boy with a red ball. Robert Belyk shared accounts in *Ghosts: True Tales of Eerie Encounters*. The TV show *Creepy Canada* featured the house in 2002, as did CTV News Vancouver Island in 2011, *Nanaimo Daily News* in 2009, and *Nanaimo News Bulletin* in 2014.

Like many reputedly haunted locations, the stories evolved over the years. Once more, *Creepy Canada* was especially inconsiderate of historic facts and provided fictional accounts of encounters. Most of the Beban House segment included convincing testimonial evidence from witnesses, however, even if the facts surrounding the original story had been manipulated or misconstrued.

It is generally stated that a Chinese boy died in the house. While the spirit is said to be a young child, later accounts have claimed that a "young servant killed himself." Peterson in *Harbour City: Nanaimo Transition 1920–1967* said that the Bebans had one Chinese cook who also helped the family with the gardens. The family had no maids. In *Ghosts*, Belyk said that the son of a Chinese servant died in the house. If this is true, then the child would have to be the cook's.

Tourism Nanaimo staff had told Belyk about the apparition of a Chinese boy seen by children at the daycare. The child had a long black braid, wore a white nightgown, and was playing with a red ball.

Interviewed by *Creepy Canada* in 2002, "Publicity Officer" Farren Ferguson said that the child's spirit had come to light during the mid 1980s. A four-year-old at the daycare had drawn an unusual picture of a child playing with a red ball. The caretaker was shocked to recognize the same image another child had drawn four years earlier. The boy in the picture had a long strip of hair and wore white as well. When questioned, the daycare child said that this was a friend he had been playing with.

The boy in white does not speak. His dark brooding eyes stare widely at the innocent, breathing child. He passes the red ball to him, then waits to have it rolled back. He does not smile but instead fixes his gaze on the ball as it is passed back and forth, over and over again.

Six Tourism Nanaimo officials have made public statements to various sources about activity they experienced while working in the building. These include footsteps on the stairs and floors above them, water faucets turning on, cupboards opening, items disappearing and reappearing, doors or windows being locked or unlocked, and an "unseen" presence. *Nanaimo Daily News* reported in 2009 that a newly arrived house cat had also been let out of a locked room overnight.

A woman's apparition has been seen on the upper floor of the building as well. In 2011, Tourism Nanaimo Executive Director Mark Drysdale told CTV News that a woman in a white dress had been seen looking out an upstairs window. The woman was mentioned as having been viewed by a witness "out of the corner of her eye." When she turned to look at the figure it had vanished. The woman was one of the tenants that rented an office from

Tourism Nanaimo. "People are terrified," Drysdale said. "Everyone has a story."

The RCMP had an office in the building as well. Belyk in *Ghosts* said that one of the police officers claimed he saw a woman standing in front of the former master bedroom. This account and many of the others is also shared in *If More Walls Could Talk: Vancouver Island's Houses from the Past.*

Lee Mason, who worked in an office rented to the United Way, told *Creepy Canada* that one of her employees had complained that a yellow powder was falling from the ceiling. When Mason went to check the woman's workspace, she saw the yellow substance all over her desk. Neither woman could determine where the powder had come from, so they cleaned the office and Mason went back to her own work area. The employee called her back almost immediately, saying that the powder was falling once more. As soon as she returned to the area the activity ceased. The ladies cleaned off the desk for a second time, and the bizarre incident never recurred.

Director of Tourism Richard Hudson told *Creepy Canada* that during a Halloween event in 2001 he left a phone off the hook as "part of the décor." The next day, when he returned to work, he noticed a message on his phone. When he listened to it he could hear thumping, people running, and laughter.

Caitlin Blakey, one of my friends who grew up in Nanaimo, said that she had an experience in the Beban House sometime around 1990 when it was still a daycare. She was three or four years old at the time, and it is her only memory of her time in the building. There was no red ball, and she does not remember details about the boy's appearance.

A Chinese boy in traditional dress has been seen in the Beban House.
PHOTO BY JOHN THOMSON

Caitlin said she was playing with "a truck or something" upstairs with a little boy. The daycare worker came to get her, and when she turned around the boy had vanished. She never heard the house was supposed to be haunted until she was a teenager. I was able to talk to her father, Dan, who confirmed the story. He told me that when he picked his daughter up she told him that she had seen a ghost. The memory stuck with him. He said he learned much later that the house was supposed to be haunted as well. When he did, he thought, "Holy shit. I exposed my kid to that."

Vancouver Island University's theatre is believed to be haunted by a former professor.
PHOTO BY SHANON SINN

Vancouver Island University's Theatre Ghost

NANAIMO

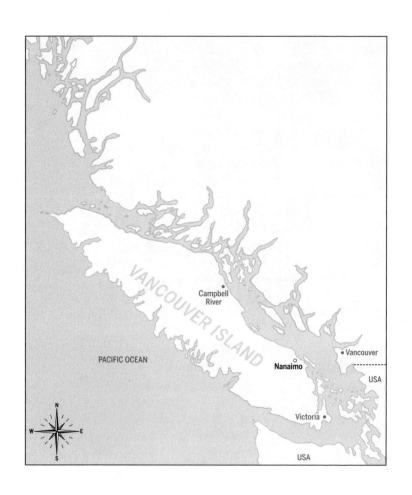

SOMETIMES, A GHOST STORY EXISTS where a person least expects it. When I first heard that the theatre building at Vancouver Island University (VIU) was said to be haunted, I was surprised. I could not think of a single reason why anyone would falsely claim there was a ghost on campus. The story was not public knowledge either. In fact, it was almost a department secret, barely known among students in other programs.

The building was also relatively new. Its first play, *Ring Around the Moon*, was performed in the fall of 1976. There had never been another building on the location the theatre had been built on.

If the theatre was haunted, it would not increase ticket sales or bring the type of tourists that would be welcome. A non-campus "paranormal investigator" looking for a chance to whip out an electromagnetic field detector would likely get a kick in the pants. There would never be an official statement about it, and critical-thinking students would be the first to look for an alternative explanation to any activity—artistic types or not. The transient nature of the student population also means that someone would have an experience and then graduate. New students would then arrive and have experiences themselves. According to what is informally known as the "telephone game" effect, the story should have evolved without the original contributors around. It had not, however. To make matters even more interesting, instructors believed they knew who the spirit was.

Interviewed in 2017, Theatre Chair Leon Potter said he remembered hearing about the haunting when he began to work at VIU twelve years earlier. When he first heard the story, he did not take it very seriously. Shortly after he started, people were taking pictures at opening night. In one of them "a glowing orb" was behind him. That was only the beginning.

Leon heard that the spirit was a former technical director, the same position he had taken. When something unexplained would happen, they would say, "that's just Neil."

Neil Rutherford was born in 1946 and raised in Northern Saskatchewan. His father took a job with the CBC and moved the family to Vancouver in 1957. After graduating from high school, he studied design in England at the Wimbledon School of Art. He then completed his degree at Simon Fraser University. Vancouver Island University was still called Malaspina University-College when the Theatre Department was founded.

Rutherford took a position in 1977, at twenty-nine years old, teaching stagecraft and design. The *Mainly Malaspina* newsletter said that *Dark of the Moon*, his first play, promised he would deliver "a set that has to be seen to be believed." Rutherford was credited as "Design" for almost twenty VIU plays between 1978 and 1984. Following in his father's footsteps, he returned to Vancouver in 1985 to work for the CBC. He's listed as an art director for at least one episode of the TV show the *Odyssey* (based on the Greek myth) and was involved in many other projects as well.

On January 29, 1994, Rutherford was returning to Vancouver from Seattle with friends when their vehicle was involved in an accident. He was killed. The group had gone to Seattle to see a play.

The Phantom of the Opera reflects the belief that many theatres are haunted.
PUBLIC DOMAIN, COVER OF 1921 EDITION OF *LE FANTÔME DE L'OPÉRA* BY GASTON LEROUX

Activity in the theatre is said to have started almost immediately, but why there? Rutherford had not passed away in the building or been working in it at the time. Could his return have had something to do with the play he had just seen? Could he have been reminiscing about his Malaspina days when the accident occurred? Could there have been staff members he was close to still working at the theatre?

Many theatres on Vancouver Island are believed to be haunted, including the Langham Court Theatre, the Royal Theatre, and the McPherson Playhouse in Victoria. This should come as no surprise, as theatres all over the world abound with ghost stories. Before coming to VIU, Leon had worked at the Stanley Theatre in Vancouver. There, he also had an experience he can't explain. He was alone one morning when someone knocked on his office door. He opened it, but no one was at the door. This happened a second time. He said out loud that he knew the presence was there. There were no more knocks after that.

Then he came to VIU. One night, Leon had his children with him in the theatre as he was finishing up for the day. His seven-year-old daughter asked him who else was working. He told her no one was because it was late. His daughter then pointed up to the booth and said, "So who's that?" Leon saw a shadow figure. "That's Neil," he responded, "that's the ghost of the theatre, he takes care of the place."

He wanted to be honest, but he also wanted his children to know the presence was nothing to be afraid of. This was partially because his daughter had already had an experience a few years earlier in Vancouver. She had started to talk about a "reflection man" she had been "telling stories" to. When her parents asked her why she called him that, she gave a description while gesturing toward an empty hallway. Leon and his wife were able to ascertain that the man was around "six-foot-three or six-foot-four," dark-skinned and glowing. She thought he was cool because she could see through him. Leon walked down the hallway to investigate. It was like walking into "a wall of ice." Like the presence at the Stanley Theatre, he acknowledged it and asked for it to go away.

To Leon, the presences feel real, but "foreign" and somewhat creepy. He has his own theories as to why theatres are often said to be haunted. "There is a huge amount of catharsis that goes on, laughing and crying and joking, and passion, in a very concentrated space." A theatre then might be a natural magnet to emotional energy. He said he often thinks that ghosts might be an echo of emotion from a specific person's life as well. Wherever they put most of their love and attention while they are alive might be what they are drawn to in death. Theatre ghosts are so common, he said, that they have inspired plays like *The Phantom of the Opera*.

In the case of the VIU theatre building, Leon said between two and three people report incidents every year. The presence most often plays with the lighting board until it is acknowledged, but can be felt throughout the building. The stories never grow, and never feel exaggerated or blown out of proportion. Only some of the students are scared. The haunting has become "kind of a known thing" in the department.

Former VIU student Manda Chelmak took several pictures during opening night of *The Merchant of Venice*. She was looking through them several days later when she came across a strange image in one of the corners. Manda had taken several pictures of another student. In the background of one of them were a man's head and face. He was not in the picture before or after. The image gave her chills and "charged" her with emotion. She could see curly hair, details of the face, and a "ruffle" neck. The image faded out at the shoulders. For someone's face to be in the picture where the image had appeared, he would have had to be eight feet tall. Manda reported the image to instructors who told her about the haunting. It was the first time that she had heard about it.

The photo circulated through email among the students and some of them began trying to contact Neil. One night, Manda and some of the other students asked for the spirit to turn the lights on and off. He did. They couldn't believe it. The students who did believe thought the presence moved throughout the building. Some thought the control area above the booth was particularly haunted, as was the corner where the picture was taken. Some of the females felt uncomfortable being alone in the woman's washroom.

As Rutherford had not died in the building, some began to wonder about an alternate explanation for the haunting. Could another entity have been responsible? It was not surprising then when information began to surface about the old Nanaimo Indian Hospital, which had been less than two hundred metres (an eighth of a mile) away. Located on the other side of Fifth Street, the Department of Indian Affairs took over a military hospital in 1946 and began to use it for tuberculosis treatments. It closed in 1967 and was demolished in 2004. In *Harbour City*, Jan Peterson said that staff described it as a friendly place. Other reports have used terms like "eugenics," "holocaust," and "crimes against humanity." According to former United Church minister Kevin Annett, there was an active effort made to destroy official records about what really happened. Victims have come forward, lawsuits have been launched, and horrendous accusations of torture and murder have surfaced. Even if partially true, this makes the history of the theatre's neighbourhood a scene of horrendous suffering. Unmarked graves are known to be just east of where the hospital once stood. Perhaps waiting for legal resolution, no memorial plaque has ever been put in place to honour the First Nations people who were buried there. The land is an unused section of a fenced-off area that faces the university. Fifty years after the hospital has closed, it is difficult to understand why. Some former students, including Manda, have proposed that the spirit might be connected to this site across the road, and not be a former instructor at all.

The disrespect of the First Nations dead might explain some of the incidents, but not all of them, as some of it seems very theatre specific, like the activity in the booth and above it.

In October of 2016, a Victoria tour company ran a contest for real ghost stories. One of the accounts caught my eye. It was from a woman claiming to be a former VIU theatre student. In her post, she claimed that she and two other students had been working the lights in the gantry above the booth during a show. Suddenly, someone touched her and one of the other women on the shoulder. It felt calming. They could clearly see that no one else was there, as that person would have had to climb a ladder up to them. She had heard the theatre was supposed to be haunted but had never experienced anything herself.

"I figure he was just there giving us a pat on the shoulder," she said in her story, "saying we were doing a good job with the lights and the rigging."

Manda has kept her old computer tower in the hopes of retrieving the image from it, which she promised to share if it is recovered. "It is the only reason we've kept that thing," she said, "for that one picture." She hopes that one of the other students might still have it in a saved email as well.

Manda now owns a small theatre company that sometimes uses VIU's theatre space, bringing her back into the building. Last year, she had a group of younger children with her when one of them pointed and said, "That corner is creepy!" She was surprised because it was the same corner the picture had been taken in. The young students had never been told that the theatre was haunted. Her own staff has made comments about the building to her, as have VIU's technicians. "They still say goodnight when they leave," Manda said. "They feel obligated to say goodbye at the end of every day."

Qualicum Heritage Inn prepped for renovations (2013).
PHOTO BY SHANON SINN

QUALICUM
HERITAGE INN

QUALICUM BEACH

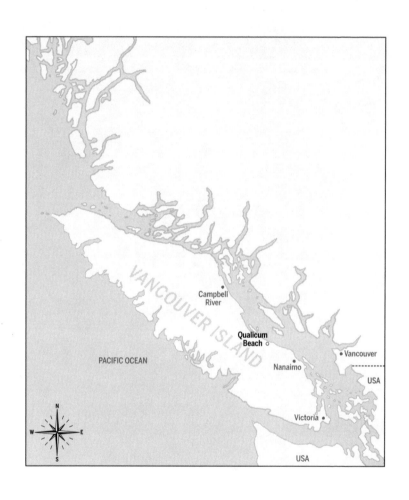

THE QUALICUM HERITAGE INN ON Vancouver Island has long been reported to be haunted. Robert Belyk found the stories so compelling that he opened *Ghosts, True Tales of Eerie Encounters* with over ten pages of the inn's haunted past. *Creepy Canada* also featured the inn during the third episode of season one. Additionally, previous inn guests have left tales of paranormal encounters on various hotel travel review sites, while former staff members have made public statements regarding their own personal experiences online and to print sources, as well.

Fifty kilometres (thirty-one miles) north of Nanaimo is the town of Qualicum Beach. According to the town's website, Qualicum in Coast Salish means "where the dog salmon run." Beautifully situated near the Strait of Georgia, Qualicum's claim to fame is that it has the oldest average age of people in Canada. In 2011, Statistics Canada reported that the median age was nearly sixty-four years old.

While Qualicum might be Vancouver Island's mellowest community, it has still received a lot of attention over the years for being home to one of the island's most haunted locations: the Qualicum Heritage Inn.

The Homeroom: British Columbia's History of Education Web Site says that the building was constructed as a boy's college in 1937. The Tudor-style school continued to operate as a centre of education for the privileged until it closed in 1970. This was the result of elitist-style schools becoming increasingly unpopular during the "Age of Aquarius."

The building became the Qualicum College Inn and then the Qualicum Heritage Inn. According to the Town of Qualicum Beach's website, the building was eventually designated a Municipal Heritage Site in July of 2007 for historical and architectural reasons. In 2008, the Qualicum Heritage Inn closed, was boarded up for several years, and then began to be converted into condo suites. Developers made several concessions before continuing the project, but according to the *Parksville Qualicum Beach News* fell short on some of them. Most of the agreements between developers and the community involved the protection, restoration, and upkeep of the heritage site, which is a smaller—yet central—portion of the overall condo development.

Interestingly, as the developers listed condos for sale online, they chose not to disclose that the former inn was reputed to be one of Vancouver Island's most haunted locations.

The list of reports from the former inn, both online and in print, is long: full apparitions have been seen of a man in an old-fashioned military uniform, of a little boy, and of a woman. Voices have been heard predominantly on the fourth floor of boys talking, a consoling woman, "crying," "moaning," and "chanting."

Belyk says that people claimed furniture had moved on its own in room 453 (later 459). The bed also looked to have been slept in when no one had access to the room. A man's voice was also heard, while blankets had been pulled off at least one person who was sleeping.

Elsewhere, lights had turned off and on by themselves, while a

TV was turned on similarly. At least two different workers reported hearing a piano on the main floor playing by itself when no one was in the room. Multiple people also claimed that they felt "watched."

One commenter, Clarissa, on the Living Library blog shared her experiences from 2003:

> After moving to Qualicum Beach, I worked at the Qualicum Heritage Inn. The day I was let go, I experienced two unexplained incidents at the inn. I was cleaning on the third floor, the original part of the Boy's College it had once been. The old wooden door to the suite was propped open by my large bin of cleaning supplies. While in the room, the door slammed shut, nobody else was on that floor with me, no other patrons, just me. I continued on and was on my hands and knees washing the bathroom floor when the toilet flushed without a thing touching it. It was a memorable day indeed, I didn't feel as if it were hostile, but I wasn't too upset to find out later that day that I wasn't needed there anymore.

There have been sounds of people running and doors slamming when witnesses could clearly see no one was there. One individual even claimed that an "invisible" person ran by them on the stairs. They had to move out of the way.

Previous staff members named one ghost "Buddy." Buddy, they claimed, would throw things around the main floor and make a mess. This same spirit was also blamed for the phone, printer, and other electronics having "disturbances." According to other statements, a boy's laughter was heard following the incidents.

As to who may be haunting the building, it is a mystery. Belyk said in *Ghosts* that groundskeeper Bert James died in the building sometime before it closed, though I have been unable to confirm this. School matron Wendy Register also passed away without warning, around the same time the school closed in 1970. Belyk mentions that some of the boys who went to school at Qualicum College left to fight during the Second World War and that some were killed. The suggestion, of course, is that they could have returned to haunt the building as well.

There was a massacre of a Qualicum First Nations village in 1856, witnessed by early explorers Adam Grant Horne, Iroquois guide Thomas "one-armed Toma" Quamtany, Francis Cote, and others—but this was several kilometres away from where the inn would be built. Jan Peterson in *Black Diamond City* said that the men witnessed "a large fleet of Haida canoes" enter the Qualicum River where the village was located and then leave shortly after displaying severed heads in each of their canoes. Upon investigation, the group found headless corpses and buildings on fire. They also discovered an older woman who died while they spoke to her and later learned a young boy had escaped into the woods. Everyone else had been killed.

As these types of raids were somewhat common during Vancouver Island's early recorded history, it is entirely possible that the Qualicum College was built on, or near, such a location.

One thing is clear: the Qualicum Heritage Inn is not known to be the site of any violent deaths or great tragedies. Fortunately, it never became a haunted tourist destination either; making it unlikely

Physical education class at Qualicum Beach School,
which became Qualicum College in 1949.
IMAGE I-68637, COURTESY OF THE ROYAL BC MUSEUM AND ARCHIVES

previous owners promoted stories of activity in the building. Why the Qualicum Heritage Inn might be haunted is another one of Vancouver Island's great mysteries. It will be interesting to learn if activity continues to be reported once tenants move into the newly converted suites.

Paper Mill Dam Park no longer allows overnight camping.
PHOTO BY SHANON SINN

THE LADY WHO
WALKS ON WATER

PORT ALBERNI

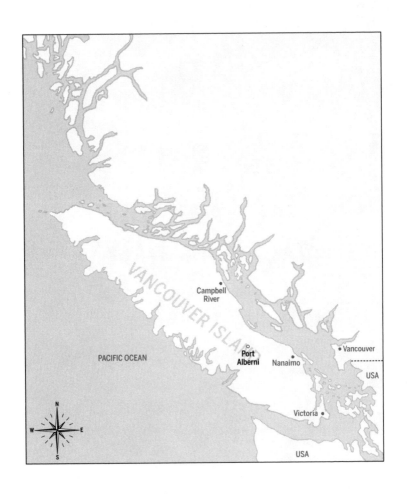

ADAM GRANT HORNE, ONE-ARMED TOMA, and the rest of their party made the trek across Vancouver Island from Qualicum to present-day Port Alberni. They did this by following a rough-hewn path used for trade between the Salish and the Tseshaht Nuu-chah-nulth living on the shores of the Alberni Inlet. After making contact and engaging in trade, the group returned to Victoria to report the success of their mission.

A paved road makes journeying across the island to Port Alberni much easier today. Many people pass through as they travel toward the Pacific Rim National Park Reserve and the vacation village of Tofino. Like other communities on Vancouver Island, Port Alberni has its fair share of haunted locations only known locally. Its most unique ghost, however, is a woman who is seen on, or nearby, the Somass River at the Paper Mill Dam Park.

According to Jan Peterson in *The Albernis: 1860–1922*, British Columbia's first paper mill was built at the site in 1892. The original construct from the year before had been destroyed and swept downriver by heavy rain. This second project was fitted with used papermaking machinery from Scotland. The mill began to produce paper by 1894, but the woodchips were not suitable for making a quality paper product. It ceased operations the following year. The Paper Mill Dam was destroyed and removed in 1915 to make way for spawning salmon and boat traffic.

Paper Mill Dam Park is on the east side of the river, while

Tseshaht First Nation land is on the west side of the river. The Somass River is a favourite swimming hole for Port Alberni locals. It is also a popular place for tubing—floating down the river on a tire inner tube. At night, the park was a popular drinking place for generations of teenagers. In more recent years, a gate has been put in place as a deterrent. A sign warns park users that camping is not permitted and that the gate will be locked from "dusk" until eight o'clock. There are no signs—literal or figurative—indicating the location is believed by many to be haunted.

Port Alberni residents claim that the haunting is old. One commenter on my blog, Nelda Jackson, said that her grandmother—eighty-two years old in 2014—remembers hearing about the ghost when she was "a little girl." If true, this would make the tale as old as the late 1930s or early 40s at the very least. Nelda shared two second-hand stories of encounters: one on my site at Living Library (2014) and the second on the Real Haunts website (2015). She used the term "the lady who walks on the water," which resonated as a good name for the spirit. The following comment was taken from my site:

> I heard stories about the Paper Mill Dam from many people since I was a little girl. The first person I knew that saw the ghost of the lady who walks on the water was my late sister, who was a teenager when she told me about it. She was with a couple of my cousins at the dam in the early morning hours (3am) one summer and they were enjoying the warm evening air with a little dip in the river. My cousins had decided to go to

shore as they were finished swimming, but my sister wanted to stay in the water a little bit longer (she was enjoying herself). They waited on shore while she waded around the chest-high water. She had her face in the cool water when she noticed a bright glow on the river's surface (she assumed it was the glow from the moon). Then she looked up. Standing right in front of her (on top of the water) was the lady on the lake [sic]. As soon as my sister looked at her the lady said to her, "have you seen my baby?" This scared the wits out of her. My sister took off running as fast as she could toward the shore. My cousins told her that as she ran through the water the lady glided along the lake, following her (looking really angry) until she reached the shore. Then the lady disappeared.

Another story I heard about the lady was from my ex-boyfriend. He told me that he was down at the dam having a few drinks with some friends. Their discussion started to get heated so he left and headed up the trail through the woods (just across the road from the dam). He was about halfway up the trail when he saw the lady. She is usually spotted walking on the water but she was in the middle of the trail. When he looked at her she said to him, "have u [sic] seen my baby?" He said he dropped his case of bottled beer and ran back to the dam. The people there told him he was "white as a ghost" so he told them what happened. Both of these stories happened in the last ten to fifteen years.

I wondered if the entity, projection, or whatever she was, could be walking across a platform that used to be over the water when the mill was still in place. As she's been described as "a native lady" in a white dress, I began to research whether or not any female First Nations women worked at—and possibly died at—the mill when it was in operation. No one had mentioned she was in traditional clothing, so I assumed, if she existed, that she would be from the late 1800s to early 1900s.

Jan Peterson in *The Albernis* says that a First Nations woman did work at the mill. Her name was Emma David. According to census records, Emma was born in 1873 and lived until 1953, making her an unlikely candidate for a traditional haunting as the apparition appeared young.

Many people divide hauntings into two categories—though the terms for them vary a great deal. Generally speaking, an apparition will either be interactive or it won't be. A non-interactive experience, sometimes referred to as a "residual" haunting, goes about its business completely unaware that it is being viewed. These would be the kind of ghosts that walk through a wall where a door used to be, or over water where a dam walkway once stood. By speaking—which in itself is somewhat rare in the ghost world—the spirit is demonstrating a connection to the witness. To some degree, it has intelligence, though for whatever reason this often comes across as slow or sluggish in spirits other than those seen shortly after death.

Nelda isn't the only commenter that has said the woman is looking for her child. On the Real Haunts website forum, Beck posted in 2009 that he heard the Somass River was haunted. In 2010, Bud replied:

The apparition of a woman in white has been reported
on the river bank and walking across the water.
IMAGE BY LARIO TUS

I've heard of a story about a Native lady's ghost who
wanders up and down Paper Mill Dam Park on the
Somass River. Apparently she is looking for her kid
who drowned there.

His comment strongly suggests that this detail of the story is either
well established or that other people have heard the woman speak
as well. A response from QualicumGuy said he had heard the same
story, but it sounded like "an old wives' tale" to him.

Nelda's comment on the Real Haunts website shares the exact
two stories above (though she says her sister's incident was mid-
1990s) and adds a story her grandmother shared when she was in
her forties. That would make this account from the 1970s using
the age she had already indicated. In this encounter, a couple with

young children was camping when they decided to wash dishes in the river "early one morning." The apparition appeared and began to walk across the water. The man ran away in fear, jumped into his car, and took off without his family. His wife and children had to walk home, giving the incident a comedic flavour. The lady apparently never asked for her baby in this encounter.

A female spirit searching for her child is a common ghost story motif throughout North America. Sarah Jane is the suicide ghost of a mother who hid, then lost, her baby in a Texas river during the American Civil War. She then committed suicide and has been searching for her baby ever since. Stow Lake in San Francisco's Golden Gate Park has a dishevelled lady in white searching the shore for her lost child. Another woman's ghost looks for hers near a bridge in Kentucky. These spirits all ask witnesses if anyone has seen their baby.

The story of La Llorona, or the "weeping woman," is a well-known tale told in Mexico and United States. In *Teaching from a Hispanic Perspective*, contributor Joe Hayes says that La Llorona was a beautiful woman named Maria. When Maria's husband left her for a younger, wealthier woman, she drowned her children in a fit of rage. Immediately regretting her actions, she tried to recover them. Her body was found on the riverbank the next morning. Since then, she has been heard weeping and crying out, "Where are my children?" as she searches the shore. People began to call her La Llorona. This story is told to children to prevent them from going out at night, implying that La Llorona can haunt riverbanks other than the one she died at, and presumably inland as well. Apparently, she abducts and sometimes eats the children.

The 2006 census of 17,366 residents living in Port Alberni reported 980 people considered visible minorities. Fifty of them were Latin Americans. In comparison, there were 2,050 First Nations and 14,295 European Canadians. With the internet and widespread broadcasting of TV programs on paranormal subjects, the detail of the spirit asking for her child could be a modern addition to the story, but it seems unlikely the tale itself was somehow transported to the area from Latin Americans through word of mouth.

The Lady Who Walks on Water has unevolved edges as well, making me suspect it is more than an urban legend. In 2014, Kevin commented on the Living Library blog that the park has had "a lot of sightings of weird-coloured light orbs and shadow figures." He claimed he would no longer go to the park after dark.

Interestingly, the falls at Stamp River—a tributary of Somass River—also has reports of hovering ghost-light orbs.

Leah placed a post on the Real Haunts website after a daytime encounter at the Paper Mill Dam Park on July 20, 2013:

> Not that anyone has really been on here but . . . The comment about the river, that rattles me. This past Saturday I was tubing down the river with a few friends. We go from the rifle range down to the pump house. There are two main breaks in the river and if you have been down you will know what I am talking about. Anyways, at the second break, one friend and I had gone right, whereas everyone else had gone left—which didn't matter because it meets up again fairly quickly. I am one to close my eyes and enjoy the

ride down especially in the calmer areas, but for some reason I felt like I needed to open them so I did. We both saw a woman and I swear on my life she was there one moment and then disappeared. She came up from out of the water and walked up a little path. Only she didn't go up the top. About four steps up she turned to us [as] if to face us and then she was gone. I know many will not believe this but she was in all white and the thing that gets me the most was her hair looked completely dry. She climbed out of the water so how could that be? I'm just wondering if anyone else has seen this, heard of it, or any of the sorts? I've NEVER seen anything that has left me feeling so uncomfortable before.

It is important to note that the Real Haunts website only has three Canadian locations listed: Banff Springs Hotel in Alberta, the Fort Langley Cemetery in British Columbia, and the South Crescent neighbourhood in Port Alberni. The Paper Mill Dam Park comments emerged out of fifty-five others on the South Crescent thread, meaning that they were a side conversation braided throughout the original reports about the neighbourhood. I couldn't find any other comments by the same users in other posts or online elsewhere. Nelda was the only person that commented at both the Living Library blog and on Real Haunts. She left the comment on my site in February of 2014 and the Real Haunts comment in October of 2015. The two stories were consistent other than when it happened—from the mid-1990s to as late as 2004. She was kind enough to answer follow-up questions about her grandmother's age and other details.

As to who the lady might be, Nelda's grandmother said it is rumoured that the woman's baby fell out of a boat and drowned. The mother's body was found in the river a month later.

The pad of her bare foot presses against the surface of the water. She is shrouded in white, adorned with light, and methodical in her motion. Her second foot reaches out, followed by the first. She moves smoothly but gathers speed as she rushes across the river. Her beautiful cheeks are tear-streaked; the edges of her face are twisted; her mouth is open; and her eyes are wide: "Have you seen my baby?" she moans.

Staff at The Schooner Restaraunt believe the building is haunted by a former chef.
PHOTO BY SHANON SINN

THE HAUNTING OF THE SCHOONER RESTAURANT

TOFINO

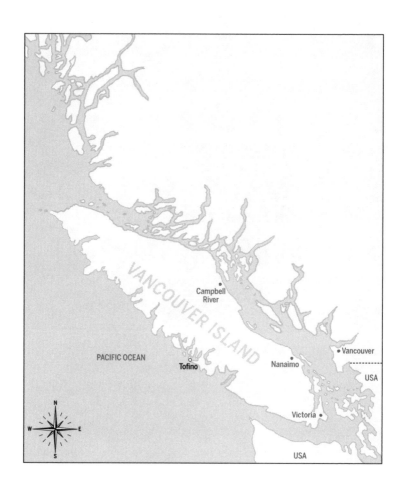

ACCOUNTS VARY FROM FULL APPARITIONS to shadowy figures, from items pitched off shelves to doors being inexplicably thrown open. As far as reputedly haunted Vancouver Island locations go, The Schooner Restaurant in Tofino—two hours west of Port Alberni—likely has the highest number of recently documented claims.

Whaylon Arthur's family has owned the building since the 1960s, when his grandmother Gloria Bruce purchased it to fulfill a long-held dream of owning a restaurant. Stories about the haunting can be traced back for decades. Most of the activity has taken place downstairs around the server station. This station is an enclosed, stylistic ship's bow fitted with stained-glass windows. Staff has often told Whaylon they had seen the shadow of a person looking at them through the coloured glass, but that when they went to investigate no one was there.

The family believes the shadow is the spirit of former Chef Morris Shank, who lived in the building. He was a close friend of the family and was well known for his chowder. The Bruces found Shank's body one morning in the early 1970s. He appeared to have died during the night of old age.

Travel blogger and friend Sean Enns and I travelled to Tofino to investigate the haunted restaurant in 2015. Sean and I have similar perspectives when it comes to investigating hauntings: be level-headed and document what is taking place. There are enough people running around pretending to "investigate" anything deemed paranormal through whimsical means. When money is involved, exaggeration or falsifying evidence is called "folklore fraud," where the details of history are moulded to better suit the story, the evidence is "discovered," and a new tale erases the real one, invalidating those who have had actual experiences.

After overhearing our conversation with Whaylon, a woman at the bar began to tell us about her own experiences. Her name is Keane Hovi, and she worked at The Schooner Restaurant for years before becoming a schoolteacher.

She claimed that the incidents usually took place in the basement in the "brown half" of the room—south of the boat-bow server station that almost divides the room in two. Keane believes there could be more spirits than just Shank responsible, as she describes the restaurant's presence as "pleasant but robust."

"It's more active in the summer," Keane said. "There are usually around three incidents a year."

When she was alone, she would often feel a gust of freezing air while cashing out. There were no doors or windows open, yet the sensation would be there one moment and gone the next. One night, a wine glass flew across the room and smashed for no apparent reason. She couldn't rationalize what she had seen.

According to *Historic Tofino: A Walking Tour* by Adrienne Mason, the building was once part of a military hospital in Tofino during the Second World War. Members of the Masonic Lodge saved the building from destruction by taking it apart and reassembling it at its current location on Campbell Street. The Masons held meetings in the building for years. The structure then became Vic's Coffee and later the Lone Cone Café. The Schooner Restaurant finally came into existence during the 1960s and was purchased by Whaylon's grandparents in 1968. The restaurant website says that the ship bow serving station was built in 1974 by three Vietnam War draft dodgers.

Long-time bartender Shaun Ingalls said he has been "touched on the shoulder," something he claimed has happened to a lot of people. He also said that he and other employees saw a stack of ten plates weighing roughly five pounds "float" from the dish pit—behind the Brown Room—and then fall to smash on the floor. Interviewed separately, another bartender, Jesse Deslippe, said he also saw the plates hover and crash.

Jesse told me that he once felt someone running past him when no one was there. Another incident happened while he was preparing to lock up one night. It was around three o'clock in the morning, and the door near the boat bow of the server station suddenly flew open.

Shaun's most intense experience took place four years ago at nine o'clock on a cold February night. "Four of us were eating. Suddenly, we look over and see a man sitting down having dinner. Everyone saw him," he said. Then the man just disappeared.

Dani Gladue, a server, said the summer before was her first year working at The Schooner. One night, she was alone with one other person in the building. She was cleaning and prepping for the next day. The Brown Room had been empty for hours. Suddenly, Dani saw a man standing and looking at her. After a moment, she realized the man was out of place and turned her head to look in his direction.

"But when I looked back he was gone," she said.

Dani hadn't yet heard that The Schooner Restaurant was believed to be haunted. When she told her coworkers what she'd seen they told her that it was the ghost of Shank.

"I don't like closing alone anymore," she said.

As the staff of The Schooner shared their personal experiences, I never once picked up signs of dishonesty from any of them; there was no embellishment, no exaggerating, no contradictions. Just disbelief. Tales told in a brutally matter-of-fact way, with a look that seemed to say: "I wouldn't believe this either, but it happened."

When we were done speaking with staff, Sean and I set up our equipment in the Brown Room and took multiple pictures. Strangely, while doing this, the full battery on my camera was suddenly drained, something that had never happened to me before. I have heard that this sometimes occurs at haunted locations—electronic devices lose their charges. I don't find this to be proof by any means, but it was strange enough to take note.

On later inspection, there was nothing unusual on any of the still images. There were no strange sounds or voices on the digital recorder either.

I inspected the door Jesse saw fly open. From the outside, it appeared to be the main front entrance. From the inside, it looked more like a back door due to the layout of the room. The old wooden door was heavy and latched closed with a large metal hook. I lifted off the weighty lock hoping to replicate what Jesse must have seen. From the inside, I pushed the door outward, but it was too solid to do so easily. I do not believe a gust of wind could have pushed the door open.

Like many other places breaking the mould of the traditional ghost story, The Schooner Restaurant left me with more questions than answers. Shank passed away in the building, but he didn't die

The Brown Room, where most of the activity occurs, is not used during the winter months.
PHOTO BY SHANON SINN

of violent causes. If ghosts are what many people believe them to be—the restless dead—then why would he haunt the building? And why does the activity mostly occur on the brown side of the room or near the boat-bow server station? Was this where Shank's room had been? No one seems to know anymore.

As the building was a part of the military hospital, maybe the spirit does belong to someone more "robust." Unfortunately, it is difficult to know if the structure was an administrative building, a morgue, or something else entirely.

Considering we were only able to interview staff working the closing shift, and that there were many other people—both past and present—who have made similar claims over the years, there were a lot of reasons for me to think something unexplained really was occurring at The Schooner Restaurant. As the story had yet to receive widespread attention, it hadn't been altered yet either. That, in itself, is always a good thing.

View of the small island from Keeha Beach, 1998.
PHOTO BY SHANON SINN

KEEHA
BEACH

**KEEHA BAY,
PACIFIC RIM
NATIONAL PARK**

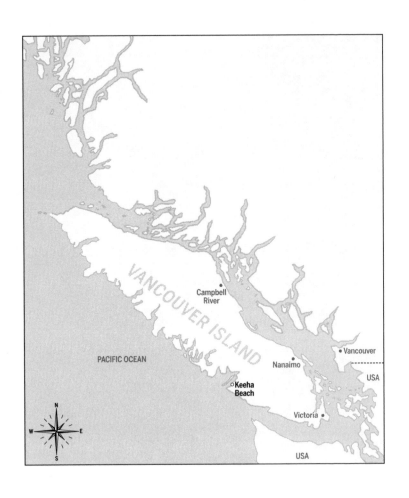

To MANY, KEEHA BEACH IS regarded as a sacred place. Hippie and New Age-type people held Rainbow Gatherings here from roughly 1992 to 1997. The site became increasingly popular as a result and word spread. I first heard about Keeha Beach in the late 1990s, after the Rainbow Gatherings had stopped meeting there. Apparently, many people had spiritual experiences on the beach. One of my friends had described the place as "life altering." It ended up being that way for me as well.

Keeha Beach is south of Tofino and Ucluelet, beyond the Broken Islands on the other side of the inlet. For this reason, to get there overland, a traveller leaves the paved highway at Port Alberni and takes the gravel road to the remote village of Bamfield on the south side of the Alberni Inlet.

A path enters the rainforest near Bamfield and the West Coast Trail head. From there, it is a two to four-hour hike to the beach. The journey is often underestimated because the trail crosses even terrain and is only a few kilometres long, but it is arduous. Travel Blog writer Natalie Myers described it as "a death march" in 2006. Outdoor photographer Matthew Lettington wrote on his Explorington blog that it is "probably the most challenging hike on Vancouver Island." Even a small amount of rain fills pits with mud. Titanic fallen trees create obstacle courses requiring crawling, climbing, and hopping. With a heavy backpack, the experience definitely has parallels to infantry training.

I first went to Keeha beach with my friends Tasha and Brian in 1998. It was only for the weekend, but I was struck by the beauty of the place. A couple of weeks later I quit a menial job, returned alone, and stayed for seventeen days.

Things had been tough. I had just returned to Canada after spending almost a year south of the border. I was in my mid-twenties, disenfranchised, and more or less homeless. I often worked unfulfilling minimum wage jobs, was angry at the world, and self-sabotaged relationships. Literally and figuratively, I was living on the side of the road with my thumb in the air. When I heard my grandfather was terminally ill, I became depressed. Something needed to change.

I had been struck by Keeha's majestic beauty and peacefulness. Since I had visited, it felt like I was being pulled back. I would think about it all of the time. I would dream about that sand beneath my feet and the rain upon my face.

A Huu-ay-aht (Nuu-chah-nulth) hereditary chief (at least I believe he was a chief) picked me up hitchhiking near Port Alberni at the start of the gravel road. I jumped into the back seat. "Spencer," he introduced himself from the passenger seat, "same as the river, same as the mountain." It was immediately clear that he had been the one who had decided to pick me up. The driver introduced himself as Barry. I told them that I was heading to Keeha beach and asked about it. There was an awkward silence at first, but the conversation started up again and shifted toward the environment. We talked about the Sioux's White Buffalo prophecy (a white calf had been born in the United States several years earlier signalling change). Spencer strongly stated that the "rape of the Earth" needed to stop. He told me that the Rainbow Gatherings had destroyed the beach. People had left mounds of garbage, were disrespectful to the land, and had destroyed the environment. He asked that I promise to respect the beach and take out all of my garbage. The conversation was important. Spencer and Barry set the tone for my journey. They dropped me off almost two hours later. I have not seen them since.

I arrived on the beach exhausted and dripping in sweat. I had seen cougar prints in the mud, and there were bear prints on the wet sand near where the surf was rolling in. I chose a place to set up camp, pulled up a tarp, and built a shelter.

There are many beaches on Vancouver Island reported to be haunted. Keane at The Schooner Restaurant told me that Chesterman Beach was haunted. Before it was developed, people would camp there and later claim they did not feel alone. Frank Island, at the south end of the beach, she said, was believed to be haunted by a "strong, powerful," force as well. The abandoned village of Kixx?in, which is thousands of years old, lies several kilometres north of Keeha. Like other abandoned village sites all over Vancouver Island, people believe there are spirits there. I did not know this at the time, but five kilometres (three miles) to the south is Pachena Point, near where the infamous *Valencia* steamer sank, killing 136 people and unregistered children. That site is believed to be haunted as well.

A Rainbower had told me that the island at the mouth of the bay at Keeha Beach was used as a Huu-ay-aht cemetery and not to go there. Like others, he said the beach was sacred, and I needed to respect it. No one told me that it was haunted.

At one end of the long sandy beach are sea caves. At the other are sea arches. The tiny island is a short distance off shore near the arches. The place is surreal. The waves crash in, the rain pounds down, the sun pierces the clouds, and if the sky is clear at night the stars are as bright as they are in the desert. It mostly rains, but the weather is cyclical. There are eagles and otters and bears and snakes. If you are lucky, you might find cougar or wolf tracks in the sand, or watch the whales come close to shore to feed or rub themselves on the rocks in the shallows.

The beach has very few people on it. I was alone most of the time before the Victoria Day long weekend in May; then there was always a tent or two in the distance. Other than saying, "Hi," most people just wanted their privacy.

A freshwater stream feeds the ocean near the rock arches. I set my camp up there. My commitment was for thirteen days, but I ended up staying for seventeen. I wrote, and I foraged, and I explored. I never felt alone. I was inspired to write. The words at times seemed to come through me and not from me:

> This is the time that dreams be forged,
> Pulled from the memory of the day.
> As brave old birds fade to a whisper,
> And the wind in the trees turns grey.
> The sky turns pink explodes and folds,
> And the moth now enters the light.
> All colours merge together once more,
> As the day gently wakes his wife.

One night, after about ten days or so, I woke up suddenly. It felt as if there was a man standing over me outside of my low-to-the-ground

My shelter and campsite, 1998.
PHOTO BY SHANON SINN

shelter. I heard his voice in my head. It was faint, but it didn't sound as if it was coming from my own thoughts; it felt similar to my experience with the writing. I had the strong sense that I was sleeping at a burial spot and that I should be extra respectful.

I got up and went outside because I thought someone might actually be there. It was like the intuitive feeling you get right before you discover someone is watching you. I saw that the night sky was clear, but no one was around.

Suddenly, I noticed that there was a light to the south of me. It was high up on the point by the sea arches. It was hovering through the trees. I watched it for a long time. I even crawled back inside my shelter for a sweater before returning to observe it again. It was just there, as real as any other light I have ever seen—explainable or not. It moved slowly but never really got closer or further away. As near as I could get in the darkness—without climbing

The foggy cliff face beneath the forest in which the light appeared, 1998.
PHOTO BY SHANON SINN

the cliff—I couldn't hear any undergrowth breaking. I watched it for so long I got tired and went back to bed. It is a long time ago now, but I am guessing somewhere between thirty minutes to an hour.

The next morning, when it was visually safe to do so, I climbed the cliff up to the forest. This was difficult, and it was hard to enter the greenery through the salal brush. I checked out the whole point. Despite it being a small area, it took me hours because my movement was so limited. There were no paths, and my feet would rarely touch the forest floor. I would move along a fallen log, then fight through more salal, and repeat over and over again. I found a bear trail, but even this would have been difficult for someone to navigate in the dark as they would have had to crawl.

I also realized that the trail was not near the cliff edge. The thick undergrowth meant the light had to have been near the cliff or some distance off the ground for me to see it. The forest on the point was also too thick to see the light from the other side if the source had been in the air. I kept checking the sides of the trees where they met the cliff edge all around the point every ten feet or so. I was looking for a trail or ledge where someone with a light could have been walking.

I also could not find a way to move silently. The ocean had been calm enough the night before that I believe I would have heard a person thrashing through the growth.

I had no rational explanation for the light. I'm still not sure what it was to this day. I told a few people over the years the story, and it gradually changed in my memory to include more than one light. When I reread my journal to research the location, I realized that

I had only seen one light. It was proof of how malleable memory is and a reminder of how beneficial journalling can be.

I do not remember feeling threatened—merely curious. The light was eerie, but I did not feel as if I was looking at something supernatural necessarily. It was just there. I never saw it again.

Several days later, I packed up and made the trip back to Nanaimo. I took a job I normally wouldn't have on a hunch. Within a year I set off on my path through Vancouver, Afghanistan, illness, and recovery.

As I wrote this book, it felt as if I was somehow completing the journey I had embarked on when I left Keeha Beach all those years ago. My whole life would have been quite different if I hadn't gone to the coast, met Spencer and Barry, meditated, journalled, cleared my head for seventeen days, and then seen that ghost light up in the trees. I did not know it then, but it was on Keeha Beach that the seed for this book was first planted.

THE PHANTOM
SHIP *VALENCIA*

PACHENA POINT

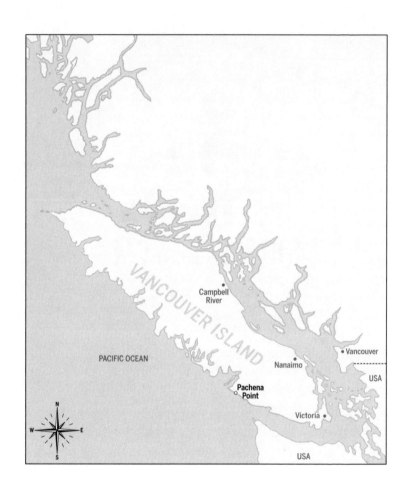

THE GHOST SHIP *VALENCIA* IS one of Canada's most famous hauntings. It has been covered on TV, in newspapers, magazines, and books. The steamship is regularly listed in online articles about phantom ships around the world, and has even been featured on the *Lore* podcast by Aaron Mahnke. It is little wonder. The wreck was tragic, claiming 136 lives, including every last woman and child, and has been referred to as British Columbia's *Titanic*. Many victims could have been saved if nearby ships and people on shore had tried harder. While many aspects of the haunting are likely contrived, other details are difficult to ignore.

The American steamer *Valencia* was en route to Seattle from San Francisco when she hit a rock near a Vancouver Island cliff face on January 22, 1906. The ship had taken over for another steamer, so Captain Johnson was somewhat unfamiliar with the route. When the inexperienced captain encountered nighttime bad weather he began to make navigational decisions based on intuition rather than common sense. The ship missed the opening of the Strait of Juan de Fuca. Believing he was further away from land than he really was, Johnson kept course. He eventually became concerned and turned outward toward what he thought was open sea. He hit land near Pachena Point between Bamfield and Port Renfrew.

The ship immediately started to fill with water. Captain Johnson tried to beach the steamer by putting her onto the rocks until help could arrive. The manoeuver was successful, leaving the ship hovering above the water. According to the American Commission on Valencia Disaster (CVD) report, many of the crew were untrained and had never performed emergency drills before. Additionally, Johnson never gave the orders one would have expected under the circumstances.

The *Valencia* was close to shore, but there was a steep, one-hundred-foot cliff face in front of her. An ocean swell created a swirling mass of violent water that twisted in the darkness. Waves pounded against the ship threatening to shake her apart or slide her off the rock. Many rushed for the lifeboats. The *Seattle Daily Times* and *Daily Colonist* reported the ensuing chaos: someone panicked and ordered the lifeboats to be lowered even though they were not full and did not have the plugs in them. Some people were pitched into the sea immediately. Other boats capsized. A baby fell into the water as a woman tried to pass it to her husband. It is estimated fifty to sixty people died during the attempted launch of the six lifeboats.

Two men from a capsized boat swam through the icy water to the cliff but were unable to climb the slippery rock. They were bashed to death against the cliff.

After brutally being tossed and spun through the water, two boats made it to a section of cliff that was more promising. There were seven survivors in one and two still alive in the other. The commission reported that the nine-person party waited in the darkness one and a half kilometres (nearly a mile) away from the *Valencia* until they could climb the cliff the next morning.

A semblance of order was restored on the ship. Flares were fired all night, and people burned whatever they could—including much-needed clothing—in an attempt to signal for help. This was unsuccessful.

The *Valencia* was beginning to come apart by the next morning. The final "work boat" lifeboat (there were still three smaller "rafts") was launched with a crew of six in order to find a spot to secure a line on shore. They could not find anywhere to land so rowed for hours until they did. The place they found was Pachena Bay just south of Keeha Beach. Discovering a trail, they chose to follow it instead of bushwhacking through impossible rainforest. The path led to the lighthouse at Cape Beale, on the other side of Keeha Beach. The other nine survivors had found their way to a telegraph line and messaged Bamfield.

The commission reported that Captain Johnson shot rescue lines without waiting for someone to be on the cliff to receive the rope. The harpoon-like safety device would have been used to secure a line between the ship and land, which could then be used to facilitate a rescue. With no one to secure the other end on shore, the lines fell into the sea.

By that afternoon, January 23, news had reached Victoria and Seattle of the wreck. Ships were sent to assist with the rescue, but none of them would find the *Valencia* until the following morning. By then, the ship was falling apart. Partially clothed and freezing victims clung to whatever they could in desperation.

The *Queen* (a steamer that authors often mistakenly call *Queen City*, another steamship operating in the area at the time) came into sight, giving the survivors hope. Owned by the Pacific Coast Steamship Company (PCSC)—the same company as the *Valencia*—she had been sent to help. The captain of the *Queen* decided it was too dangerous to approach or launch a lifeboat rescue.

A tugboat, the *Czar* (owned a few years earlier by James

Dunsmuir), arrived as well. The *Czar* went much closer than the *Queen*, but the crew claimed they could not see any survivors in the rough water. Another steamer owned by the PCSC, the *City of Topeka*, arrived with an executive of the company on board. He told the captain of the *Queen* he was "relieved" of duty and sent that ship away. The *Czar*, believing no one was still alive, left as well. It was later revealed that the *City of Topeka* did not know exactly where the *Valencia* was, but stayed nearby. None of the other ships had launched lifeboats in an effort to help, later claiming that the sea had appeared too rough.

The *Valencia* continued to break apart and flounder. Two of the three rafts were launched. None of the remaining women wanted to board them, possibly because they thought rescue was imminent. In a final act of incompetence, Captain Johnson failed to order any of them, or their children, to do so. Men boarded the rafts. Most of them were crew members. One of the rafts managed to make it past the surf and was seen by the *City of Topeka*. The ship sent out a lifeboat and rescued the eighteen men it carried. The second raft was swept away. Four men would survive from that raft and were later rescued off an island. How these rafts could have stayed afloat when the "rescuers" believed launching much more stable boats to offer assistance would have been suicide, would be a point of mystery for many.

An overland rescue party made it to the top of the cliff in time to watch the *Valencia* go under. Women, children, and other surviving passengers screamed as they were thrown into the swirling water with debris that tore many of them apart. This rescue group, which Seattle and Victoria papers criticized for not trying to lower ropes in an effort to help, left in horror instead of watching the final moments of the massacre.

According to the CVD report, there had been 173 registered people aboard the *Valencia*. Of the 108 passengers, only twelve survived. Young children were not included in the official death numbers, as they had not been recorded. Of the sixty-five crew members, forty died, including a stewardess. The thirty-seven survivors came from four different groups: nine from the two lifeboats that made it to shore, six from the work boat sent to secure the line that went to the lighthouse (the commission says seven, which would make their own numbers inaccurate), eighteen from the raft the *City of Topeka* picked up, and four were rescued from the small island the raft had made it to. There were no women or children survivors.

As details of the incompetent captain and crew and subsequent pathetic rescue attempts came to light, people were enraged. The *Daily Colonist* and *Seattle Daily Times* filled pages of their papers for weeks with accusations and finger pointing. In the months that followed, there would be both a Canadian and an American investigation as well.

Bodies were recovered for weeks. Some of them were sent to Seattle, others were buried in unmarked graves near the wreck site, and some were buried at the Ross Bay Cemetery, including—according to the *Daily Colonist*—eight unidentified victims.

The *Daily Colonist* reported the disaster's aftermath. The years that followed would see the creation of Vancouver Island's West Coast Trail and five shore stations. These unmanned stations were equipped with wireless telegraphs to be used in the event of a similar emergency. The Life Saving Association would be founded that year and would have at its disposal two life-saving motorboats by December of 1907. A lighthouse would also be built at Pachena Point. The American commission would demand changes on its side of the border near the entrance to the Strait of Juan de Fuca as well.

The west coast of Vancouver Island had always been a dangerous place. Hundreds of ships and lives were lost along its rocky shores. Newspapers referred to it as the Graveyard of Ships, and later— when the coast down to the Columbia River dividing Washington State and Oregon was included—the Graveyard of the Pacific. It wasn't until the *Valencia* disaster, however, that British Columbia finally received a proper ghost ship story.

The earliest tales reported in Victoria and Seattle newspapers were of people having had premonitions about the ship sinking. While possibly true, stress can create false memories and papers like dramatic flair so the reports are hard to take seriously.

There are two parts to the story worth noting that I've never heard spoken about in relation to the ghost story. The first is the crew of the *Czar* claiming to have not seen anyone alive at the wreck site. The *Seattle Daily Times* thought the Canadians were lying, as the *Queen*—who was farther away—could hear signals and apparently could even see people clinging to the sinking vessel. The American commission did not disclaim the Canadian officer, Captain Cousins, who testified that the *Czar* did not see the vessel. Instead, it called the opposing stories "a contradiction of evidence." The *Seattle Daily Times* claimed that the tugboat could have gotten a lot closer and helped if the stranded people had been seen. They called the actions of the crew shameful. The *Czar* crew's testimony, however, remained steadfast. According to the *Daily Colonist*, the Canadian investigating Commission of Enquiry believed they were telling the truth as well, presumably because their words were convincing. It ruled that the *Czar* could not see the *Valencia*'s victims because it was a "much smaller boat lower in the water." If any of the tugboat's crew ever confessed to lying it never received much attention. In other words, either the whole crew was made up of skilled liars committed to this mistruth for life, or they really could not see people clinging to the boat, even though they should have been able to, no matter how low in the water they were.

The second item worth noting is somewhat of an urban legend, but is important because it added to the mystery of the disaster at the time. Located at the mouth of the Strait of Juan de Fuca—on the Washington State side—is Tatoosh Island. The lighthouse there was instrumental in helping boat traffic during conditions like those reported on the night of the accident. No one aboard the *Valencia* had seen the lighthouse, but what many believed was strange was that no one heard the foghorn either. The lighthouse was equipped with a ten-thousand-dollar steam foghorn in 1872, which could be heard up to thirteen kilometres (eight miles) away. According to *Seattle Daily Times* reporters, the foghorn could not be heard by the *Valencia* because it had passed through a "silent zone," an area where sound would sometimes mysteriously stop carrying. Later in history, radio beacons—which transmitted Morse code—were reportedly not heard in these zones during similar occurrences either. Another silent zone was reported one hundred kilometres (sixty-two miles) inside the Strait of Juan de Fuca at Race Rocks

The ghost ship became sensationalized in 1910,
when this *Seattle Daily Times* story was printed.

Light near Victoria. Another was believed to occur at the Point Wilson Light located at the entrance to Puget Sound between Victoria and Seattle. Interestingly, the Race Rocks silent zone phenomenon was actually proven in 1929. According to the Metchosin Museum Society, the problem there had been the positioning of the foghorns, which were subsequently moved. As technology advanced, people slowly forgot that the Strait of Juan de Fuca once had a Bermuda Triangle-like reputation for local shipping traffic. Some believed at the time that this was the cause of the *Valencia* disaster. The American commission, however, found that the foghorn had not been sounding at all. Unfortunately, the fog had been off shore, so the lighthouse didn't even know it was there. The doomed ship had been travelling inside of it.

The story of the actual haunting, as far as documentation goes, begins in August of 1906. The *Daily Colonist* reported that a Nuu-chah-nulth man named Clanewah Tom found a lifeboat full of skeletons in a cave "less than two hundred yards (180 metres) from where the *Valencia* was lost." Although never stated explicitly, he was likely looking for valuables. Other *Daily Colonist* stories had said that First Nations men had been scavenging the area of the wreck. One story about the lifeboat said that the men were going to keep their discovery a secret until it could be recovered after they returned from hunting. Even if true, Clanewah Tom reported the find.

The cave was described as fifty-five feet high and two hundred feet deep (nearly 17 metres high by 61 metres deep). To get inside the area where the boat was, Clanewah Tom had to leave his canoe and climb over a large boulder. Once inside, he had to swim.

There he had discovered the boat with eight badly decomposed bodies in a near-skeletal state. There was also a large iron box. Several other Nuu-chah-nulth men had gone in and confirmed the find as well. The lighthouse keeper's sons went to investigate, but could not get past the boulder as the water was too rough. They did, however, observe that there was wreckage from the *Valencia* in some of the caves. Part of the third raft was found—it had "slid overboard"—but no bodies or lifeboat. From beyond the boulder where the lifeboat was supposed to be, they could smell a "bad odour" and saw numerous flies. It was believed that the tide had been unusually low and the water calm for Clanewah Tom to have been able to enter the cave at all. Gaining access again appeared impossible.

The American commission noted in the April CVD report that there was some evidence there had been a third lifeboat, which had successfully made it into the water. "If so," it said, "she probably capsized later, as no one in her survived and her fate is unknown." With Clanewah Tom's discovery it was believed the water picked the lifeboat up over the boulder when the ocean was rough and placed it back in the water deeper inside the cave. The large rock prevented the boat from floating back out. The men in the raft would have had no hope. The *British Colonist* said that they starved, but they would have frozen to death long before that as they were pummelled with icy water.

It is not known what happened to the skeletons or the iron box inside the cave. Captain Kilgor of the *Grant*, who was bringing bodies back to the United States from Bamfield, was reported in the *Daily Colonist* as having scoffed at the story, saying it was "without foundation." Clanewah Tom was brought to Victoria and interviewed. The paper reported no further efforts to recover the boat.

Surprisingly, a lifeboat was actually discovered by Captain George MacFarlane in Barkley Sound around 1933—afloat near the island that the four men were rescued from. In *The Valencia Tragedy* by Michael C. Neitzel, the captain's grandson John MacFarlane shared the story in greater detail. His grandfather had found the lifeboat twenty-seven years after the disaster. He borrowed an axe from a farmer and removed the *Valencia's* nameplate as proof of the discovery. There have been stories that the boat was in perfect condition, but John MacFarlane in *The Valencia Tragedy* said this was incorrect. He had been told that the boat was actually in rough shape.

It is unreasonable to think that a boat like this could stay afloat for so long without having rainwater bailed out of it. If one were to dismiss the impossible, it either really was in the cave and finally washed free, or someone else had been using it and lost it at high tide. A large lifeboat like this—capable of holding thirty people—would have little use for any other purpose than it was intended for. It would need to be rowed by a large crew (presumably at least four people) and would be hard to carry from above the high tide line into the water. In other words, it would have been useless as any type of private work or fishing boat.

Unable to decipher the mystery, Captain George MacFarlane took the nameplate and abandoned the boat to the elements. The nameplate was then stored in a shed until the British Columbia Maritime Museum opened in Victoria in 1955 and it was donated to the museum. There, it was packed away. In a strange series of coincidences, Captain MacFarlane's grandson John became the curator of the museum. He came across the plate his grandfather had discovered in 1987. He put it on display beside an image of the Pachena Lighthouse, which had been constructed as a result of the shipwreck. No one has ever been able to explain the sudden appearance of the lifeboat decades after the *Valencia* sunk.

The *Seattle Daily Times* reported the first ghost story in 1910. The title read: "Have You Seen the Phantom Ship? Ghost of Lost Valencia Sails Again and Again upon the Rocks Where More Than 100 Souls Met Their Doom." The paper said that "persistent" stories had been brought by sailors into Seattle of a "phantom ship seen off the dangerous coast of Vancouver Island." The ship resembled the *Valencia*, they said. People could be seen "vaguely" clinging to the rigging and mast. Sometimes, the image appeared to be stationary— as if the disaster was being replayed—but the still scene somehow followed the witness ship, until "it leaped upon the rocks where the real ship met destruction."

The *Seattle Daily Times* asked maritime historian R.H. Caulkins in 1954 why Washington State didn't have any phantom ships. Caulkins said that the *Valencia* could be a candidate, as "her whistle could be heard wailing on foggy nights as she still tried to make her way home."

"Breakers Ahead!": A History of Shipwrecks in the Graveyard of the Pacific by R. Bruce Scott is often given by authors as the source for two more ghost stories. It is important to state that this is a false source and that this information is not in the book at all. After the first writer used it, other authors claiming to have referenced the book themselves have used it repeatedly. Scott doesn't even mention the

haunting. That being said, these two stories have still become part of the overall legend.

In the first one, the *City of Topeka* carried some of the survivors to Seattle after the disaster. The ship slowed to let another passing ship know about the tragedy. In the thick, black, coal smoke, the shape of the *Valencia* could clearly be seen.

In the second tale, fishermen reported seeing a lifeboat near the site of the *Valencia*'s demise. Unbelievably, they saw a crew of skeletons manning the small vessel. It is frightening to think that even if a person does not believe in the supernatural, there might be the possibility that a lifeboat with skeletons was actually floating around the area before it was finally discovered, her deathly cargo of human remains removed by sea otters and ravenous birds, one bone at a time.

Water sloshes against the lifeboat's bow as it slowly cuts across the dark ocean's surface. The crisp night is bright beneath a full moon, but smoke-like fog raises several feet from the surface of the water to caress the lonely vessel. Oars dip gently into the inky black water, grasped tightly by skeletal hands. A scream carries across the night, and then another, and another. Smiling skull faces lean forward in unison and then back again, as they row diligently, searching for help, or revenge. They will do so for as long as the ocean continues to exist, or until their bodies are finally laid to rest.

Ahousaht welcome figure.
PHOTO BY SHANON SINN

GHOSTS AND
BLACK MAGIC

STORIES FROM CHIEF JAMES SWAN
OF AHOUSAHT

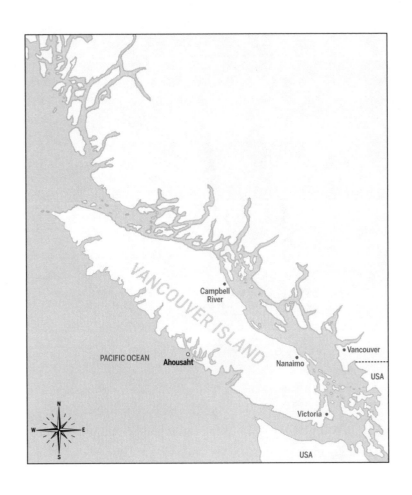

THE NUU-CHAH-NULTH VILLAGE OF AHOUSAHT is located north of Tofino on Flores Island. With mountains jutting out of the sea, foggy mists, monstrous trees, massive whales, and screaming eagles, the whole region feels like stepping into another world.

With an oral tradition stretching back thousands of years, some Nuu-chah-nulth remember a time when their ancestors lived in harmony with nature and the spirit world, an age when humans were able to harness powers unfathomable today.

I met Chief James UuKwaqum Swan in the army. Despite being a public figure and artist, he had humbled himself to the position of Private in the infantry. There is no rougher trade or lower rank in the army. Traditionally, this was the place for the lower class, uneducated, and expendable soldiers. It was these men who did the hard work, carried the heavy loads, and fought the real battles. Even today, the infantry attracts a rougher crowd than any other branch of the military. James hadn't joined as an officer but as a soldier without any rank. For him, it wasn't about ego.

James and I became friends before I learned he was a chief. It was confusing at first. He was a hereditary chief of Manhousaht, but his people lived in the village of Ahousaht and had their own chief. I asked him to explain.

According to James, Manhousaht had joined Ahousaht out of necessity to avoid an "extinct" classification from the government. Their numbers had been decimated by war and disease. The idea was not unprecedented. Other groups had joined as well. James' family was welcomed into the village and became part of a larger community. There are two other hereditary chiefs connected to Ahousaht besides James, from nations who also amalgamated. There is also one vacant seat from another nation.

As part of the Ahousaht Nation, the lineage of the Swans is one of artistic vision and respect for the old ways. It was this other side of James, the infantryman, that fascinated me. From what little I had read, the Nuu-chah-nulth were known for their intricate art, whaling and fishing, navigational skills, fierceness in battle, and long-range coastal raids. Their oral traditions had somehow survived, and their art was recognized around the world.

When I first asked James if I could interview him about the belief of spirits in his culture his response was, "I always need a fishing partner." And so, he brought me to Ahousaht in 2012 when I was still sick from cancer treatment. I was welcomed into his home, met his family and friends, and spoke to his mother, Mrs. Rosie Swan, an elder who treated me with a level of kindness that I will never forget. Then, during the day, James and I fished and talked.

James talked a lot about reel-to-reel tapes belonging to his grandfather, Luke Francis Swan, which were filled with old stories, songs, and language. Dave Ellis, who had initially recorded them, wrote a book called *Teachings of the Tides*, which is credited to both men. James possesses copies of these tapes and has committed some of the stories to memory. At times, he would attribute other teachings to his mother.

Eventually, I interviewed James on a digital recorder so that I could share clearly and accurately what he had said. My fear was

that, as much as I respected James' culture, I could also get something wrong. For ease of reading, my questions are in bold type and
quotation marks are not used.

**James, do the Nuu-chah-nulth believe in sea serpents or lake
monsters, anything like that?**

We believe in them, that's why we draw them, that is why they're
in our art. One man [says his name] was fishing alone on a herring
skiff when he saw one.

When you see something that's not normal you are actually not
supposed to talk about it for four years. When a creature or sea
serpent or anything else shows itself to you, you are supposed to ask
why it showed itself to you, because a lot of the things we see out of
the normal are something special. That person needs to go find it.
That person needs to go fast [not eat], to go up to the mountains,
to pray to the Creator and find out why that creature, that animal
appeared to that one individual or many.

[Man's name] was fishing alone and he saw a sea serpent. He
said that it was so big it could have taken out his herring skiff no
problem. He did not talk about it for four years after.

**Do animals have spirits? You have told me before that in your
culture you thank the animal when you kill it, much like other
First Nations people.**

We are taught that you pray for an animal when you kill it. Any time
you take a deer or elk or anything you thank it for its life, even a tree.

We believe, because it is alive, there is something existing within
it, so we thank them, we will actually say a prayer, and it will give

us good luck. When part of the tree is used to catch sea urchins, for example. In modern times, when you are getting a pole for your trawler, it will give you good luck and help you catch fish if you ask it.

My mom [Mrs. Rosie Swan] will also pray that I catch fish, she is my "backer" if you will, that the fishing will be good. One man stopped being a "highliner" [a person who catches a lot of fish] when his grandmother passed away. It might be psychological, but when you hear my mom talking about the Creator, this is what she means.

When we thank the salmon, we don't throw away their bones in the garbage; we throw it back in the ocean. It doesn't matter where we are, we throw it back in the ocean. But we use most of it. When we put it back in the water that's when we thank the fish so that more fish will come back.

My mom was once very upset with me because I shot a deer and put it in my vehicle and moved it before I cleaned it. It was supposed to be cleaned right there, where it had been killed. My mom said that you bring the water you are going to use after to wash your hands . . . you don't move it!

My mom is very strict. She is adamant about our teachings. My mom is strong. She's culturally strong.

There is a saying in my culture *Hishuk ish tsawalk*. It means that everything is one. If you interfere with one thing, you will interfere with everything else.

My dad [James Francis Swan Sr.] said that we couldn't have caught the fish they used to catch before with the fishing line we use today. They were too big. They would break the line today. That's how big they were.

Hishuk ish tsawalk. Everything is one.

True Reflections by Chief James UuKwaqum Swan depicts many of the Nuu-chah-nulth beliefs.
COURTESY OF JAMES SWAN

Do the Nuu-chah-nulth people believe in wandering spirits, or are there First Nations ghosts?

Whether I believe in it or not, there are ghosts. In our culture ghosts are stuck. They are souls or spirits. One of the things that I was taught is that there's another realm where our spirits go. Some people believe, like the Catholics for example, that there is a heaven [holds his hand up high] and a hell [holds his hand down low] on the other side. These people are stuck between heaven and hell.

Our souls go into another room, another realm, and are always met by three people; three other people that are a part of our family. Anyone who has died or has went slowly has seen someone like their father or even my father coming to greet them and show them the way. They were there waiting for them to show them the way.

Sometimes, people don't see good things. My grandfather talks about it. He says there is a hell, and there is a heaven, although I don't know the name for it, but it's something that my grandfather talks about.

All of the things we see, in our culture, in our heritage, he says that they happen for a reason. He also says that all of the things that you dream about can happen if you really truly believe. That's one of the things. I went down to the United States, for example, to go see a friend of mine's son who was in the hospital. I turned to one of our songs and I prayed for him, and he got up. The doctor said he wasn't supposed to do that. He was supposed to be in the hospital for the rest of his life. He got up and left the hospital. It might be psychological, but if you believe in it . . .

In society, you talk about being stubborn. When I go out hunting, or I go out fishing, and I get cold, in my mind I will say, "I am going to be warm when I get home and have a nice warm bath," and I am not cold. In the army, the first time that I had to run thirteen kilometres [eight miles] I knew I would finish it even though I had never run it before. I puked, but I did it. I am stubborn.

So when you talk about ghosts, one of the things I always tell myself is that I will believe it when I see it. Whenever I hear of ghosts, or Sasquatch or anything I think that I will believe it when I see it. But when you hear the stories of what people have experienced, of seeing my father, who was seen by one of my other relatives, I am sometimes disappointed. I think why doesn't he come see me the way he does in my dreams? That is one of the places, I believe, there is a place for our spirits. In our minds and in our dreams.

When you talk about dreams, things you've done before but you haven't—like déjà vu—or something you've dreamt about. You are wondering, for example, "I have been here before, I've done this before, I have asked this before," and it is the first time that you have ever done it for real. I believe that someone has given me that thought. Whether it's a soul, a lost soul, an ancestor, a father, a grandmother, they have gone on and have given that thought. I am not saying out-of-body, but that they are visitors that were in those places that give us those thoughts, that déjà vu.

So I really want to see a ghost. I really want to see it to believe it. When I listen to the stories of my father and my mother and everyone else talking about ghosts and spirits, these stories you can't dismiss them. You can't dismiss the elders because then you are calling them a liar and saying that they are full of shit because in my language that is what you are saying. They are not. They raised you, they taught you, they gave you everything they could, and told you stories of their life and maybe their story of a ghost.

There is actually one; she was actually dressed like a witch in Ahousaht. There are two different stories about this witch dressed in black. We call her a witch because she was dressed in black. She had a black hat on. There is no face. We know it's a girl even though it has no face on it. My grandfather saw it.

The first time I ever heard about this thing was when my grandfather saw it. There was a house fire at my mom and dad's house, and it burnt to the ground. My grandfather had been burnt inside, and he went to my sister's house. He had half his face burnt in the fire. The house burnt down when I was about sixteen years of age. What happened was that my grandfather was out on the deck—at my sister's—and he was looking down the hill. He said that he saw somebody then running away from that black hag, and my grandfather saw it yelling at them.

Another person experienced the same thing around the same time. They got so terrified that they jumped into the nearest house. They smashed a window and jumped in a bunk in the nearest house. That was probably about thirty years ago . . . quite a while ago.

One woman talked about a thing too. She was reaching up into the attic once to grab an item she was going to sell—that she shouldn't have—and a hand grabbed her wrist. She was fighting to get her hand out of there. It scared the bejesus out of her, and she never did it again.

I also have a story of Jenny's Beach [Shelter Inlet]. There was an old lady that lived there, and she lived there all by herself. They used to say that she used to talk to somebody and that somebody would carry wood and water for her. People witnessed the water and the wood come in there by itself so that she was taken care of. That was a long time ago. My grandfather would talk about it.

Have you ever heard of stories about possession? Can a person become possessed by spirits in your culture?
Like I said before, my grandfather said we had a name for hell so my answer would be yes. I don't think our people ever had possession before, though. Our culture was really strong before Europeans came.

One thing, people were not allowed to watch us during our

cleansing—whether we were in the ocean or up a mountain we never told anyone where our cleansing spot was. We never told them when we were going to go out and when we were going to come back. It was something that we did on our own—going up the mountain, finding our own pond or pool or going into the ocean in the morning in our own spot.

We used to pray this way to get things right. Someone would pray to use the medicines to make him stronger, or to make him more powerful, or to conquer a whale, to kill a whale or a fur seal, or to do something that he wanted like being a warrior. These were the types of things he had to do to prepare himself. He had to fast for four days in order to do the stuff that he had to do when it comes to cleansing himself. In some cases, you would see visions, which would tell you something like what to do with your life, or how to do something, or give you songs in some cases or dances. All through fasting.

If somebody was watching you, one of the things we had to do was actually kill that person. This is because all of their bad stuff will be absorbed into us. You were talking about being possessed, possession. That is one of the things that I understand. Our culture tells us we should not have been there, that we should know better than to watch or to observe what that other person was doing to get things right.

Do people still fast?
I fast. It's really hard not to eat for four days especially when we consider what we eat today. Back then it could have been easier because every day you had to go out for food, but we usually had nothing. Back then we could smoke our fish, but there was no refrigeration or anything.

I think if we don't believe something our elders taught us we are really missing something. It is important that we do not get off so easy. Otherwise you can become weak minded because we are missing something in our life. Our teaching is *Hishuk ish tsawalk*, "everything is one." It doesn't just mean the resources we have, it means the stuff we have inside of us too.

If we don't deal with things like grief the right way, it will leave a hole inside us and make us vulnerable. By dealing with things the right way, by having *yatsu-yatsu* [prayer song] and having the dance, we deal with things the right way.

In the Nuu-chah-nulth culture are there such things as curses or people who can give you the evil eye?
They talk about black magic. Nobody likes to talk about them—I don't know why—they are scared of them. One of the things we are told is that even a hair . . . My grandfather said to me, "Every time you cut your hair, you put the hair in the garbage, and you tie it! You put your own hair away, and you don't trust anyone else!"

They will put a curse on you or hex you or whatever you want to call it. That's the kind of thing my grandfather said to me in real life. I heard him saying this, and I heard other people talk about it.

Like when you put your name on a container, like one on my boat that has "James Swan" on it. If somebody took something like that and they did something with it, well, it had my name on it and it belonged to me and was mine. One of the things we are always taught is not to put your name on stuff you own. If somebody wants it bad enough, they can take it.

That must have been difficult in the army!

[Laughs] Yeah! I have my name on everything!

Do you think anyone still believes in these things or practices them anymore?

Yeah, they do because they say that even some people in Ahousaht practice black magic or witchcraft or whatever you want to call it. Some people in our culture do.

All we are told is to pray if something bad happens. Pray for the people that you think are doing bad things. You never pray or wish them the same bad luck. You never do that because it will come back to you three times. So, if they do it to us you will see things happening to them really bad, and that is how you know it is them.

They pay a price for sending something off.

James, you were talking about letting the spirit of a person go after they've died by practicing what you called "dealing with things the right way."

In our culture we have a song called the *yatsu-yatsu* and it lets the spirits go. We can't have bad thoughts about a person, even from a photograph, or we will hang onto them. So we sing the *yatsu-yatsu* and it lets the spirit go.

We will also have a memorial ceremony, a potlatch. It's really tough for people when a loved one has passed—to let them go—because we always want to have that person close to us forever.

Even with my dad's death. He is always with me, my father [James Swan Sr.]. Half of what he was is always with me. Same with my mother, I am half of what she is. So my father, or my mother, will never be gone. I look at my daughter and I say to her, "Make Grandpa James" and she goes like this [makes a face]. Jessie will make a frown on her face, and when you will see it, it's just the way he would look. So he's always going to be around. All of his grandchildren and great grandchildren, they know who he is from his pictures, as well. His memory will always be around.

By putting pictures away when someone passes on we let their spirit go as well. When my dad passed away, all of the pictures of him we put away for one year after the memorial service. Usually, this is for four years, but our elders said only to do it for one year because all of our songs and dances were really popular back then and they wanted to have them back. They didn't want them gone for four years, so we took them back one year after he passed away.

We had a memorial potlatch and took the pictures and songs back after we did the *yatsu-yatsu*. After all of the songs and dances were finished, we did ours and took them back that day. This was after the songs had been gone for one year. It was one year after my dad passed away.

In our belief, if something was really loved by a person we would also send that item with them when they died. We would take that special item, and we would put it in a grave or in a cave with them. Nowadays, even if you went to our cemetery, there are items there like somebody's sewing machine. The sewing machine will be sitting on top of the grave of the person that loved that item they cherished so much. It is not very often that this happens anymore, though.

So do people in your culture bury the deceased?
We do now, but I'm not going to be. I am going to be put up in a

tree for one whole year waiting for my body to decay. I then want my bones put into a cave.

A cave? Is this the traditional place to be buried?
In caves, yes it is. The cave I want to be put in is in Manhousaht territory.

The old way.
Yes, the old way. Some people might say it won't matter because I'll be dead, but I want it done this way. It's all in my will.

I've noticed that a lot of places in Ahousaht have paintings of the thunderbird on them. Can you tell me a bit about that story?
What we are told, from a long time ago, is that when you hear the thunder rolling out—when you first hear that thunder—it is actually rolling out to the ocean. It means that the thunderbird is actually going out to capture its prey, the whale.

Shortly after, you will hear it rolling back in, so if you listen very carefully, you will hear the thunder roll, or rolling. It will roll out toward the ocean and it will come back in after it captures its prey. Every time you hear the thunder going out that is the thunderbird that is going out hunting.

[According to Nuu-chah-nulth lore, the thunderbird sometimes carries the sea serpent with him out to sea, and it is he who creates the lightning in the sky. Lightning is not very common off the coast of Vancouver Island.]

One of the things that we're told is that there was this man that followed the thunderbird. He went over four mountains following the thunderbird. He saw the thunderbird going into a cave. The man followed it into the cave. The man then saw another man coming out of the chest of the thunderbird. So that is one of the reasons why you will see a man's face on the thunderbird's chest in our First Nation art.

So the man, is that the spirit of the thunderbird or a separate being? I don't know what it could be. It could be anything from the first visions and sightings of airplanes, or it could be something else. When some people talk about UFOs that's something that somebody actually saw. That is where that legend or tale came from in regards to that man coming out of the chest.

Even when I think about it, I think about a hanger. I think about an airplane when they say he got out of the chest of a bird. I think of an airplane with wings. That is kind of what I think of when I hear that story.

A long time ago our people went down to Victoria. They got into a canoe and went that way before we had motorboats and everything else. They went down there and they got scared because they heard this loud whistle. They found out later that it was from the train. So that's where that whistle came from.

Our people heard that whistle for the first time, and it spooked them. They came back. They never made it all of the way to Victoria.

A lot of people in Ahousaht are Christian or Catholic. There used to be two churches, but your mom says that one burned down and now there is only one. Would you say that most people are now mixing the old beliefs with Christian traditions?

I think that there are a lot more coming back to the First Nations' way. We don't have a priest that stays in Ahousaht, but we have one that comes to Ahousaht. A lot of the old-timers, especially the ones who had it really rough in the residential schools, had it shoved down their throat—Christianity and religion that is. My mom talks about it.

My mom prays to God and Jesus and I don't disrespect her for that because I'm 100 percent First Nations. I pray to Naas. I pray to the Creator. I don't have any disrespect for Jesus or for God. I don't have any disrespect for Allah or for any other religion or belief that anyone else has. I'm not saying it's wrong.

What I believe in, in my culture, I practice to the best of my ability. That is what I have.

JAMES' STYLE OF responding to the interview questions was often layered and indirect. Each answer would hold a great deal of information though. When I asked James a question, he would sometimes seem to change the subject at first. He would then wrap around the topic slowly, before eventually responding to the question directly.

When I asked him about Ahousaht ghost stories, for example, he explained his own skepticism—delicately—but articulated that he felt honour-bound by tradition to believe in the stories of the elders. Following this introduction and explanation, James went on to tell the original tale to the best of his recollection.

When applicable, James would usually say the name of the person he had heard the story from and who they in turn had heard it from. This method of storytelling allows the teller of the original story to be sourced. The tale can then be linked to another person, living or dead. It seems like a small thing, but it is this system of information-sharing that held many communities together for thousands of years. It's easy to forget that reading and writing hasn't existed on the West Coast for very long. The Nuu-chah-nulth, like the Celts, had a strong surviving oral tradition instead. This included a belief in spirits and ghosts. The First Voices website lists 1,275 Nuu-chah-nulth words. Of these, three pertain to ghosts: One means "ghost," another means "to see a ghost," and a third is to be "ghosted in a dream"—presumably either by a relative or an enemy spirit.

As I wrote out responses from the recordings of the interview with James, I would sometimes realize that there were things he had said that I hadn't picked up on the first time. When talking about black magic, for example, he had a certain compassionate contempt for those who practiced this form of sorcery. James had listed personal items—things with his name on them—that a dark practitioner could theoretically steal and put a curse on. He did not seem to care if anyone tried. I say "compassionate contempt" because contempt alone doesn't suit the philosophical stance James seemed to be taking. He had a genuine pity for these dark practitioners. He believed they would receive three times the negativity that they had directed at him. Much of the specific wording, such as where his labelled items could be found, I left out. James laughing about the army labels was left in to demonstrate his overall lack of concern, or perhaps unshakeable faith. Besides, it was true. We really did have our names on everything.

A lot of suffering has been inflicted upon the people of Ahousaht and other Vancouver Island First Nations communities by agents of government in the not-so-distant past, from colonialization to murder. There has been publicity in recent years regarding the treatment of Indigenous children in Catholic-run residential schools especially. Men, in the name of religion, committed atrocities on schoolchildren ranging from torture to rape. In 2013, Ian Mosby published the report *Administering Colonial Science: Nutrition Research and Human Biomedical Experimentation in Aboriginal Communities and Residential Schools, 1942–1952*. Along with other Canadian residential school locations, Port Alberni on Vancouver Island was named specifically. It is little wonder that residential school sites across the island are thought to be haunted. If ghosts are "stuck" spirits, as James said, then it would make sense that these grounds would hold the restless dead. Innocent children being abducted and tortured in mass numbers sounds like the fictional plot of some foreign horror film, and yet this happened all across the island, in other parts of Canada, and to Indigenous cultures throughout the world, all in an attempt to force people to assimilate.

Much of the old lore might still be forgotten or lost. James had told me during the interview that his mother was the last one in his family who remembered how to speak their language, as there are distinct differences from the Ahousaht dialect. Sadly, Mrs. Rosie Swan passed away in 2015, taking an important piece of history with her.

In 2012, James had told me that the passing of time "had really brought a lot of healing" back to the people of Ahousaht. A return to the old ways helped. Problems like addiction or bootlegging became community issues to be dealt with by the elders instead of an excuse to cast members out of society forever. Nuu-chah-nulth art, history, dancing, and storytelling continues to give the next generation something to be proud of.

It would seem that when people have to grow, gather, or hunt their own food that they are more thankful—in general—and able to find a greater meaning from the natural world around them. When a person relies on the life of a fish from the sea—instead of a breaded piece of food taken out of a box to be dipped in sauce—it comes with a certain sense of understanding, respect, and gratitude. Idealistically, the animal or tree's spirit is thanked for its sacrifice, and us humans can, in turn, remain humble.

The Nuu-chah-nulth belief that everything has a spirit resonates with me. The law applies to all things on Vancouver Island, from the spider to the wolf, from the darkest storm to the brightest day, from the twisted ancient tree to the brightest-coloured songbird. The teaching is *Hishuk ish tsawalk*, and it means everything is one.

Wild Woman of the Woods mask at the Royal BC Museum.
PHOTO BY SHANON SINN

FORBIDDEN
PLATEAU

COMOX VALLEY

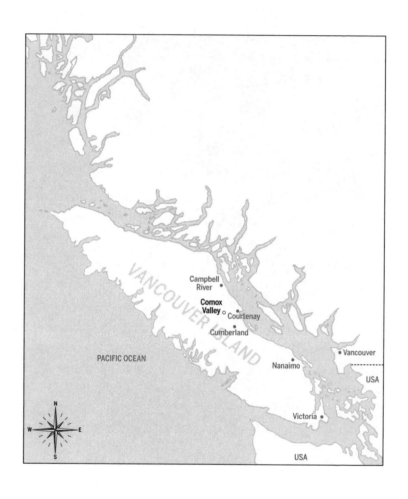

BACK ON THE EAST SIDE of Vancouver Island, north of Qualicum Beach, is the furthest reaches of Coast Salish territory: the Comox Valley. Most of the valley's population lives in the city of Courtenay, or the more or less attached town of Comox. The village of Cumberland has several thousand residents as well. Like many other places on Vancouver Island, the region has its fair share of ghost stories, but none of the tales are as persistent as Forbidden Plateau.

A 1968 *Comox District Free Press* article told two versions of the legend: the first claimed that the K'omoks (anglicized as Comox), "fought a battle to the death" with their enemies on the plateau. Everyone disappeared afterward. The second—and much more popular version—said that the K'omoks were about to be attacked by the Cowichan. They sent all of their women and children to hide on the plateau until the battle was over. When the fighting was finished, the warriors went to Forbidden Plateau to retrieve their elders, wives, sons, and daughters. There was no sign of them anywhere. Forever after, the area was off limits to the K'omoks. An earlier 1927 *Vancouver Daily Province* newspaper article had said that some believed a powerful enemy "sorcerer" had put a curse on the land.

In 1969, Philip and Helen Akrigg said in *British Columbia Place Names* that Forbidden Plateau was given its name because the First Nations people believed "evil spirits" inhabited it. Whether the result of a curse, or something far more ancient and foreboding, the evil spirit belief has widely been accepted.

Forbidden Plateau is a recreational area of Strathcona Park, located southwest of Mount Washington and northeast of Mount Albert Edward. The area is about 250 square kilometres (97 square miles). A 1954 Report of the Provincial Museum on the BC Geographical Names website said that only a small region of the park is plateau-like at all. The area "consists of a series of ridges, sloping wet meadows and open park land at various elevations ranging from 3,500 to 4,000 feet." The same website says that the name Forbidden Plateau has been in use officially since 1939.

In 1864, Robert Brown led the Vancouver Island Exploring Expedition down the Puntledge River to Comox Lake, and beyond toward Port Alberni. One of his men was the legendary one-armed Toma who had assisted Adam Grant Horne in the over-island trek from Qualicum almost a decade earlier. Brown's journal has been used as a source to promote the Forbidden Plateau legend.

John Hayman's edited version of *Robert Brown and the Vancouver Island Exploring Expedition*, paints a clearer picture. On August 22, 1864, Brown wrote: "These Indians like all others have only a few places where they have gone for years, and the slightest deviation from the beaten track fills them with fear." On August 31 he added: "I was certain that they would not go higher than the lake at the river source, the old fear of getting outside their circle being dominant." As the salmon run was also beginning—a busy time of the year for all Vancouver Island First Nations—the expedition was forced to make their way without any local guides.

The *Comox Argus* published several stories about the legend. In

1922, Sasquatch-like creatures abducted a man. Other sightings of hairy men were reported as well. The snow was said to turn pink in certain areas, the result of a rare moss that the K'omoks people had interpreted with superstition.

Forbidden Plateau was the epicentre of an earthquake that was felt as far away as Washington State on June 23, 1946. According to the CBC News in 2014, the 7.3 magnitude earthquake was the largest earthquake recorded in Canada at the time. (There have since been three more powerful earthquakes in the Haida Gwaii archipelago north of the island, which are less populated areas.) The *Daily Colonist* reported that the event rocked the Comox Valley and was "the worst earthquake ever experienced" in Port Alberni. Chimneys collapsed all over the island. One man was killed in Qualicum when a wave overturned the raft he was in. Another death sometimes attributed to the earthquake was a heart attack. Several whales were found dead shortly afterward as well. The earthquake happened on a Sunday, so no children were killed when a Courtenay school's chimney collapsed into a classroom. Several homes were thrown off their foundations. A house slid off a cliff, a beach disappeared, and a thirty-foot wave swept over Comox Lake, pushing a floating work camp "one hundred feet up on shore." No one in any of the buildings including six bunkhouses and a residence had been injured. The story was the same all over the valley: major destruction, but miraculously no one was killed. When it was discovered that the epicentre had been in Forbidden Plateau, the reputation of the land being haunted by evil spirits grew even greater.

Usually seen alone, three cougars were captured on video surrounding a man in his truck on a Forbidden Plateau road in 2016.

He shared the video on YouTube. There have also been several unusual deaths over the years. According to the *Comox Valley Echo*, the ski lodge shut its doors forever and was abandoned following fires, a collapsed roof, and vandalism. Evil had prevailed. Some legends are impossible to ignore, even if they are without foundation.

A scrapbook of newspaper clippings and articles by Ruth Masters at the Courtenay & District Museum titled *History of Forbidden Plateau 1920–86* said the stories were created for tourism purposes. She called them "tourist promotional bunk."

In the 1920s and 30s, several backcountry men built cabins in the area. One of them was Clinton Wood. In 1967, Wood confessed to having made up the initial legends to attract recreational users for himself and other residents in the region to profit from. The 1927 *Vancouver Daily Province* story was written by Ben Hughes, who had written the *Comox Argus* stories as well. Wood promoted the original tale, and then Hughes ran with it. Apparently, the newspaperman loved to tell a good story, regardless if it was true or not. Even the legend of the snow turning colour had been completely made up.

In *CV Collective* magazine, Ryan Stuart said in 2016 that the "promotional efforts worked." Wood offered horse and hiking tours, at first, then founded the ski hill. Eventually, Forbidden Plateau became part of Strathcona Park, even as its reputation continued to grow.

Hughes, and others, used Brown's journals as a source for the stories. There are several problems with this theory, however, the primary one being that Brown didn't go to Forbidden Plateau. The route he was taking was believed to be a lesser-used First

A 1934 *Daily Colonist* article mentions some of the legends attached to Forbidden Plateau.

Nations trail, not off the beaten path or into the mountains. His expedition also found human remains, even more evidence that the path had been used in the past. Brown mentioned "Indian" paths across Vancouver Island frequently in his journals. Vancouver Island First Nations groups didn't just stick to the coast, as many people believe. They hunted elk and deer, foraged, fished freshwater fish, and sometimes sought out spirit aids in secluded mountain pools. What Brown had been frustrated about was his inability to find any guides. He said that they were afraid to go where the terrain was unfamiliar. If true, this would have been anywhere, not just the Forbidden Plateau area. Going into the wilderness alone would be power-seeking, which only occurred under certain conditions. Positive places of power were either already known, or could be sought out at a specific time for a specific purpose. Brown also admitted in his journal that there were other reasons for not acquiring guides, such as the start of the salmon season.

There is one more point worth adding. Everyone was terrified of Toma. Brown mentions several times that many First Nations people on Vancouver Island were especially afraid of him. It is hard to gauge a man we know so little about, but the few facts we have are sobering. Having just one arm, Toma was still the man Brown sent out day after day to hunt for the party's food. Brown admitted that he himself was afraid of Toma when he was drinking, even though Brown had become close to him, as he listened to him recount First Nation myths late into the night often. Brown was not, however, afraid of other members of his rough crew, including the man who pulled a knife on another—at least not enough to write about it.

Toma was also smart. He was able to speak a number of Vancouver Island First Nations languages. And there was more. A year before, Toma had been charged with killing his wife but had been released for lack of evidence. Brown's notes suggest that he thought Toma might not have done it and that this was the reason he was angry and drank, but that Toma was still not a man to be taken lightly. More than once, Brown stated that other First Nations men feared Toma. This could be a more likely reason young men might have been afraid to join the expedition party, even if Brown hadn't connected those dots himself.

Is Forbidden Plateau home to spirits as the Coast Salish understands them? The answer would be "yes," because spirits were—and are—everywhere. That was what few settlers understood, and few understand about most Indigenous people who follow their traditional beliefs today.

Robert Brown had a fascination with Vancouver Island's First Nations cultures, so many of his observations contained insights into a belief in spirits haunting wild places. "Every living thing had a superstition," he said. He expressed concern that the people who knew these traditions were "dying out" and that their knowledge would be lost within a few years. He wrote:

> There are Pans and Driads—Gods of the woods and the groves, the running streams and the fountains. I have seen the women sitting for hours listening to the God of the Waterfalls.

And in regard to spirits of the dead he said:

The figure of the owl occurs frequently, the bird of
Athens [Athena] among the Indians as among the
Greeks being a bird of superstition. It is, they say,
the spirit of the dead. And they will crowd closer
around their campfire as they hear the solemn hoot
in the gloomy pine forest and wonder if they have
offended the dead by talking about anyone in the land
of spirits. Among them it is a breach of etiquette to
mention the dead.

The Forbidden Plateau area was undoubtedly believed by the
K'omoks to be a land of spirits. Oral and recorded history from across
Vancouver Island claimed these spirits exist. A person was always
expected to tread lightly in the wilderness in order to not offend
them. The largest hole in the legend theory, however, is that—as
a place—it never even existed. Forbidden Plateau is a drawn-out
area on a map made by settlers. As a named location of its own, it
wasn't real before white people said it was. This does not mean, of
course, that the area was not believed by the K'omoks to be haunted,
only that these spirits would not be confined to fictional boundaries.

In its early days, Forbidden Plateau had become a place for prospectors seeking fortune and for outdoorsmen escaping civilization.
This did not always work out very well. The *History of Forbidden
Plateau* scrapbook lists several tragic deaths. In 1926, the skeleton of
a miner missing since 1913 was found. The cause of death: unknown.
Another man went missing in December of 1933. His naked body
was found beside an unfired shotgun the following summer. There
have been other deaths connected to the area as well, including the

suicide of an outdoorsman living on Forbidden Plateau in 1930 after he became hospitalized. In 1937, the body of another man was found partially submerged in a stream. He had suffered a head wound. The survey party he was with found his dead body, but did not witness what had happened to him.

One after another, the cabins on Forbidden Plateau were abandoned and fell into disrepair. By 1962, it had become a part of Strathcona Park. Eventually, even the ski lodge was abandoned.

Forbidden Plateau is not the only area on Vancouver Island to remain untamed. It is the only one, however, to have maintained such a strong reputation as being home to "evil spirits." There are those who believe that spirits wander the wilderness still, but who would scoff at the idea they would be confined to the imaginary lines of a park. These spirits—both good and bad—are everywhere.

The Heriot Bay Inn, the third hotel on this site, was built in 1912.
IMAGE 7676, COURTESY OF THE MUSEUM AT CAMPBELL RIVER

INVESTIGATING THE HAUNTING OF THE HERIOT BAY INN.

QUADRA ISLAND

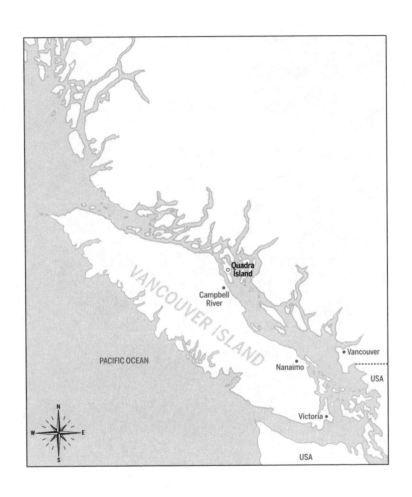

J UST TO THE NORTH OF the Comox Valley is the city of Campbell River. It is located on the shore of the Discovery Passage, which meets the Strait of Georgia nearby. It is the northernmost city on Vancouver Island, and the only city located within Kwakwaka'wakw traditional territory.

Campbell River's stories of hauntings are considerably light compared to other municipalities on Vancouver Island. Truthfully, reports of the unexplained are more often in regards to mysterious lights in the sky or Sasquatch-like creatures seen on remote back roads. This does not mean, however, that the area has no notable hauntings.

The 120-year-old Heriot Bay Inn is located on Quadra Island, only a few kilometres from Campbell River by ferry. The inn holds the region's most notable ghost story, and one of Vancouver Island's most persistent. The haunting was the first investigation that Sean Enns and I conducted together.

Hosea Arminius Bull, an immigrant from Missouri, established the Heriot Bay Inn sometime around 1895 in a protected bay, facing east toward Cortez Island. His clients were loggers and the island's first settlers. According to Jeanette Taylor in *The Quadra Story*, a fire burned the original building to the ground a few years after it had been built. Another fire destroyed a second building in 1911. The present inn was constructed in 1912.

The Heriot Bay Inn is a relatively small, L-shaped building. The short portion of the "L" faces the bay, while the longer portion runs parallel to the shoreline. For unknown reasons, owner Charles Webster removed the smaller half of the building during the late 1920s and made the remaining piece his private home. Later owners restored the building. In 1946, the chimneys collapsed during the Forbidden Plateau earthquake. No one was hurt, but the structure required significant repairs.

It was a rough place. The inn was a retreat for local loggers and those who wanted to get away from Campbell River. Miners and fisherman frequented the establishment as well. One tale in *The Quadra Story* speaks of two men who had gotten into a disagreement. Tempers had flared as they prepared to have a pistol duel. The locals tricked them separately, getting each of them so drunk that they ended up passing out. The two men woke up tied to, and facing, one another. They were so furious that they threatened to join forces and kill everyone involved. Somehow, nothing came of this. A more tragic incident occurred in 1907 when a First Nations woman was murdered (off the property) following a masquerade.

Current inn manager and co-owner Lois Taylor believes the building's location could have something to do with the haunting. A First Nations midden containing layers of seashells lies beneath the inn, providing evidence of the site's ancientness. Like Campbell River, Quadra Island is Kwakwaka'wakw territory. It originally belonged to the Salish, but the Kwakwaka'wakw migrated into the area in the eighteenth century and absorbed the remaining Coast Salish members.

Lois first started to work at the inn in 1974 when she was nineteen years old. She said that by then, the inn's reputation as being haunted was already well established.

According to Lois, there are two spirits believed to haunt the inn. One is thought to be an old lady, sometimes seen knitting, with white-grey hair up in a bun. She's primarily seen in room fourteen (where I would sleep). She's also been reported "more than once" in the dining area. Room fourteen's bathroom window was once found pushed out of the grout and lying on the grass unbroken below. To be clear, that means the glass had no frame to protect it from its fall from the upper floor. Lois said that on another occasion, a guest ran into the lobby and told a former staff member that an old lady was leaning outside of the room's window shouting. To them, it looked like she was going to fall or jump. The staff member told the witness that there was no one staying in the room. They verified this by looking at the guest book and by checking room fourteen physically. No one was there. A psychic at one point told Lois and other inn staff that the old woman's spirit was waiting for her husband to return from sea.

Once, another employee said he was walking by the stereo near the fireplace in the dining room when it suddenly turned on. The unexpected blast of noise startled him. The stereo was located next to where the old woman had been seen knitting by the fire, so the activity was attributed to her. According to a 1997 news article in the *Campbell River Mirror*, reporter Tanya Storr—a former employee at the inn—was another witness who saw the old woman over the years.

The second apparition is said to be a murdered logger. His clothing has been different in various versions of the story, such as suspenders in one account or a long overcoat in another. He's usually described as having a moustache, but might also sport a beard. He is said to walk up and down the upstairs hallway and is also seen inside the pub. The only pattern in any of the inn's accounts is that his loud hallway walking usually happens in the early morning (around "six-ish" or earlier).

Many people claim to have seen him come into the pub or have had him stand beside them. When they then turned to look at him he was gone. One bartender told us she thought that her manager was beside her, but when she looked that no one was there. In a Vancouver Island CTV News story, housekeeper Eileen Anastacia-Peters said that a man in old-fashioned clothing peered around the corner at her in room twelve. When she went into the hallway to look no one was there.

In the province's two regional BC ghost books (by Joanne Christianson and later Barbara Smith), the story is that the logger was murdered after a bar fight and then was put into an unmarked grave. Lois said that she does not know where this story came from, but that the version she heard originally was that the man was the murderer and not the victim.

There have been several times when the pub's stools have been put up for the night but found shortly after back on the floor. A housekeeper and a separate bartender both told us that they often had feelings of not being alone. The bartender said she felt as if she was in an old lady's presence. A second-hand account from a non-present staff member was of a bathroom stall door that had been slammed shut when she was alone in the washroom.

The visiting psychic had said that room nine had a female spirit in it as well. (This was the room my co-investigator Sean Enns would sleep in.) She said that this spirit did not like males.

Unexplained occurances are common in the bar, including the front
of a bottle somehow becoming detached and falling to the floor.
PHOTO BY SHANON SINN

Lois told us that room eight had two separate reports where a
square of intense white light had been seen. Both parties initially
thought that the light was coming through a grate connected to the
next room. The sightings took place in 2014, "within a year" of our
investigation. The witnesses discovered in the morning that there
wasn't a grate there, and if there had been it would have only led into
the room's bathroom. All of them reported feeling annoyed when
they initially saw the light.

The loft (room five) has sometimes had furniture inexplicably
moved as well. Lois and another manager once heard this occurring
when no one else was in the inn. They started to go up the stairs
to investigate, but changed their minds and left the building. Sure
enough, all of the furniture was found out of place the next day.

A final, rather interesting, story happened in the pub in 2014. Lois was present during this incident along with other staff members and customers. It had been "open mic" night, and Lois was singing the Bob Dylan song "You Ain't Going Nowhere" with the lyrics "tomorrow's the day that my bride's going to come." Someone noticed that the floor was wet behind the bar. The bartender discovered that the front of a bottle of Amaretto—the raised square glass portion around the label—had somehow "popped out." Strangely, the rest of the bottle had remained intact; it was still high up on the shelf and had not fallen over or moved in any way. There was no explanation they could find. Lois said that they all had an eerie feeling at the time. They opened a new bottle of liquor and poured out shots before collectively toasting the ghosts.

I had checked into room fourteen before we had conducted any of the interviews. Lois had told me then that it was supposed to be one of the haunted rooms. I returned to my room at nine o'clock. I immediately sensed I was not alone and felt a grandmotherly presence. I noticed that the bathroom window—which had been slightly open when I left the room—was closed. I was overwhelmed with emotion and tears came to my eyes. (This was a strong and uncommon reaction for me.) Later, Sean observed that I was sick with a cold. What he had suggested was that maybe this grandmotherly presence had been looking out for me by closing the window.

It was an old window. When I opened it, it took a significant amount of jostling to get it to come back down again. It had been open since early morning when the cleaners had been in the room. There was a wooden block on the window ledge, used as a stopper. Playing with the window, I found that the block would have likely only been used when the window was open just a crack. In this position, the window would not stay open on its own, but when opened further, it would. I went and asked Lois about access to the room. No one had been in my room since housekeeping had, and they had left for the day much earlier. Interestingly, I never felt this overwhelming grandmotherly presence again during the investigation in any other location or in the room.

I set the window up in the same way again. I then placed a video camera on it for the duration of our two-night stay. I discovered the window closed the following afternoon. Reviewing video, I discovered that at 1:32 PM it sounded like there was someone in the room. At 1:33 PM the window slammed shut. No one touched the window. It sounded like someone was still in the room after it closed, ruling out the possibility of outside noises through the previously opened window. (This video is on my YouTube channel.) This time, the window had become different. It would no longer stay open on its own without the block. It was as if the force of it closing had somehow sanded down the rough paint and wood that had allowed it to stay open previously. I would later learn that it was the glass from this same window that had been found on the ground.

I woke up at 2:22 AM on the second night, which I documented by taking a photo with my camera phone. I'm not sure what woke me up, but a translucent orb was coming through the door. It hovered for a moment at the foot of my bed and disappeared. I did not feel scared. I have woken from a dead sleep to see a spider suspended near my face before, an early waking hallucination, but this felt different. There were parallels to the green cloud I had seen years earlier, but that had felt eerie and remained visible for several long moments where this did not. I don't recall ever having had a similar incident with an orb before.

We had other experiences worth noting during our investigation. We walked around with an audio recorder and asked questions out loud. The idea is that sometimes a voice can be heard answering a question when the recording is played back later that could not be picked up by the naked ear at the time. When captured, this is called an Electronic Voice Phenomena, or EVP. Out of all the pseudo-scientific research methods available to the ghost hunter, the audio recorder is the only one I feel has any merit. Ghost boxes scanning radio channels, electromagnetic measuring devices, and Ouija boards are at best instruments of eccentric curiosity. At worst, they are tools of deception, misinformation, or "reality TV" performance aids. I can sometimes be a hard sell, but when it comes to EVP, I have heard convincing samples. Many are available online. It turned out we were lucky enough to capture one of our own.

Near the fireplace in the dining room I asked the question: "Do you like Lois?" Later, while reviewing the recording I discovered a sound I was unable to otherwise rule out. I believed it was an EVP as it had a distinctly whisper-like sound. A voice answered that at first sounded like "Huh-huh," though today it sounds more clearly like "yeah," almost as if the recording had changed. It sounded like there were quieter voices speaking before and after the EVP as well. There were other background noises throughout the investigation, but this clip stood out and did not sound like any other recording. The quality wasn't the greatest, but I eventually posted it on YouTube for others to listen to and scrutinize. The "huh-huh" sounds very faint right before the "yeah."

Sean recorded many hours of audio while he was asleep in room nine. He said that some of it sounded strange to him, but it was hard to decide conclusively if it was relevant—the bedrooms had thin walls and noise carried. Catching sounds from an adjacent room might have been possible and so could not be ruled out. He posted his findings on his blog, The Offbeat Traveler.

Like our investigation at The Schooner Restaurant, the most compelling evidence was staff members' testimonies of their own encounters. I noted no obvious signs of lying, though some members at this location did not come across as skeptical as the Tofino restaurant crew. I found it especially interesting talking to Lois, as she had had experiences, or been told about others' experiences, since 1974. This is important, as she becomes the one measurement of consistency. She knew, for example, that the story of the logger's ghost was that he originally was the murderer. That does not fit into the traditional idea of a ghost, however, so storytellers turned him into a victim. Ah Heung in Victoria's Chinatown and Peter Kakua would, of course, be murderer ghosts as well, so the idea is not completely novel. Lois also remembered the psychic providing details that added to the story. Room nine is haunted only because the psychic said a man-hating ghost was there. There is nothing else to corroborate this. She also added the detail that the old lady was waiting for her husband to return from the sea, which is similar to the White Lady of Thetis Point. There is no evidence for this other than the psychic's word either. Heriot Bay is not a port. It only had a dock for resource management. Additionally, the population was small and people kept track of others and what they were doing. It is highly unlikely an unknown older woman died waiting for her husband to return from a lengthy sea voyage.

The Heriot Bay Inn is fascinating to me because I believe it is haunted by whatever it is that leads people to believe in ghosts. Like many others, I do lean toward the belief that these are spirits of the dead—only because it is the most logical answer—but I am still not completely convinced either. I only know that the experiences themselves are real.

As a final act, Sean and I went into the pub and asked to be poured a shot of Amaretto. It felt ceremonial as I rarely drink. We then toasted the spirits, honouring the Heriot Bay Inn's newest tradition, the friendly staff who work there, and, of course, the ghosts themselves.

Rain splatters against the window as lightning flashes across the sky. The dark, empty barroom lights up for a long moment and then another. Thunder shakes the old inn's beams. Bottles rattle behind the bar. The man slowly steps out of the darkness and onto the wooden floor in rubber gumboots dripping with water. A heavy axe is suspended from his right arm. From beneath his old-fashioned raincoat hood, dark, unblinking eyes stare menacingly. A handlebar moustache crowns a snarling shadowy grin. He begins to pace back and forth, over and over again across the floor and down the halls, searching for his prey.

This 1858 house post depicting Tsunakwa is on display at the Royal BC Museum.
PHOTO BY SHANON SINN

THE WILD PEOPLE
OF THE WOODS

VANCOUVER ISLAND

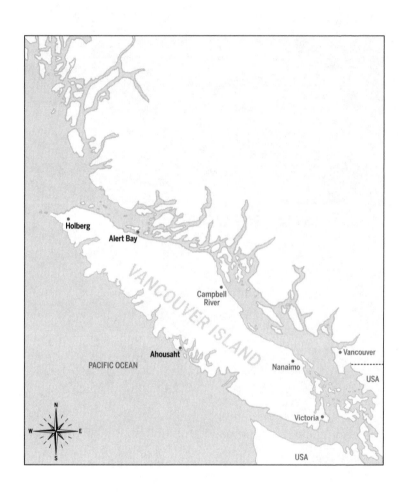

PEOPLE LIVING ON VANCOUVER ISLAND often refer to Campbell River and Ahousaht as part of the North Island. On a map, however, a line drawn across the island from just above each location merely divides it in half. This northern portion is sparsely populated and heavily forested. The region is Kwakwaka'wakw territory on the east and north, and Nuu-chah-nulth on the west. It is a land of remote fishing villages, logging, and outdoor adventure. The terrain is mountainous, crisscrossed with creeks and rivers, glaciers, and mountain lakes. Some areas receive over three metres (ten feet) of rain annually. Wildlife is abundant: elk, bears, wolves, and cougars. These unhabituated regions are so unforgiving that the History Channel filmed the first two seasons of the reality TV survival show *Alone* on the west coast.

There are plenty of rational things to be afraid of in the wilderness of Vancouver Island, let alone those that science does not accept as being real. Like other types of hauntings, individuals claiming to have had Sasquatch encounters are met with skepticism. The term is loaded because even though it is taken from Coast Salish, it now implies an undiscovered man-ape. The footprints are the most compelling pieces of evidence, but the lack of more substantial proof speaks for itself. Those who live in cities like to think there are wide regions of wilderness completely unexplored, but this is not true. Humans searching for precious metals and virgin lumber have visited even the most remote locations. There are now thousands of outdoor cameras set up across Vancouver Island, used by branches of government, scientists, and hunters. There are car dash cameras, information-gathering planes, drones, and satellites, and yet, there is still no proof of an uncategorized ape. This is a problem. A breeding population would need a certain number of individuals or would become inbred and die out. Enough, in fact, that they could not rationally have avoided detection for this long. Yet, credible witnesses report Sasquatch encounters on Vancouver Island every single year, just as First Nations people did before colonial contact.

The term Sasquatch was first used by Canadian newsman J.W. Burns in the 1920s. It is believed to have come from the Coast Salish word *Sesquac* (sess-k-uts), which was the name for a legendary large hairy wild man. The term Bigfoot is used in the United States, but Sasquatch is more popular in Canada. In 1967, filmmakers Roger Patterson and Robert Gimlin shot the infamous short clip of Bigfoot now known as the Patterson Film. Strangely, there is still a debate as to whether or not the footage is real with compelling arguments on both sides. Faked or not, that image now represents what Sasquatch is supposed to look like. Amateur investigators on reality TV shows stand at the edges of well-used logging roads and make howling noises trying to attract the "Squatch." They and their fans use pseudo-scientific language to promote the illusion that the creature is more or less already discovered and fully understood. And so, the legend continues to morph and to change.

The Pacific Northwest has the highest number of these types of reports anywhere in the world. Sightings are so common on Vancouver Island that in 2009 the History Channel's *MonsterQuest* called it "Mysterious Ape Island," on an episode dedicated entirely to Vancouver Island. Wildlife biologist Dr. John Bindernagel moved from Ontario to the Comox Valley in 1975 to study the creature as well. He had become convinced that Sasquatch was real, and that this strategic placement would grant him the easiest access to all areas of the island.

Bindernagel has written *North America's Great Ape: The Sasquatch* and *The Discovery of the Sasquatch: Reconciling Culture, History, and Science in the Discovery Process*. He was featured on "Mysterious Ape Island" and has appeared on many other documentaries as well. Bindernagel's position is that there is already evidence Sasquatch exists, and we are currently engaged in a discovery process whether we accept it or not. The scientific community as a whole, however, refuses to look at this evidence because of the stigma attached to it. As I have mentioned, the footprints are the most compelling pieces of evidence as they are often found randomly in extremely remote locations where a hoax would be unlikely. The anatomical human-oid/ape correctness, size, and weight depth of many of them also make fraud unlikely. It is these footprints, not the sightings, which stump hardcore skeptics. The sightings are rare in comparison, but they do occur.

Bindernagel writes that resource explorer Michael King was inland from the mouth of the Campbell River sometime around 1900 when he had an encounter. (*MonsterQuest* inaccurately reported the location as the Forbidden Plateau.) In 1904, King had reported to the Vancouver *Province* that he had come across a "man-beast" washing some edible roots in a water hole. His body was covered in "reddish-brown" hair. Later inspection of the area revealed tracks that were human-like with wide-spaced toes. King claimed his Kwakwaka'wakw guides had refused to go into the area with him. This sighting is believed to be the earliest documented encounter on Vancouver Island.

Canadian Sasquatch pioneer John Green wrote *On the Track of the Sasquatch* in 1968. Following the Patterson Film, it was generally believed it was only a matter of time before proof of Sasquatch was found. Royal British Columbia Museum Director Clifford Carl wrote the foreword for the book. He began by questioning whether or not the sightings were real or a hoax. All of the facts pointed to them being real, he claimed, but without a specimen there was no certainty. In his opinion, Green's book was a collection of all of the evidence to date:

> The publication of this up-to-date factual account will help greatly to publicize the "Sasquatch Problem" and may speed the day when scientific proof is at last made available.

Fifty years later, a specimen has still not been recovered, even though the public was told this was inevitable. So, with nothing more than a video that sort of looks like a man in a suit, and a handful of experts saying "any day now" for nearly fifty years, the Sasquatch has become a mainstream part of our culture's belief system. Our ancestors had stories of giants in myth and legend, now we have found a semi-logical way to believe in them as well. Sightings have become much more common in the last fifty years, whether it is because it feels safer to report them, or for some other undetermined reason like misidentification, hopefulness, hoax, etc.

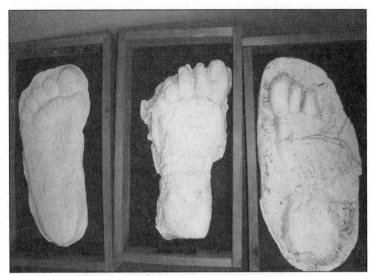

Unidentified foot casts from Dr. John Bindernagel's private collection.
PHOTO BY SHANON SINN

MonsterQuest's "Mysterious Ape Island" explored several modern sightings through convincing testimonial evidence. Ted Storey recounted an incident where his recreational vehicle was shaken with him in it in Strathcona Park. Rob Wilson Storey (their identical surnames are never addressed) said he saw a Sasquatch leaning over water and reaching into the Kennedy River near Tofino. This sighting was from his car. Most convincing, James Dean Beaulieu and Jo-Jo Christenson shared their encounter near Alert Bay. The two witnesses spoke on behalf of a larger boat crew.

The village of Alert Bay is located on Cormorant Island in the waters between Campbell River and the northern tip of Vancouver Island. The island is largely 'Namgis Kwakwaka'wakw reservation land, though many who live in the village are of European descent.

Dzunukwa by James Halliday. There are many stories of Tsunakwa stealing children in the woods, putting them in her basket, and eating them later.
IMAGE BY JAMES HALLIDAY

The crew that Jo-Jo and James Dean were a part of was fishing for crabs and prawn. One evening, they noticed a strong smell from an island near the boat. A spotlight was turned on, and they saw a Sasquatch eating cockle clams. They watched for an hour before the creature took "three strides" and disappeared into the woods twenty-seven metres (thirty yards) away.

The Alert Bay area has more Sasquatch reports than anywhere else on or near Vancouver Island. Kwakwaka'wakw member, commercial fisherman, and "bushman" Thomas Sewid gave a three-part interview on the podcast *Sasquatch Chronicles* in November of 2016. Alert Bay, he said, has the "highest concentration of Sasquatch carvings in the world." Claiming multiple personal sightings and encounters, Sewid spoke about his own experiences and those of others. Under Bindernagel's guidance, Sewid has become a part of the Sasquatch investigation scene. His knowledge of both Kwakwaka'wakw lore and the area makes his perspective unique in many regards. Sewid has a theory, for example, that Sasquatch contracted smallpox from settlers when First Nations people did, devastating their populations as well. Pre-contact, he said, Sasquatch had interacted with people. There were even stories that insinuated rape. He believes smallpox deaths could be the cause of a decline in sightings and the reason that these sightings have now been increasing again as their numbers recover. Interestingly, Sewid also said Sasquatch eats cockle clams.

In September of 2015, several television news teams visited Alert Bay after a rash of sightings and other reports had been made on the island. Though a tourist destination for those interested in 'Namgis Kwakwaka'wakw culture, it is important to mention that the community has never used Sasquatch sightings as a way to attract tourists. Sewid, however, does offer Sasquatch tours that include learning about First Nations lore. His wife has a similar company in Washington State.

There have been sightings all over the island, but some garner more attention than others: Sewid shared a third-hand account from a 1976 encounter on the *Sasquatch Chronicles* podcast. A logger claimed to have hit one with his truck on a back road. Although the creature was not killed, Sewid believes this was covered up because the company did not want to stop logging—which could have happened if scientists or other citizens had called for a protection of the elusive creature's habitat. In 2002, the *Alberni Valley Times* reported that people had claimed to see Sasquatch along the highway between Port Alberni and Tofino, at Radar Hill, and on Long Beach. It was believed that the creature had been searching for water, as the year had been particularly dry. In 2011, Shaw TV Nanaimo reported another sighting in the Cowichan Valley from a "couple years" earlier, where a man came forward not wanting to keep his experience secret anymore. By the time *MonsterQuest's* episode aired in 2009, Bindernagel said he had collected more than eighty eyewitness reports. Many encounters have never been covered by the news.

One problem is that there is no one place to make a report if a person does decide to come forward. Other than police or news sources, there are multiple sites that collect testimonials from witnesses, including two on Facebook for Vancouver Island alone. Vancouver Island Bigfoot Encounters is a less active page, while Vancouver Island Sasquatch Investigation Squad has three thousand members.

When I asked James in 2012 if the Manhousaht had stories about Sasquatch he told me he didn't know of any, but that he knew of a place where hunters had found tracks from a creature with one big foot and one small foot. I couldn't help but wonder if a tracker could somehow mistake footprints from a juvenile and an adult creature walking together. Then, in 2014, James' nephew Luke Swan Jr. reported seeing one. This was covered by multiple news sources. Luke is a fisheries officer, making him a credible witness. He had been on a beach when an "eight or nine"-foot creature appeared. "It scared me," he admitted to reporters. He got off the beach as quickly as he could, got his father, and returned to find tracks measured as forty centimetres long and between eighteen and twenty-three centimetres wide (sixteen inches long and between seven or nine inches wide). This would make the feet size 26 by North American shoe measurements. I was with James when I met Luke Jr. in November of 2016. He told me he had seen the creature again since the news story had initially run. It had been watching him from the treeline on shore.

MonsterQuest claimed Meares Island, a short water taxi away from Tofino, had "more reports than any other place." During the program, two investigators walked along the beach and found a stack of clamshells they thought looked like a feeding site. Meares Island is regularly trafficked by boats and easily accessible to tourists and locals. It is the kind of place that looks rugged in a documentary to someone who lives in a city, but isn't that remote at all. At least the shore isn't. What is interesting, however, is that the Ahousaht Nuu-chah-nulth believe Meares Island is the land of Sasquatch as well. When they recently opened Lone Cone Hostel & Campground, its logo was the image of a contemporary Sasquatch. This Ahousaht-run campsite's website has a page whose sole purpose is to inform tourists that they are in "Sasquatch Country." This page claims there have been sightings of the creature in recent months.

The Ahousaht call it "Buc Miss" (pronounced book-mees). While the contemporary or "white" version of Sasquatch is that of a great ape or primitive man, the traditional Buc Miss story is of a spirit being. The site says that to see Buc Miss is to gain good luck and spiritual strength. The Maquinna (head chief) of Ahousaht says that a person should not be afraid because Buc Miss is a protector of the land. It is a being who moves back and forth between the spirit world and the physical realm, or the "seen and unseen" worlds. Maquinna's mother had told him that the creature was gentle, shy, and misunderstood. To gain the creature's powers, a person just had to run at Buc Miss, "wrestle with her, tickle her and roll around." It's a good thing to learn, as I would have never thought to do this on my own.

Indicating that Buc Miss is female is interesting because the Kwakwaka'wakw determine this as well. Though there are many different anglicized spellings, the giantess is named Tsunakwa and is known as the Wild Woman of the Woods. The male is called Bukwas. He is only a few feet tall, however, and has sharp teeth. This means that the legends don't usually fit modern perceptions of Sasquatch as well as many claim.

Chief James Wallas in *Kwakiutl Legends* told several stories about "Big Figure," hairy men with sunken eyes over six feet tall with families of their own. The stories were from the northeast part of the island, the Holberg–Winter Harbour area occupied by the Quatsino Kwakwaka'wakw people. Big Figure is the closest fit to Sasquatch on Vancouver Island that I am aware of.

Sewid believes that Tsunakwa and Bukwas are two different unidentified creatures. In the *Sasquatch Chronicles* interview, he sometimes refers to Tsunakwa as a male as a result, even though this does not fit with the traditional story. As for the legend, Sewid said that Tsunakwa was seen as primarily positive, but that there were also stories about her abducting children in her basket to eat them. This is a type of boogeyman tale used to frighten children into submission. This giantess, or ogress, who steals children, is also known among the Salish, Nuu-chah-nulth, and other Pacific Northwest First Nations people.

The Bukwas story is very different. Despite his small size and similar monkey looks, he is something to be feared. He is "the King of Ghosts," especially those who have drowned at sea. Sewid said that Bukwas is "in command of the spirit world." When a person gets lost in the forest, Bukwas will leave out ghost food. If the person eats it they will become confused and never return to their village. The modern-day version of the Bukwas, he said, is the drug dealer who inadvertently prevents a person from ever returning home. The idea to make this connection was originally from his cousin. Sewid claimed that the Salish have a "little one" like this as well, though he does not name it.

Brian David Thom in *Coast Salish Senses of Place* names Sasquatch as a *Stl'eluqum* specifically, which makes it a spirit being to them as well. He does mention "little people" elsewhere but does not describe them in any detail.

A lesser-known Sasquatch theory among contemporary believers is that the creature really is a type of spirit being or ghost. This would be closer to the First Nations legends on Vancouver Island.

It would also explain certain encounters and attributes that might otherwise not make sense. These include specific recurrent themes in encounters such as a nocturnal nature, glowing red or orange eyes, an odour of death or sulphur smell, an ability to shapeshift, and the overwhelming feeling of fear or experiencing something supernatural in the Sasquatch's presence.

Thomas said that it is more common to see them near old abandoned village sites. The Alert Bay sightings in 2015 were especially strange because there isn't any wildlife larger than raccoons on Cormorant Island, not even deer. Children had seen the creature near the 'Namgis Big House—a large ceremonial building—and it was reported in the totem pole-inhabited cemetery as well. Several witnesses came forward, and one provided a recording of it howling on his phone. If Sasquatch is an undiscovered, elusive, shy ape, why would it swim to a small island that is essentially just a village? Why would it let its presence be so well known by loudly howling? Why would it visit the cemetery?

Strangely, sightings of Sasquatch in cemeteries have been noted often enough that it has come up among amateur investigators regularly. The team on Animal Planet's *Finding Bigfoot* mentioned it, there have been blogs written about it, and even two discussions on the Bigfoot Forums. The first was titled "Sasquatches Often Hang Around Cemeteries" and the second was "Bigfoot and Cemeteries."

If the creatures on Vancouver Island collectively referred to as Sasquatch really are spirit beings, as First Nations groups traditionally believe, then it would explain why they have remained so elusive to discovery, why there has never been a physical specimen recovered, and why there never will be. If Bindernagel, Sewid, and many others are right, there are uncategorized creatures not yet catalogued living in the wilds around us. If that is the case, then it is only a matter of time before we have answers. Until then, Sasquatch remains a creature of folklore, much like the similarly reported sea serpent.

As this Nahant, Massachusetts, illustration depicts, sea serpents
were reported in North American waters by settlers as early as 1639.
COURTESY OF MASON HAMMOND/NAHANT HISTORICAL SOCIETY ARCHIVES

SERPENTS AND
SHAPESHIFTERS

VANCOUVER ISLAND

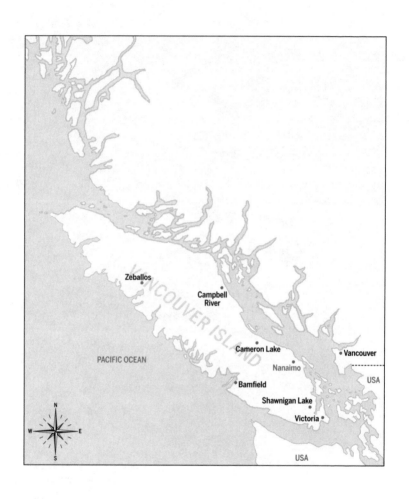

SEA SERPENTS HAVE NOT ONLY been reported near Vancouver Island but wherever there is ocean. To the ancients, they were dragons of the sea, fierce protectors existing at the edges of the known world. To explorers and pioneers, they were obstacles to overcome in order to tame savage and forbidden lands. Radical colonial scientists thought that they were uncategorized creatures awaiting discovery and classification. Then, between the World Wars, serpents became all the rage, drawing tourists to places like Victoria in the hopes of glimpsing one themselves. Strangely, sightings have continued ever since. Cryptozoologists believe—like their Victorian counterparts—that the serpent is an undiscovered animal. Vancouver Island First Nations, however, contend that they are powerful supernatural beings.

The *British Colonist* reported sightings as early as the 1890s. Multiple Vancouver (mainland) witnesses came forward in 1895 claiming to have seen a serpent in English Bay and the Granville Island inlet. They described it as "terrifying." In 1903, the serpent again made the newspaper. Several officers at the Bamfield cable station near Keeha Beach reported a sea serpent that had been seen by "almost everyone in the area." The officers had received reports from First Nations, but had dismissed them until they saw the "forty to sixty feet in length" (twelve-to-eighteen-metre) creature themselves. In 1911, the *British Colonist* said that the steamship *Leebro* found a decomposing carcass in Esperanza Inlet on the west coast of

Vancouver Island (near present-day Zeballos). Everyone from "the Japanese cook's mate to the master" had seen it. The steamer had been replacing beacons when it made the discovery. What makes this story unique (as most bodies recovered have been ruled out as "misidentified") is the description: the top of its head was covered in coarse hair.

Besides the hair—or mane—often described on its head, there are several other physical characteristics repeatedly reported. The head itself has been described as camel-like, giraffe-like, horse-like, or moose-like. It is sometimes said to have what look like whiskers on the sides of its mouth, or bumps resembling horns. If a real creature, this could indicate a difference in the sexes or a seasonal change. It is often said to have a hump-like appearance as it swims. The serpent also has large sharp teeth, giving it a frightening aspect. While the serpents are often monstrous in size, individuals have claimed to see serpents smaller than a metre (three feet) in length with these same visual details. This could, of course, indicate a juvenile. Interestingly, the art of the Pacific Northwest First Nations often depicts the sea serpent as having a horse-like head and teeth, and sometimes long hair on its head. In *Teachings of the Tides* by David Ellis and Luke Swan (James' grandfather), the Manhousaht sea serpent dance mask is described as having strips of red-dyed cedar bark to represent hair growing from the serpent's head. These specific details are what connect modern sightings to First Nations legends.

In October of 1933, the *Daily Colonist* and other Victoria news-papers reported a sighting at the Chatham Islands (where Staqeya the wolf would appear eighty years later). Major W.H. Langley, a law clerk of the Legislative Assembly, said he saw it with his family.

This led to the story being published, which included a sighting from the previous year by Mr. F.W. Kemp, a BC Archives employee, and his family. A woman came forward after the story was published saying that she had also seen the creature, but in nearby Cadboro Bay. Within a few days, people had dubbed the creature "Caddy" after the bay, and then Cadborosaurus. The *Victoria Daily Times* kept the story running as more witnesses came forward. In less than a month, postcards and other items were being sold to promote Victoria as a sea serpent tourist attraction. Two weeks later, a seven-and-a-half-metre (twenty-five-foot) replica was built and set out on the rocks as a publicity stunt. The paper offered a reward for convincing photographs. A craze had begun.

There have been several books written about Caddy, including *Cadboro: A Ship, A Bay, A Sea-Monster* by Ursula Jupp; *Cadborosaurus: Survivor from the Deep* by Dr. Paul H. LeBlond and Dr. Edward L. Bousfield; and *Discovering Cadborosaurus* by Paul H. LeBlond, John Kirk, and Jason Walton. Many other books, such as *Monster! Monster!: A Survey of the North American Monster Scene* by Betty Sanders Garner, have dedicated whole sections to Caddy. Countless newspaper stories, magazine articles, and TV shows have investigated Caddy as well. In 1962, Campbell River decided it wanted the serpent that had been sighted there to have his own name and dubbed it "Klamahtossaurus." Oyster River (twelve kilometres, or seven and a half miles, south) had tried the same thing in 1942 when they called their monster "Klato."

To put the mania into perspective, it is important to keep in mind that the Ogopogo in Okanagan Lake in the interior of British Columbia had just become a sensation in 1926. Only months earlier, the Loch Ness monster photograph from Scotland swept the world and made "Nessie" a star. This image has since been determined a fraud.

While it is hard to take anything that becomes a tourist sensation seriously, there have been advantages. Vancouver Island having its own independently named sea serpent makes it easier for me to seek out reports specifically from our region. Both of the Cadborosaurus books LeBlond has been involved with provide lists of reports by date. Every year, there is usually between one and three. A lot of them are hard to dismiss. Unlike Sasquatch, the serpent is often seen by groups of witnesses. In 1958, the *Daily Colonist* reported that Arnold Webb, then-secretary manager of the Victoria Chamber of Commerce, had seen the serpent near Qualicum Beach. He proposed Victoria create a three-person committee to investigate the reports of thirty-five believable witnesses—many who had chosen to remain unidentified for fear of ridicule. Every few years, someone credible will talk to the media about their sighting. In 2016, Discovery Channel's *Sea Monsters: The Definitive Guide* dedicated a large section to Caddy, which included LeBlond and Galiano Island witness Lisa Lake. With reports of it being up to twenty-four metres (eighty feet) long, it is easy to see why the creature has attracted so much attention.

James had told me that the fisherman from Ahousaht said that the serpent he saw was so big it could have "taken out his herring skiff, no problem." The man would not speak about it for four years afterward, because the serpent was a supernatural being and that was protocol. This particular sentiment is echoed throughout Pacific Northwest First Nations lore: the sea serpent is spiritual in nature.

Nuu-chah-nulth totem pole sea serpent detail near Port Alberni. Created by Master Carver Tim Paul and apprentices Willard Gallie II, Gordon Dick, Tobias Watts, and Samuel Albeny.
PHOTO BY SHANON SINN

While all beings in the cosmos of the Vancouver Island Indigenous belief system have transformative power, the sea serpent is especially magical. It is a master of all of the elements. It could go on land, swim through saltwater and freshwater, and even fly (usually with the aid of the thunderbird, but sometimes it would grow wings).

The First Nations of Vancouver Island often depict the sea serpent as double-headed in their art, with a man's face in the middle. The Kwakwaka'wakw name for this image, the *Sisiutl*, has been adopted by anthropologists and other First Nations groups to refer to similar images throughout the Pacific Northwest. In *The Northwest Coast Sisiutl* by Roderick Paul Paterson, it is said that the creature is "a central figure in the Northwest Coast cosmos." The Sisiutl is the mediator between the physical world and the supernatural world. The face in the middle, whether a person or, more commonly,

Sisiutl, the double headed serpent. Late 19th-century
Haida baby cradle at Antique Gallery in Anchorage, Alaska.
PHOTO BY SHANON SINN

another supernatural being, represents someone connected to
both of the realms. Sisiutl brings both wealth and death and
helps the shaman heal. Like the Medusa of Greek myth, it has
the power to turn mortals who gaze directly at it to stone, so it is
protective as well. Paterson says that the Sisiutl is seen as a lord
of the supernatural, so much so that the Tlingit (non-Vancouver
Island First Nations) call it "the chief of shamans." It is the carrier
of prayers to other supernatural beings and a protector of mighty
warriors. The Transformer—a Christ-like creator-god—wore the
Sisiutl as a belt, which gave him many additional powers. The
symbol of the Sisiutl is so powerful that it adorns many ceremonial
objects, including masks and canoes. To find a single scale—now

thought to be shards of mica—from the creature was to possess great power.

There are no sea snakes on record in the Vancouver Island region, but there are two families of land snakes, including the sharp-tail snake and three types of garter snake. Katie Bell in "Sssnakes on Vancouver Island" wrote that garter snakes on Vancouver Island can have a wide range of colours or patterns, called polymorphism, making them difficult to identify at times. Garter snakes can swim, and the Western Terrestrial Garter Snake is often found near water and will feed on small fish and amphibians. All of the snakes on Vancouver Island are smaller in size though, making it uncommon to find a species longer than a metre (three feet). None of them are considered poisonous.

In *An Illustrated Encyclopaedia of Traditional Symbols* by J.C. Cooper, there is a lengthy entry on the serpent as a metaphor: as the serpent sheds it represents death and rebirth; it is androgynous; a killer and a healer; living beneath the earth it is connected to the underworld, but above ground, to the sun; coiled it is the cycles of manifestation; it is "secretive, enigmatic, and intuitional"; and it represents both the forces of light and dark.

No surprise then, that great power could be obtained through encounters with the physical manifestation of the greatest snake of all, the sea serpent. In *Teachings of the Tides*, James' grandfather, Elder Luke Swan, states this directly. For those unfamiliar with the book, its subtitle is *Uses of Marine Invertebrates by the Manhousaht People*. This is important because it is not a book of mythology, but primarily a book of marine and shore foraging. The sea serpent stands alone as a "supernatural creature" in the book. Mr. Swan says that the serpents were not seen often anymore, but that their usual length was only between two and three metres (seven and eight feet) . There was one that lived at Sharp Point by Hotsprings Cove north of Ahousaht. His father had seen another one further north at Hesquiat Peninsula. He shot an arrow at it but missed. The other man he was hunting with was terrified and would not help him kill it. This would have made him a powerful man, he said, as no one on the west coast of Vancouver Island had ever killed a sea serpent before. The beast fled onto a beach and into the forest.

A sea serpent seen on land is not unprecedented. In *Ahousaht Wild Side Heritage Trail Guidebook* by Stanley Sam Sr., there is a story of a beach where a man saw two sea serpents crawl across the sand dunes and go into the water. The man then found where they had been lying and recovered some scales, which made him powerful. There is an image of the sign located on the trail; it depicts two serpents that appear to have horse-like heads. In Franz Boas' 1895 *Indian Myths & Legends from the North Pacific Coast of America* there is a Comox-area Coast Salish story of a serpent crawling through the forest. In *Teachings of the Tides*, Mr. Swan shares his uncle's story of a sea serpent scraping the bark off a spruce tree as it climbed up before it grew wings and flew away. There are also contemporary reports as well, including one LeBlond and Bousfield shared in *Cadborosaurus: Survivors from the Deep* from 1991. The sighting took place on Johns Island near the city of Sidney in the Greater Victoria area. Phyllis Marsh claimed to have found one less than a metre (two feet) long, which she described as a "baby dinosaur." She claimed she picked it up with sticks and threw it into the water, though the reasons for this are never stated.

The sightings of the serpent on land are strange, but if it is a real unidentified creature, this might possibly explain another mystery. There have been serpent sightings in lakes on Vancouver Island, including Cowichan Lake and Shawnigan Lake specifically. Stone carvings, or "petroglyphs," depicting mythological-like lake monsters are found along a stone rock face at Sproat Lake. The most famous lake serpent on Vancouver Island, however, has been reported at Cameron Lake—a small shallow lake once rumoured to be "bottomless"—on the road between Qualicum Beach and Port Alberni. According to a 2009 CTV News story, locals had claimed to see something in the lake for years—since the 1980s at least—before a woman captured a "fuzzy" photograph. While the sea serpent has been seen in rivers near the ocean, it would be unlikely it could swim upstream through waterfalls to Cameron Lake without the ability to traverse land as well. It is even more unlikely that the small lake is big enough to feed or hide an unidentified creature of any size permanently. Curious about the lake's shoreline and whether or not I could see the creature, I decided to paddleboard around the perimeter of the lake in 2015. I did this in only a few hours.

If the serpent is merely a physical being as so many believe, then why was there traditionally so much fear of it among First Nations people? The Sisiutl can transform into many forms in lore, including animal and human. This is a trait shared by other serpents in stories as well.

Brian David Thom recounts a Vancouver Island legend in *Coast Salish Senses of Place*, attributed to late Elder David Page. It was a story his grandparents had told him.

Between 1883 and 1886, the E & N railway was being constructed from present-day Nanaimo to Victoria. It was Robert Dunsmuir who had won the contract and who would profit the most from the railway's construction (even though his political position aroused suspicion). Chinese labourers and other cheap workers were hired to complete the task. One particular stretch of railway was constructed along Shawnigan Lake, a forested area believed to be haunted by a powerful *stl'eluqum*. When the work was being conducted people began to disappear.

> Lots of people would go there in the evenings. They go
> for a walk and they disappear, they never come back.
> [Chinese men] all kinds of people that works there.

Elder David Page said that people would go and search for the missing men, but that nobody could find them anywhere. The disappearances initially started at the north end of the lake. When the railway line made its way to the south end of the body of water people began to disappear once more. Mr. Page said that the trail was just a wagon path at the time, and that this was how people would travel to Victoria: by foot or by wagon. One day, a man was walking and he saw a beautiful First Nations woman. She was calling him over to her, enticing him, saying, "Come to me." He was tempted to approach her, because she was so attractive, but there was something strange about her so he slowly backed away and left. Frightened, he told others. Some of them went to investigate. One man returned distraught. He claimed he had seen a large serpent transform itself into a beautiful woman who began to call to him. He had then run away. Shortly after, a tunnel near the lake was being created using explosives. Mr. Page said that "all kinds" of human bones were found near where the woman had last been seen.

> [The serpent] turns into a woman and then takes the men away. Ate them up or whatever they do. Yeah. At the other end, south end of the lake there. Solid rock there where they were blasting.

There is no indication whether people stopped disappearing once the creature's lair was discovered, or if the serpent woman haunts the Shawnigan Lake area still. The implication as to the motive for the killings, however, seems to be vengeance for the defilement of the land by the railway company. Perhaps the men simply provided her with an easy meal.

The stories of serpents—both contemporary and legendary—are widespread here. From the snake that lived in Tzouhalem's hair to the shapeshifting beautiful woman, the sea serpent roaming the coast to the power beings found hidden in mountaintop pools, the serpent is the most prevalent secret identity for supernatural beings on Vancouver Island. Maybe this is why the Sisiutl, the double-headed snake, master of all elements, is the communicator between the land of the living and the land of disembodied spirits? For if there is one spirit that haunts Vancouver Island above all others, it is the serpent, perhaps aptly named Sisiutl, chief of all shamans.

Shanon Sinn in a CTV News image from the Heriot Bay Inn Investigation.
PHOTO BY GORDON KURBIS

CONCLUSION

A GHOST STORY DEVELOPS IN SEVERAL stages. The first stage is the actual event or events. This is the sighting of the entity or the paranormal occurrence. The second stage is the sharing, telling someone else what has occurred. Then there is the third stage, the passing of the story to others, and the evolution of the story. The fourth stage is the writing down or recording of the tale, often by a third party, so that it becomes set in stone—at least at that moment—and can be found and shared by others in the future.

There are several problems with this process. In the first stage, memory is malleable. That is, a person cannot remember an event exactly as it occurred, especially if it was traumatic. Then, the oral telling of a story becomes somewhat like the telephone game, in which details will get altered even if it was never a teller's intention. Because ghost stories are somewhat like fisherman's stories, they become exaggerated and distorted intentionally as people try to one-up each other. In the case of hauntings, making the tales as frightening as possible is often seen as a good thing. By the time the experience has been recorded, it has usually been altered to some degree.

When people begin to profit from a story it often becomes even more damaged. The profiteer purposely adds details to suit their needs so that directly or indirectly they make more money off it. Aaron Mahnke on the *Lore* podcast was the first person I heard use the term "folklore fraud," and this is an apt description. Unfortunately, Vancouver Island has its fair share of this. While researching this book, I even came across incidents where the stories had damaged the official historic record. At first, it would hold me back for a few days as I checked and rechecked my findings, to make sure my version was closer to the truth than the one commonly promoted, but then I became used to it. This is a huge reason why this book relies on sources so heavily. While I enjoy the spooky nature of Halloween as much as the next person, I believe these incidents deserve to be looked at with some seriousness, especially because so many people claim to have experienced them, and because they are a part of our collective culture.

In March of 2017, paranormal investigators offered, "a spooky two nights investigating the historic, enigmatic and haunted Heriot Bay Inn" for several hundred dollars. The price included accommodation so it was not unreasonable. There are several problems with weekends like these, however. As I did not attend this specific event, I am making my point broadly as similar-themed seminars are common everywhere.

First of all, it is not an investigation if a place has been officially—by an investigator—labelled as haunted. An investigation requires an open mind. That includes openness to other possible explanations. There is no proof as to what these events actually are, even though there are many who claim to have the answers both in books and on TV. Many investigators promote their opinion of what a ghost is as fact. The statement "Ghosts are . . ." is a personal belief based on an unfounded opinion. TV shows promote a mainstream view about ghosts that resembles a cult. If embraced, the dogma then becomes a search for supporting evidence and not investigative at all.

Second, there is no expertise in the equipment people are using. Take an electromagnetic field (EMF) reader for example, which is intended to diagnose problems with electrical wiring and detect unhealthy levels of radiation from power meters and appliances. Assuming this device really could pick up spirits, a person would need to be familiar with every item already emitting EMFs in the building to use it to detect something unusual. Electricians trained in using these devices would also be making claims of unexplained readings, which doesn't seem to be the case.

I have no doubt investigators are usually well-meaning, but am stating often-overlooked considerations for those who choose to use reality TV personalities as scientific mentors. In the introduction, I mentioned the PSICAN guidelines used by many groups. These rules adhere to transparent and ethical standards I wish everyone followed. The basic principles revolve around respect for other people, their property, and the acceptance that we do not have all of the answers. The stance an investigator should take, belief-wise, should be neutral. What one chooses to believe on their own time is, of course, one's private business. This is the mark of a professional in any practice.

In the case of the Heriot Bay weekend, the paranormal group advertised that research recruits would participate in a séance as well. This is also more common than one would imagine. Unfortunately, it is a practice that has always been associated with fraud and/or making hauntings worse. It is not something I would personally encourage for both of these reasons. It would make more sense to me if an investigation and a séance were on separate weekends, completely removed from one another.

A person should be especially wary of events like these that ask for a large amount of money, or of TV shows that rely on ratings. As long as ghosts are a commodity, the product (evidence) cannot be trusted, if only because it needs to be produced over and over again, even if it does not exist. Anything a paid investigator finds is suspect. A real discovery will sound made up. A lack of anything happening will tempt that same investigator to claim they found something when they did not. If they say they never captured any evidence, then they are a failure in an industry that demands recurring proof. In places where ghost tours are offered, at least the only thing they need to provide is the legend, and the same one can be told over and over again. Evidence on demand is problematic. If one out of every five people has had a paranormal experience, we need to start looking at these incidents more seriously in search for possible causes. Together, we should be able to demand a higher level of professionalism from those who claim to be providing it.

I do believe that there is a case to be made for using psychics in investigations, but this is very conditional. Psychics are intuitives. By their nature, they cannot be relied upon to provide evidence. The belief is that they get impressions that can help them see things more clearly than most people can. Besides experiences with my own intuition, I have first-hand experience with card readers. In Saskatchewan, it was Kathy's Kards. In Nanaimo, I went to see Liberty Harakas who owns Lobelia's Lair. Both of these women have impressed me by seeing things I thought unlikely, but that later happened. Of course, there were also things that did not. I trust both of them though, as they do not claim to have all of the answers or to be able to see everything. As I have come to understand it, the gift of intuition is cultivated and made stronger with use. When a psychic goes into a haunted place—as Liberty has—they say something to the effect of: "this is what I see." This can be helpful in an investigative sense to point a person toward physical proof. Whether it be a police case, a missing person, or a haunting, a psychic's intuition is not the evidence itself. What they see should never become a part of a story without it being stated that it was a psychic's intuition. In almost every case on Vancouver Island, writers and investigators have made this clear, but it is still a point to keep in mind. No psychic has ever been right all of the time.

To me, the less-evolved stories are the most believable. Clichés might exist because they are repetitive elements in many hauntings, but non-conforming details might hold more answers, especially because they are outside of what we would expect someone to make up. Why would a worker at Craigdarroch Castle only be able to see a woman's feet on the stairs? Why would the Headless Woman of Mount Sicker sometimes be seen with her head? Why would the April Ghost wear different clothes during the day than at night? Why would the Ahousaht Witch have no face? I believe it is in details such as these that the mystery of ghosts will one day be solved. When this happens, we might be surprised to discover that the giants who roam our forests and the sea serpents who lurk in our waters are more closely related to ghosts than we had imagined.

In the introduction, I spoke about the idea of the *tulpa*. By its very nature, this entity would require a more established or defined story to exist. People start to believe in something specific, and then it manifests. Though usually thought to be a hoax, this would explain the Thetis Lake Monster—near Victoria—reported in 1972, which resembled the monster in the movie *The Creature from the Black Lagoon*. Several witnesses claimed to have seen the beast; it became a sensation, and the RCMP conducted an investigation. A witness from the first sighting later claimed that he and a friend had lied. As a result, the public assumed that other witnesses must have lied as well. At least two of them still claim to have seen the monster though. Could the collective belief in a lie have created something more substantial? Could this exact same thing have happened throughout history, giving rise to all manner of sightings? Could our ancestors who believed in shapeshifters and blood drinkers have been more intelligent and honest than we usually give them credit for?

During the summer of 2015, a young woman in Ucluelet told me another strange tale that the concept of *tulpa* might be able to explain. There were stories, she said, of teenagers seeing a black-eyed child on the bicycle and walking path that stretches from the village to the junction. I was surprised for several reasons. First of all, there have been cougar, wolf, and bear encounters in the area, and yet teenagers were still more afraid of a supernatural child than they were of the animals most city people would fear. Second, the urban legend of black-eyed children can only be traced back to the late 1990s. They have supposedly been reported all over the world since. The child is usually small and sometimes barefoot. They will hitchhike or will approach an adult or older child to ask for help. What makes them distinct is that their eyes are completely black with no white in them. The black-eyed child will try to get invited into the home or car of the witness. The legend suggests that something bad will happen to the victim, but it is never clear exactly what that would be. Interestingly, the stories resemble pre-Christian tales from all over the world. But what could they be? An overactive collective imagination? A *tulpa*-like apparition that we have essentially created? Or an entity with its own agenda that appears how and when it chooses to?

Canadian journalist Joe Fisher wrote several books on the paranormal between 1980 and 2001 from an investigative perspective including *Hungry Ghosts: An Investigation into Channelling and the Spirit World.* Channelling is what happens when a spirit speaks through a living person, usually a psychic. Fisher initially intended to expose hoaxes but came to believe that spirits being channelled were real. He later claimed that he had been satisfied as to their authenticity when they were able to provide information later verified as true. The most compelling was a spirit named William, who said he had been a member of England's 99 Squadron during the Second World War. Fisher confirmed that the bomber squadron existed and found living former members who could verify many of the details provided by the spirit that would have been unavailable to anyone outside of the squadron. Another spirit was a Greek woman who claimed to have been Fisher's partner in previous lives. She spoke what was later verified as Greek and also knew things the psychic could not have. Other witnesses claimed to have seen these events as well, and Fisher provided documentation in the book. Imagine everyone's surprise then, when it was revealed that William had never existed nor had the village the Greek woman said she had lived in. Fisher claimed that he then learned that this theme was consistent with all of the spirits he investigated. They provided many details that were true, but their identities had been made up. Fisher's stance was that the types of spirits that wanted to communicate with the living were deceitful and could not be trusted. In 2001, at age fifty-three, Joe Fisher committed suicide by jumping off a cliff in Ontario. VisionTV's *Supernatural Investigator* aired a two-part special on his life and death. They said that witnesses claimed that he had made statements shortly beforehand that spirits wanted to hurt him for exposing them. There was evidence that he may have been pushed off the cliff, but there was a counterargument that he was on a type of psychiatric medication that has, in some cases, been reported to cause suicidal thoughts. Joe Fisher's story is sobering, if only because it could suggest that spirits are real, and that some of them may want to hurt us.

If spirits are independent beings, I find it difficult to believe that they all have a dark agenda. Perhaps the spirit world is as varied and diverse as the "real" world. There are spirits who are angry, others who just want attention, and those who are benevolent. Some feel protective to those around them like the old fire hall's ghost in Nanaimo or the spirit at VIU's theatre. Others seem to be on a mission to promote a connection to the natural world, or a belief in life after death. If one considers the Songhees beliefs, then this could be the purpose of the wolf Staqeya. It could also explain a similar set of events involving a killer whale that was known by the public as Luna.

The story is told in the acclaimed documentary *The Whale*. Born east of Victoria in American water, a one-year-old whale dubbed Luna disappeared from the area during the end of 2000 and the early part of 2001 and was thought to be dead. This was noticed because he had been part of a pod that was being monitored by scientists. They thought he was dead because he had gone missing at the same time as other adults did. That July, however, he showed up, alone, in Nootka Sound north of Ahousaht.

Luna began to interact with humans more and more, appearing to be seeking social contact. By the time he started to visit the docks at Gold River, he had become a controversial media sensation. Officials with the Department of Fisheries and Oceans wanted him left alone for his own safety, while many other people thought there was something profound about him. The Mowachaht/Muchalaht, who are Nuu-chah-nulth, thought that he represented their chief who had just passed away.

In *The Whale*, witnesses with many different perspectives and beliefs all described how he would come up to their boats and look directly into their eyes. There is footage of this on the film. Strangely, he also liked to play and be touched. Luna has been described repeatedly as uncanny. People—even scientists—felt a connection with him that went beyond anything that could be described as ordinary.

A plaque at Muchalet Inlet tells his full story:

> Tsu'xiit—Luna—L98
> September 19, 1999–March 10, 2006
>
> Tsu'xiit was born near the San Juan Islands on September 19, 1999, and was found alone in Nootka Sound in July of 2001, three days after the passing of Tyee Ha'wilth Ambrose Maquinna.
>
> Maquinna had told Ha'wilth Jerry Jack that he would return as a kakawin (killer whale). Luna's arrival

was seen as a spiritual reflection of his deep love of his people, community, and hahoulthee (traditional territory). Luna was named Tsu'xiit in his honour.

The controversy surrounding Luna's presence in Nootka Sound peaked in the summer of 2004 when the Department of Fisheries and Oceans were confronted by Mowachaht/Muchalaht canoes, determined to keep Tsu'xiit free. Tsu'xiit was recognized as the return of Ha'wilth Ambrose Maquinna consistent with the cultural beliefs of the Mowachaht/Muchalaht First Nations.

"Since time immemorial we've stood by each and every animal and living thing within our territory. For the past few years, we've been honoured by the presence of the whale. We have a lot to be proud of as Mowachaht/Muchalaht people, for withholding our beliefs of letting nature take its course, and keeping Tsu'xiit free."—Chief Michael Maquinna

For 18 months, various stewards watched over Luna as the controversy continued. Then on March 10, 2006, it all ended. The young whale was killed instantly after being pulled into the prop of the *General Jackson*, a 30-metre [one-hundred foot] tug pulling a fully loaded log barge.

The name "Luna" was heard around the world. He touched a lot of lives and brought a community together, united with strong cultural and historical ties with the kakawin.

As tradition dictated, the Mowachaht/Muchalaht people had held a memorial potlatch for their chief in November of 2005, four years after his death. Speaking in *The Whale*, Chief Ambrose Maquinna's granddaughter Brenda Johnson said that "a lot of us" knew that the whale was going to leave afterward. She said they did not know if he would be killed or if he would leave the territory on his own, only that his time felt to be coming to an end. Several months later, Luna was killed.

In *The Whale* the killer whale, or orca, is described as a sacred being to the Mowachaht/Muchalaht people, associated with "truth and justice." The wolf is one of the most revered animals on land, they claim. His counterpart in the ocean is the killer whale.

As modern contemporary humans, we often like to believe we have all of the answers. We do not. For many, ideas of supernatural beings or life after death are nothing more than a curiosity. To those who believe in a spirit world, however, there are realms that exist parallel to our own. As for me, I am not yet old enough or wise enough to claim to have the answers. There are things I have witnessed, however, that have led me to believe that there is much more to this world than immediately catches our attention or that we can possibly understand. So, I sometimes burn candles in memory of those who have gone before me, I speak with nature, and I give thanks for all of the gifts I have been given. If I had not had my own experiences, I would not have written this book. If I had not broken bread with, laughed with, and shared stories with the people on Vancouver Island and the islands that surround her, you would not be reading this. For the sharing of these tales is an act of communion that unites us all despite our differences. Whether you believe in ghosts or nature spirits is fundamentally irrelevant. This land is an entity of its own. Anyone who lives here or visits here can sense that it has its own unique personality. My intellect might always struggle to fully accept that this is true, but my heart knows it is. Whatever spirits really are, they exist here in abundance. Perhaps we just want to believe there is more to life than science can explain, or maybe on some level we know there is. Either way, Vancouver Island is a place haunted unlike any other. I, for one, am proud to call this land home. To all of the spirits who live here and visit here, *haychka*, I am thankful to have become a part of your journey and grateful you have become a part of mine. *Hishuk ish tsawalk.*

ACKNOWLEDGEMENTS

This book would not have been possible without the help of many people. However, I would first like to acknowledge Vancouver Island's Coast Salish, Nuu-chah-nulth, and Kwakwaka'wakw people, whose traditional territories Vancouver Island is a part of. Thank you for sharing your stories with me both directly and indirectly. As a resident of Nanaimo, I am especially grateful to the Snuneymuxw Nation for allowing me to call this place home. *Haych'qa Siem.*

Many thanks to James UuKwaqum Swan, hereditary chief of Manhousaht, for sharing his family's stories, for accompanying me on the quest to find Staqeya, and most of all for being a solid friend and brother ever since we first met in the army. I am truly blessed to have you in my life, *Kleco* brother. Thanks also to your mother, the late Rosie Swan for opening her home to me and for sharing the Manhousaht/Ahousaht culture. You are a special lady, Mrs. Swan, and I am honoured to have met you. Thank you also to Heather, Jessie, Kora, Heidi, Iva, and Tyler for welcoming me into your home and treating me like family. Thanks also to Luke Swan Jr. for sharing your experiences with me regarding Buc Miss. I am glad to have met you as well.

I am also very thankful for Sean Enns, not only for organizing the investigations to the Heriot Bay Inn and The Schooner, but also for bailing me out when my website crashed. You've been a good friend for almost twenty years now. Your support with this project stretches back as far as anyone's. More than a few people thought this was an impossible dream; you, on the other hand, rolled up your sleeves

Chief James Swan aboard the *Amanda Ann* with Victoria in the background.
PHOTO BY SHANON SINN

and tried to help. Thank you brother. Thanks also to Alexandria Stuart, who I met through Sean. Your ever-constructive feedback and encouragement has been a blessing for as long as I've known you—as the associate editor of the *Navigator* at Vancouver Island University (VIU), as a classmate, and as a friend. Many thanks for agreeing to edit my manuscript especially. Thank you to Gabriel as well, who always warms my heart. You are a special (not-so-) little dude.

Thanks to Aimee Greenaway of the Nanaimo Museum for allowing me to take on the role of research assistant for the museum's lantern and cemetery tours, for much information about our region's ghost stories, and for being so supportive with the book. I appreciate all that you have done for me, Aimee. Thank you.

I am very grateful to VIU's Theatre Chair Leon Potter for meeting me on such short notice regarding the department's ghost stories. Thank you for sharing your family's experiences as well. Thanks also to Headliners School of Performing Arts owner/director and former

Sean Enns during an investigation at the Heriot Bay Inn.
PHOTO BY SHANON SINN

VIU student Manda Chelmak, for taking time out of your busy schedule and for your enthusiasm for the project.

I would also like to thank Willow Friday of Iron Oxide Art Supplies. I am always grateful for your optimism and friendly sprit. Thank you for taking time while you were so busy to speak to me about the presence you had felt in your business. Thanks also to Willow's daughter Ocean and artist Danielle Dickson for telling me about their experiences and observations.

A special thank you to my friend Caitlin Blakey and her father, Dan Blakey, for telling me about their incident in regards to the Beban House. A chance encounter in Tofino led to Caitlin and her partner, Dan Senft, becoming good friends of mine. When we realized we were all from Nanaimo and that there was a ghost story to share, it was almost unbelievable. Thank you, Caitlin and Dan Blakey, for all your support. Thank you, Dan Senft, for being a solid friend as well.

Thanks also to Lois Taylor and the staff of the Heriot Bay Inn for opening up your business, showing Sean and I around, and for telling us your many ghost stories. Thanks to Whaylon Arthur and Mare Bruce of The Schooner Restaurant for the same reasons. Thanks also to Schooner staff Shaun Ingalls, Jesse Deslippe, and Dani Gladue, as well as former employee and Schooner family friend, Keane Hovi. All of you were instrumental in this book becoming what it did.

I am also very grateful for Nelda Jackson. Without your stories and patience with all my questions there wouldn't have been a chapter on the Somass River. You called the spirit the "Lady Who Walks on Water," which has now become her unofficial/official name. I appreciate all you have done for me. Thank you. Similarly, I would like to thank Larry Baker for sharing his experiences in regards to the Headless Woman of Mount Sicker. Thank you, Larry.

Special thanks to Heather McKenzie and all of the other members of the British Columbia Ghosts & Hauntings Research Society (BCGHRS) who have also been instrumental in this process. Thanks to you especially, Heather. Also, thank you to fellow Vancouver Island member Catherine Gordon and mainland members Brian and Tara Wells McKinney, Tracey Gambin-Mah, and Meridith Bramham. My heartfelt appreciation for Paranormal Studies and Investigations Canada (PSICAN) member and leader Susan Demeter-St Clair. You are an inspiration to all of us.

There were many other people who left comments on my blog or who gave me information semi-anonymously. Thanks to all of you as well. I would also like to express my gratefulness to the woman in Ucluelet who told me about the black-eyed children. I'm sorry that I never got your name. If you ever read this, please get in touch so I can properly express my gratitude.

There are also those I would like to thank in regards to the actual writing and publishing of these stories. As many people at VIU can tell you, I have been working on this project for years. Many have helped.

It often feels as if higher powers conspire to make things happen. This was the case when TouchWood Editions' publisher Taryn Boyd came to speak to our writing class at Vancouver Island University (VIU). I went and spoke with her afterward about the idea for this book. My professor, Joy Gugeler, who had brought Taryn to the class, said something to the effect of "this is the student I was telling you about." Taryn asked for a book proposal—which Joy was teaching us how to prepare—and here we are. I was able to convince Taryn that Vancouver Island was hungry for a regional book on ghost stories. Thank you, Taryn, for helping make this dream become a reality. I could not have done this without you. Thanks to Joy, as well, for both believing in me and for providing such an amazing opportunity. Thanks also to TouchWood's in-house editor, Renée Layberry, for your attention to detail while preparing the final version of this book, and to designer Pete Kohut who is responsible for the cool-looking final product. I am very grateful to both of you.

As for the actual writing: Susan Juby has taught me more about this craft than anyone ever has. Two of the stories in this book were workshopped in your classes specifically. Not many writers have this kind of support when they're starting out. You have always pushed us to find that fine balance between hard work and creativity. You have also accomplished many things as a writer; I hope to one day as well. You are an inspiration to me, Susan, and I am grateful to have had the opportunity to learn from you, and I hope to continue to have the ability to do so for many years to come, directly or indirectly. You once said that you would like to write a horror novel one day. I honestly can't wait.

Thanks also to Spenser Smith, who helped with the Staqeya story in another class. Not only did you edit the first drafts of that chapter, but you were in the workshop groups for the other two stories as well. You have been a good friend and solid supporter from the beginning, so it's always exciting to hear about your writing projects and accomplishments as well. Thanks, buddy. I'm also grateful for Spenser's fiancée, Sarah Packwood, who took the author image for this book. You have been encouraging from the moment I met you. Thank you, Sarah.

Professor Frank Moher also worked on the Staqeya story, adding final touches and giving me much-valued feedback. Thank you for everything, Frank; your feedback, attention to detail, and willingness to help are always appreciated.

Students who workshopped the two stories in Susan's class were Sheena Robinson, Carly Harstad, Chynna Moore, Cole Schisler, Caileigh Broatch, Shauna Andrews, Joe Blackburn, Chantelle Nazareth, Phoenix Courtney, Jesse Wilson, Heather Froese, Karina Geipel, Justin Shankaran, Ashley Mann, Rhyly Bell, and Connor Cambrey. It was truly a gift to have so many talented writers looking at my work. A sincere thank you to each and every one of you.

I would also like to thank professor Janis Ledwell-Hunt who helped me solidify the idea for this book during a business proposal assignment. Thank you, Janis, for your encouragement and guidance during this project's infancy. You really helped me put things into motion.

Heartfelt gratitude to VIU First Nation Studies professor and chair Laurie Meijers Drees. Thank you for allowing me to register for classes that as a writing student I technically didn't have prerequisites for. Through you, I have been exposed to elder teachings, learned protocol, and became much more aware of the importance of preserving oral histories. I have also met many of my favourite people in your classes. Thank you so much, Laurie. Thanks also to retired professor Melody Martin, who has been an invaluable resource and beacon of support. Also, thank you to professor Camie Augustus for teaching me about First Nations representation and misrepresentation, hopefully helping me not to make the same types of errors other writers and artists have in the past. I appreciate you answering my many questions, knowing I was working on this book. Thank you, Camie. To all of you, and to all the amazing elders at VIU, I would like to say *Haych'qa Siem*. Words cannot fully express my gratitude.

I would also like to thank Auntie Geraldine Manson, VIU Elder in Residence, specifically. Thank you, Auntie, for all your support, and for telling me about your own ghost experiences. Even though I met you after the editing process had already begun, your teachings have helped me see a bigger picture when things have been difficult along the way, and you have expanded my understanding of spirits. The challenges you have overcome in your own life are an inspiration to many people including me. I am very grateful to have met you and to know you. *Haych'qa Siem*.

I'd like to express my appreciation for Christine Meutzner at the Nanaimo Community Archives, for answering so many questions, for helping me find information and images for both the Lantern Tours and the book, and for being such a solid resource in the community. Thank you, Christine, for your generosity.

A huge thank you to Dr. Leanne Campbell who has been hugely supportive of my dream to write this book. There were many times when it felt as if by tackling this project I was biting off more than I could chew. Your encouragement often came during moments where it felt like this task was hopeless. Thank you very much, Leanne. I am very grateful to know you.

When it comes to day-to-day encouragement, there really are too many people to name. I would, however, like to give a huge thank you to my family. I was committed to a January 15th deadline, so Christmas was especially difficult as I kept my head down and was writing most of the time. I'm especially grateful that my nieces and nephews understood. Thank you, Aiden, Hailee, Kol, Avaleigh, and Drake. Each of you occupy a place in my heart, so it's hard when writing cuts into hanging out and playing games. Thanks also to my Grandma Fenske. I always feel like your belief in me is unshakeable, and I am very thankful for that. I love all of you.

I have many friends who have been extremely supportive of the writing of this book, most notably: Scott Boyd, Chad Ledgebokoff, Greg Guspie, Brianna Deimart, Lana Unger, Chantelle Spicer, David Quinn, Shawn Ruste and Caitlin Blain, and Joseph and Tamara Waugh. Thank you for being here for me in so many ways. I am also grateful to many other friends, especially all of you who have kept in touch online. Thank you for believing in me.

May the spirits that teach me, nourish me, protect me, and guide me, know my eternal gratitude. May I walk my path with honour and make you proud. May I learn from the darkness but never succumb to it. May my voice be clear. Thank you for these stories.

BIBLIOGRAPHY

Akrigg, Helen B. and G.P.V. Akrigg. *1001 British Columbia Place Names*. Vancouver, BC: Discovery Press, 1969.

Arnett, Chris. *The Terror of the Coast*. Vancouver, BC: Talonbooks, 1999.

Audain, James. *Alex Dunsmuir's Dilemma*. Sunnylane Publishing: Victoria, BC, 1964.

Bayor, Ronald H, ed. *The Columbia Documentary History of Race and Ethnicity in America*. New York, NY: Columbia University Press, 2004.

Boas, Franz. Bouchard Randy and Dorothy Kennedy, eds. *Indian Myths & Legends from the North Pacific Coast of America*. Vancouver, BC: Talonbooks, 2002. First published 1895 in German by Verlag von A. Asher & Co.

Belyk, Robert C. *Ghosts: More Eerie Encounters*. Victoria, BC: TouchWood Editions, 2006.

Belyk, Robert C. *Ghosts: True Tales of Eerie Encounters*. Victoria, BC: TouchWood Editions, 2006. First published 1990 by Horsdal & Schubart.

Bindernagel, John A. *The Discovery of the Sasquatch: Reconciling Culture, History, And Science in the Discovery Process*. Courtenay, BC: Beachcomber Books, 2010.

Cartwright, Peggy. *Black Pioneers in Gold Rush Days*. Victoria, BC: Manning Press, 1993.

City of Nanaimo. *City of Nanaimo Community Heritage Register*. Nanaimo, BC: City of Nanaimo. March 14, 2011. PDF file.

Commission on Valencia Disaster. *Wreck of the Steamer Valencia: Report to the President of the Federal Commission of Investigation*. Washington, DC: Department of Commerce and Labor, 1906. PDF File.

Cooper, J. C. *An Illustrated Encyclopedia of Traditional Symbols*. London, UK: Thames and Hudson, 1978.

Cryer, Beryl Mildred and Chris Arnett. *Two Houses Half-Buried in Sand: Oral Traditions of the Hul'q'umi'num' Coast Salish of Kuper Island and Vancouver*. Vancouver, BC: Talonbooks, 2008.

Ellis, David W. and Luke Swan. *Teachings of the Tides: Uses of Marine Invertebrates by the Manhousaht People*. Nanaimo, BC: Theytus Books, 1981.

Evans, Albert. *A La California: Sketches of Life in the Golden State*. San Francisco, CA: A. L. Bancroft & Company. 1873. PDF file.

Fisher, Joe. *Hungry Ghosts: An Investigation into Channelling and the Spirit World*. Toronto, ON: Doubleday Canada, 1990.

Garner, Betty Sanders. *Monster! Monster! A Survey of the North American Monster Scene*. Surrey, BC: Hancock House Publishers, 1995.

Green, John. *On the Track of the Sasquatch*. Agassiz, BC: Cheam Publishing, 1968.

Green, Valarie. *If More Walls Could Talk: Vancouver Island's Houses from the Past*. Victoria, BC: TouchWood Editions, 2004.

Harrison, Eunice M. L. *The Judge's Wife: Memoirs of a BC Pioneer*. Vancouver, BC: Ronsdale Press, 2002.

Hayman, John. *Robert Brown and the Vancouver Island Exploring Expedition*. Vancouver, BC: University of British Columbia Press, 1989.

Jupp, Ursala. *Cadboro: A Ship, A Bay, A Sea Monster 1842 -1958*. Victoria, BC: Jay Editions, 1988.

LeBlond, Paul H. and Edward L. Bousfield. *Cadborosaurus: Survivor from the Deep*. Victoria, BC: Horsdal & Schubart, 1995.

Leland, Donald. *Aboriginal Slavery on the Northwest Coast of North America*. Berkeley, CA: University of California Press, 1997.

Lillard, Charles and Robin Skelton. *The April Ghost of the Victoria Golf Links*. Victoria, BC: Published for the Hawthorne Society by Reference West, 1994.

Marshall, Daniel Patrick. *Those Who Fell from the Sky: A History of the Cowichan Peoples*. Duncan, BC: Cowichan Culture and Education Centre, 1999.

Mason, Adrienne. *Historic Tofino a Walking Tour*. Tofino, BC: Postelsia Press, 2011.

Masters, Ruth. *History of Forbidden Plateau: 1920—1986*. Campbell River, BC: Campbell River Museum, n.d.

Merilees, Bill. *Newcastle Island: A Place of Discovery*. Victoria, BC: Heritage House Publishing, 1998.

Mussio, Russell. *Vancouver Island BC Backroad Mapbook: 6th Edition*. Coquitlam, BC: Mussio's Ventures, 2011.

Mussio, Russell. *Vancouver Island BC Fishing Mapbook: 3rd Edition*. Coquitlam, BC: Mussio's Ventures, 2015.

Neitzel, Michael C. *The Valencia Tragedy*. Victoria, BC: Heritage House Publishing, 1995.

Norman, Michael and Beth Scott. *Historic Haunted America*. New York, NY: Tor Books, 2007.

Old Cemeteries Society of Victoria. *Favourite Stories from Lantern Tours in the Old Burying Ground*. Victoria, BC: Old Cemeteries Society of Victoria,1998.

Oliphant, John. *Brother Twelve: The Incredible Story of Canada's False Prophet and his Doomed Cult of Gold, Sex, and Black Magic*. Toronto, ON: McClelland & Stewart, 1991.

Parnia, Sam. *What Happens When We Die? A Groundbreaking Study into the Nature of Life and Death*. California, CA: Hay House, Inc., 2006.

Paterson, T. W. and Garnet Basque. *Ghost Towns and Mining Camps of Vancouver Island*. Victoria, BC: Heritage House Publishing, 1999. First Published 1989 by Sunfire Publications.

Peterson, Jan. *The Albernis: 1860 – 1922.* Lantzville, BC: Oolichan Books, 1992.

Peterson, Jan. *Black Diamond City: Nanaimo – The Victorian Era.* Victoria, BC: Heritage House Publishing, 2002.

Peterson, Jan. *Harbour City: Nanaimo in Transition 1920 – 1967.* Victoria, BC: Heritage House Publishing, 2006.

Reksten, Terry. *More English Than the English: A Very Social History of Victoria.* Winlaw, BC: Sono Nis Press, 2011.

Reksten, Terry. *The Dunsmuir Saga.* Vancouver, BC: Douglas & McIntyre, 1994.

Sam, Stanley Sr. of the Ahousaht First Nations. *Ahousaht Wild Side Heritage Trail Guidebook.* Vancouver, BC: Western Canada Wilderness Committee, 1997.

Scott, R. Bruce. *"Breakers Ahead!" A History of Shipwrecks on the Graveyard of the Pacific.* Victoria, BC: R. Bruce Scott, 1970.

Skelton, Robin and Jean Kozocari. *A Gathering of Ghosts: Hauntings and Exorcisms from the Personal Casebook of Robin Skelton and Jean Kozocari.* Saskatoon, SK: Western Producer Prairie Books, 1989.

Taylor, Jeanette. *The Quadra Story: A History of Quadra Island.* Madeira Park, BC: Harbour Publishing, 2010.

Whitaker, Pamela and Chief James Wallas. *Kwakiutl Legends: As Told to Pamela Whitaker by Chief James Wallas.* Surrey, BC: Hancock House Publishers, 1989.

OTHER PUBLICATIONS

"About the Nuu-chah-nulth People." *First Voices.* Accessed December 28, 2016. http://www.firstvoices.com/en/Nuu-chah-nulth

BC Museum Association & Nanaimo District Museum. *Is the Bastion Haunted?* August 20, 2004. Screen shot.

Bell, Katie. "Sssnakes on Vancouver Island." *Habitat Acquisition Trust: Victoria's Local Land Trust.* May 18, 2016. http://www.hat.bc.ca/i-want-to/news-and-events/470-sssnakes-on-vancouver-island

"British Columbia." *The West Shore.* February, 1881. PDF file.

Britt, Robert Roy. "Higher Education Fuels Stronger Belief in Ghosts." *Live Science.* January 20, 2006. http://www.livescience.com/564-higher-education-fuels-stronger-belief-ghosts.html

Bruce, Maré. "1949 – 2016 Celebrating 67 years of Amazing Food, Friends, Family and Community." *Schooner Restaurant.* Accessed March 6, 2017. http://www.schoonerrestaurant.ca/history

Bryan, Dan. "Chinatown's Sex Slaves – Human Trafficking and San Francisco's History." *American history USA.* February 17, 2013. https://www.americanhistoryusa.com/chinatown-sex-slaves-human-trafficking-san-francisco-history/

Cass, John. *The Beginning of the Nanaimo Fire Department: Prepared for the Radio Series "Files of Yesteryear", Presented Over Radio CHUB, January 11th to January 19th, 1968*. Presented to Fire Department, January 22, 1968. PDF file.

Coleman, Loren. "The Sudden Death of Joe Fisher (1947-2001.)" *The Anomalist*. May, 2001. http://www.anomalist.com/milestones/fisher.html

Counter, Rosemary. "The 'Rock Star' Wolf of Juan de Fuca." *Maclean's*. March 12, 2017. http://www.macleans.ca/news/canada/the-rock-star-wolf-of-juan-de-fuca/

Courtney, Stan. "Cemeteries and Squatches, Pt. 1." *Stan Courteny* (blog). June 10, 2009. http://stancourtney.com/cemeteries-ghosts-squatches/

Duffus, Maureen. "Vancouver Island History: Thetis Cove's Earliest Subdivision." *Maureenduffus.com*. Accessed May 9, 2017.

Dunae, Patrick A. "Qualicum College." *The Homeroom: British Columbia's History of Education Web Site*. Accessed March 6, 2017. https://www2.viu.ca/home-room/content/schools/Private/qualicum.htm

Enns, Sean. "The Haunting at Heriot Bay." *The Offbeat Traveler* (blog). March 27, 2015. http://offbeattravel.ca/the-haunting-at-heriot-bay

"Forbidden Plateau." *British Columbia: BC Geographical Names*. Accessed March 6, 2017. http://apps.gov.bc.ca/pub/bcgnws/names/12978.html

Guide to: Mount Sicker. Cowichan, BC: Municipality of North Cowichan. PDF file.

Hayes, Joe. "La Llorona – A Hispanic Legend." *Teaching from a Hispanic Perspective: A Handbook for Non-Hispanic Adult Educators*. May, 1996. http://www.literacynet.org/lp/hperspectives/llorona.html

Illerbrun, W.J. "Kanaka Pete." *Hawaiian Journal of History*. Vol 6, 1972. PDF file.

Kase, Aaron. "Science is Proving Some Memories Are Passed Down From Our Ancestors." *Reset.me*. February 20, 2015. http://reset.me/story/science-proving-memories-passed-ancestors/

Lettington, Mathew. "Keeha Bay & Meeting my Hero." *Explorington* (blog). May 17, 2015. http://explorington.com/2015/05/keeha-bay-meeting-my-hero/

Lipka, Michael. "18% of Americans say they've seen a ghost." *Pew research Center: Factank*. October 30, 2015. http://www.pewresearch.org/fact-tank/2015/10/30/18-of-americans-say-theyve-seen-a-ghost/

McKinley, John. "Cross Returning to Tzouhalem Lookout." *Bclocalnews.com*. December 17, 2014. http://www.bclocalnews.com/news/285991871.html?mobile=true

Montgomery, Monty. "The Nanaimo Tank Farm Fire." *Canadian Coast Guard Association Newsletter*. Winter, 2012. PDF file.

"Mount Tzouhalem." *British Columbia: BC Geographical Names*. Accessed March 6, 2017. http://apps.gov.bc.ca/pub/bcgnws/names/54721.html

Mosby, Ian. "Administering Colonial Science: Nutrition Research and Human Biomedical experimentation in Aboriginal Communities and Residential Schools, 1942 – 1952." *Social History*. Vol 46, May 2013. PDF file.

Myers, Natalie. "Keeha Death March." *Travel Blog* (blog). December 3, 2005. https://www.travelblog.org/North-America/Canada/British-Columbia/Vancouver-Island/Bamfield/blog-29749.html

Nanaimo Campus Communication Department. "Malaspina Loses Two Friends." *Mainly Malaspina… The Malaspina University-College Newsletter*. February, 1994. PDF file.

Nature Conservancy Canada. "Chase Woods Nature Preserve." *Natureconservancy.ca*. Accessed December 22, 2016. http://www.natureconservancy.ca/en/where-we-work/british-columbia/featured-projects/chase_woods.html

Norrell, Brenda. "Mass Graves Revealed of Indian Children in Canadian Schools." *The Narcosphere*. April 18, 2008. http://narcosphere.narconews.com/notebook/brenda-norrell/2008/04/mass-graves-revealed-indian-children-canadian-schools

"Our History." *Four Mile House Restaurant*. Accessed December 21, 2016. http://fourmilehouse.com/press-room/

"Paranormal Studies and Inquiry Canada: General Information – Ethics and Codes Version 4.0." *Psican.org*. May 16, 2016. PDF file.

Paterson, Roderick Paul. "The Northwest Coast Sisiutl." Master's thesis, University of British Columbia, 1972. *UBC Library Open Collections*. Accessed December 9, 2016. PDF file.

Pilkington, Mark. "The Fear Frequency." *The Guardian*. October 16, 2003. https://www.theguardian.com/science/2003/oct/16/science.farout

"Sasquatch Country." *Lone Cone Hostel & Campground*. Accessed March 6, 2017. http://www.loneconetrail.ca/sasquatch-country

Smart, Amy. "Cross Put Back Atop Cowichan Mountain." *Times Colonist*. January 14, 2017. http://www.timescolonist.com/news/local/cross-put-back-atop-cowichan-mountain-1.1731351

Steckler, Gerard G. "The Case of Frank Fuller: The Killer of Alaska Missionary Charles Seghers." *The Pacific Northwest Quarterly*, Vol. 59, No. 4. October, 1968. PDF file.

Stuart, Ryan. "Finding Forbidden." *CVC Collective*, Vol 5. Winter, 2015. http://www.cvcollective.ca/finding-forbidden/

Thom, Brian David. "Coast Salish Senses of Place: Dwelling, Meaning, Power, Property, and Territory in the Coast Salish World." Doctorate thesis, McGill University, 2005. *McGill Library and Collections*. Accessed October 19, 2016. http://digitool.library.mcgill.ca/R/?func=dbin-jump-full&object_id=85209&local_base=GEN01-MCG02

Wolfenden, Madge. "Tod, John." *Dictionary of Canadian Biography*. University of Toronto. Accessed December 21, 2016. http://www.biographi.ca/en/bio/ tod_john_11E.html

MIXED MEDIA

Alone (seasons 1 & 2). Leftfield Pictures. History Channel, 2015 & 2016.

Creepy Canada. Created by William Burke. Outdoor Life Network (OLN), 2002 – 2006.

Lore (podcast). "Adrift." Aaron Mahnke, November 16, 2015.

Monsterquest. "Mysterious Ape Island." Directed by Leo Singer. History Channel, April 29, 2009.

Sasquatch Chronicles (podcast). Episodes 274 – 276. Wes Germer, November, 2016.

Sea Monsters: The Definitive Guide. Directed by Mark Bridge. Discovery Channel, March 28, 2016.

Supernatural Investigator. "What Killed Joe Fisher Part 1 – The Trap is Set." Directed by Doug Williams. VisionTV, February 10, 2009.

Supernatural Investigator. "What Killed Joe Fisher Part 2 – The Trap is Sprung." Directed by Doug Williams. VisionTV, February 17, 2009.

The Whale. Directed by Suzanne Chisholm and Michael Parfit. Mountainside Films, 2012.

NEWSPAPERS

Alberni Valley Times

Campbell River Mirror

Comox Argus

Comox District Free Press

Comox Valley Echo

Ladysmith Chemainus Chronicle

Nanaimo Daily News

Nanaimo Free Press

Nanaimo News Bulletin

Parksville Qualicum Beach News

Seattle-Post Intelligencer

Seattle Daily Times

Vancouver *Province*

Victoria *British Colonist*

Victoria *Daily Colonist*

Victoria *Daily Times*

Victoria *Times Colonist*

OTHER NEWS OUTLETS

A News Vancouver Island
CBC News British Columbia
CTV News Vancouver
CTV News Vancouver Island
Shaw TV Nanaimo *Go! Island*
Shaw TV Nanaimo News

WEBSITES

Ancestry.ca (database)
Archive.org (database)
Bigfootforums.com (forums)
Chinatown.library.uvic.ca (Chinatown Chronology and 1891 fire maps)
Library.viu.ca (database)
Livinglibraryblog.com/haunted-landmarks-of-vancouver-island/ (comments)
Livinglibraryblog.com/haunted-locations-of-victoria-vancouver-island/(comments)
Nanaimoinformation.com (forums)
Open.library.ubc.ca/collections/bcbooks (database)
Ourroots.ca (database)
Realhaunts.com/canada/south-crescent/ (comments)
Search-bcarchives.royalbcmuseum.bc.ca (database)

INDEX

SHANON SINN is the author of *The Haunting of Vancouver Island* as well as several shorter pieces of fiction and nonfiction. He is currently working on a sequel that focuses on ghost stories and folklore from the West Coast of British Columbia. Sinn earned his Creative Writing degree at Vancouver Island University where he received the Barry Broadfoot Award for Journalism and the Gisele Merlet Creative Writing Award. His focus at VIU was on Indigenous topics including Elder teachings and field school at the University of Fairbanks in Alaska (learning oral history recording guidelines). Find him online at shanonsinn.com.